Family Business:
Human Dilemmas in the Family Firm

Family Business:
Human Dilemmas in the Family Firm

Text and cases

Manfred F.R. Kets de Vries
Clinical Professor of Management and Leadership
Raoul de Vitry d'Avaucourt Professor in Human Resource Management
INSEAD, France

INTERNATIONAL THOMSON BUSINESS PRESS
I(T)P An International Thomson Publishing Company

London ● Bonn ● Boston ● Johannesburg ● Madrid ● Melbourne ● Mexico ● City ● New York ● Paris
Singapore ● Tokyo ● Toronto ● Albany, NY ● Belmont, CA ● Cincinnati, OH ● Detroit, MI

Family Business: Human Dilemmas in the Family Firm
Copyright © 1996 Manfred F.R. Kets de Vries

First published 1996 by International Thomson Business Press

I(T)P   A division of International Thomson Publishing Inc.
The ITP logo is a trademark under licence

British Library Cataloguing-in-Publication Data
A catalogue record for this book is available from the British Library

First edition published by ITBP 1996

Typeset in Times by LaserScript, Mitcham, Surrey
Printed in the UK by TJ Press (Padstow) Ltd., Padstow, Cornwall

ISBN 0–415–11462–4

International Thomson Business Press
Berkshire House
168–173 High Holborn
London WC1V 7AA
UK

International Thomson Business Press
20 Park Plaza
14th Floor
Boston MA 02116
USA

To Abraham Zaleznik, mentor and friend

Contents

C. Envy, Spite, and Sibling Rivalry

D. Multigenerational Issues

Acknowledgments

When you see a turtle sitting on a fence post, you know he did not get there alone. The same can be said about the making of this book. I am indebted to the many people who helped to make this undertaking on family business possible. I would first like to thank a number of my previous research associates and students who have helped me in developing selected cases presented in this book. Brian Baxter, Robert Dick, Nelleke Hennemann, Henk Luykx, Jane Petrie, and Daphna Zevadi were instrumental in preparing some of the included material. I would also like to thank Didier Anzieu for his willingness to let me adapt his article "Observation Clinique d'un Groupe Malade" *Bulletin de Psychologie*, published in October 1968, which led to the Dunor Company case. Mark Turek was very helpful in providing me with information pertaining to the Roland and Stone case. The consultant in the Fashion Shoe Company case was my old mentor Abraham Zaleznik, to whom I have dedicated this book. Since I have taught this case many times to illustrate irrational processes in organizations, the case has become an "old friend," and I therefore decided to include it in this book. I would like to thank both Abraham Zaleznik and the Harvard Business School for their permission to use the case.

I am particularly appreciative of the help of Lawrence Nadler, who often played the role of guide through the labyrinth that many family businesses represent. The Nadia and the Chantel cases could not have been written without his help. His request that I join him on some of his consulting assignments was the catalyst for these case projects. I often miss the lively discussions that we had after visiting a family firm, trying to make sense out of the problems presented by the various protagonists. I regret that our physical separation has limited these opportunities for collaboration.

I would also like to thank Arnold Steinberg for encouraging me to write a case about the company of his uncle. His insights into the turn of events surrounding that company and his commentary on the film *After Sam* (part of the National Film Board of Canada documentary *The Corporation*) were instrumental in getting this particular case project off the ground.

Last but certainly not least, I deeply appreciate the various executives who, through their comments (whether included in the text or not), contributed to the cases presented in this book. Whatever their motives may have been, it is not always easy to open up and talk to outsiders. Their participation represented a willingness to expose their own vulnerability. I am indebted to them for their courage to do so and hope that others may learn from their wisdom and their mistakes.

In getting the book to its present form, I have benefited from the editorial help of my old friend Ardis Burst. She enthusiastically took on what turned out to be quite a difficult assignment. Her comments are remembered and very much appreciated. Her good cheer and positive criticism helped me overcome many a dark hour working on the book. While preparing the final draft, I also profited greatly from the editorial advice of Kathy Reigstad – an editor's editor – who put the book into its final shape.

I would also like to acknowledge the help of the department of R&D at INSEAD – particularly the members of its research committee and its former and new associate deans, Yves Doz and Landis Gabel, who have always stood behind my research, although it must at times have seemed strange at a school of management. After all, psychoanalysts – particularly the kind that meddle in business – are not exactly a regular feature at business schools! I would also like to thank the former and present deans of INSEAD, Ludo Van der Heyden and Antonio Borges, for being so encouraging about the kind of work I do.

I am also grateful for the help of my present research associates, Elizabeth Florent-Treacy and Katharina Balazs, who gave me many valuable suggestions on integrating a collection of diverse materials. They contributed to the teaching notes, added case vignettes, did library research, checked out sources, and untiringly cleaned up draft after draft. I owe my appreciation to them for helping me make clearer what I wanted to say and pointing out what I had forgotten to include. I am thankful not only for their efforts but also for their ideas. Throughout the making of this book, with the help of my secretary, Sheila Loxham, they kept me organized, a feat that is not always easy to accomplish.

Finally, I am grateful to the editorial staff at Routledge for their patience and good spirits in handling the author. Dealing with academics requires special skills, which they certainly seem to have acquired over the years.

The English Nobel laureate T. S. Eliot, in his poem *Four Quartets*, says, "What we call the beginning is often the end. And to make an end is to make a beginning. The end is where we start from." That is the way I feel about this book. The little I know, I owe to my ignorance and curiosity. I hope others will follow my example and use some of the ideas in this book as a point of departure for further reflection on the vicissitudes of the family business.

The Author

Manfred F. R. Kets de Vries holds the Raoul de Vitry d'Avaucourt Chair of Human Resource Management at the European Institute of Business Administration (INSEAD), France, where he is clinical professor of management and leadership. He did a doctoral examination in economics (Econ. Drs) at the University of Amsterdam (1966) and holds an ITP certificate (1967) from Harvard; in addition, he has a master's degree (1968) and a doctoral degree (1970) in business administration from the Harvard Business School. In 1977, he undertook psychoanalytic training at the Canadian Psychoanalytic Institute, and in 1982 he became a member of the Canadian Psychoanalytic Society and the International Psychoanalytic Association. He is a practicing psychoanalyst. He has held professorships at McGill University, the École des Hautes Études Commerciales, Montreal, and the Harvard Business School.

Kets de Vries's main research interest lies in the interface between psychoanalysis, dynamic psychiatry, and management. Specific areas of interest are leadership, cross-cultural management, career dynamics, organizational stress, entrepreneurship, family business, and the process of corporate transformation and change. Kets de Vries's books include *Power and the Corporate Mind* (1975, new edition 1985, with Abraham Zaleznik), *Organizational Paradoxes: Clinical Approaches to Management* (1980, new edition 1994), *The Irrational Executive: Psychoanalytic Explorations in Management* (1984, editor), *The Neurotic Organization: Diagnosing and Changing Counterproductive Styles of Management* (1984, new edition 1990, with Danny Miller), *Unstable at the Top* (1984, with Danny Miller), *Prisoners of Leadership* (1989), *Handbook of Character Studies* (1991, with Sidney Perzow), *Organizations on the Couch* (1991), *Leaders, Fools, and Impostors* (1993), and *Life and Death in the Executive Fast Lane: Essays on Irrational Organizations and Their Leaders* (1995). In addition, Kets de Vries has published over one hundred scientific papers either as articles or chapters in books, and his books and papers have been translated into ten languages. He has written numerous case studies, including three that have been named best European case of the year.

Kets de Vries is a member of many editorial boards and a founding member of the International Society for the Psychoanalytic Study of Organizations. He is also an occasional newspaper columnist and a consultant on organizational design/transformation and strategic human resource management, and he has done extensive executive development work with many US, Canadian, European, and Asian companies. He has received INSEAD's distinguished teacher award five times.

Part I

Conceptualizations

Chapter 1

Introduction

As the year 2000 approaches, more people than ever are becoming interested in entrepreneurship and family businesses. New entrepreneurial enterprises are growing at an ever-increasing rate, with annual start-ups running at 1,400 percent of those of forty years ago (Birch, 1988). This increase in entrepreneurial ventures will not only mean more family businesses but will also further the growing awareness of the vital importance of entrepreneurial and family businesses for economic development.

The number of new businesses is increasing in part because our attitude toward work is changing. Cultural historians and psychiatrists who suggest that we live in a narcissistic age (for example, Kohut, 1971; Kohut and Wolf, 1978; Lasch, 1978) identify narcissistic behavior as a way of coping with the tensions and anxieties in our postmodern society. Tom Wolfe's "me generation," a group of people who seem much more self-absorbed than their parents were, has come of age. Many people in today's workforce are determined to "do their own thing," to have greater control over their lives and their work. Just making a salary is no longer good enough; the "me generation" wants a piece of the action. And what better way to get there than by starting one's own business?

The rise in entrepreneurial and family businesses has also been a result of the fallout from downsizing, business process reengineering, and corporate transformation programs. Many executives have been laid off through these various efforts. Corporate loyalty has become a relic of the past, while the "organization man," the one-time mainstay of the large corporation, is rapidly becoming extinct. Frightened by these developments, executives are looking for other ways to obtain control over their lives. One obvious approach, particularly for someone who finds him- or herself suddenly unemployed, is to start one's own business.

These entrepreneurial and family businesses are not, however, something new. Over 80 percent of the businesses in the United States are privately owned (Zeitlin, 1976), and in Europe the percentages range from 52 percent (the Netherlands) to more than 80 percent (Germany and Austria) (Donckels and Fröhlich, 1991). Furthermore, family firms are a prime source of employment growth in the United States and Western Europe, employing over 50 percent of the total workforce and accounting for about 40 percent of the national income.

Statistics on family businesses refer not only to the corner grocery store. On the contrary, a family business can as easily be a multinational corporation. One third of the companies included in the Fortune 500 list are family controlled, as are some of the world's most successful firms, including Michelin in France; Tetrapak and IKEA in Sweden; Lego in Denmark; Fiat, Olivetti, and Benetton in Italy; C&A and Heineken in the Netherlands; Cadbury Schweppes, Marks & Spencer and Guinness in the UK; Mars, Anheuser-Busch, Bechtel, and Seagram in North America; and the Swire group and Hyundai in Asia.

The importance of entrepreneurial and family enterprises is often underrated, in part because privately owned companies are not always easy to study. Many family enterprises are quite secretive, jealously guarding their privacy and wary of communication with outsiders. Because these businesses are privately held, the usual reporting regulations do not apply to them, and little information is available to the public. Furthermore, for reasons of taxation, ownership is often disguised through a complicated web of legal arrangements and offshore companies and trusts.

Difficulties in obtaining information notwithstanding, interest in family and entrepreneurial businesses is on the rise. Academics, founder-entrepreneurs (and subsequent owners of family businesses), and people working for family businesses – management consultants, investment bankers, tax accountants, lawyers, investment counselors, and other professionals who serve these businesses – are beginning to realize that entrepreneurial and family businesses possess certain unique qualities, problems, and challenges. There are specific legal, tax, and financial skills directly relevant to these companies, and, less obviously, there are also certain psychological processes that are fostered in the often closed environment of the family firm. In fact, many people working with and for these firms have discovered that traditional management theories are not always applicable.

Among the host of issues unique to entrepreneurial and family firms are the following: the dilemma of family members in management positions for which they are not qualified; the question of how to deal with family members who, though not in operating or ownership positions, try to influence the business; the quandary of role conflict (a person has the role of parent, son, or daughter, for example, but at the same time is an executive trying to run a business); and the vexing issue of differences in intergenerational goals.

And these issues, difficult though they may be, are only the beginning. What can be said about the "inner theater" – that inner script, based on lifelong experiences, that forms one's character and directs one's life – of the founder-entrepreneur and subsequent owners from within the family? Are there any differences between the wishes, motivations, and needs of these people compared to those of executives managing publicly held enterprises? How adaptive is the leadership style of people running entrepreneurial and family businesses? How should problems concerning succession and transition be dealt with? What makes certain entrepreneurial and family businesses succeed while others fail? Are there certain dangers family businesses should be aware of?

   The intertwining of family and business concerns is at the core of the issues and questions that surround family businesses. What makes entrepreneurial and family firms so different is such factors as the strong identification of individuals with the business itself, the unusual family dynamics, the intensity of emotion among the participants, and the existence of specific kinds of conflict that revolve around the challenge of establishing a balance between family and business concerns.

   For these firms, competing successfully with the outside world is only the beginning. Intra- and interfamily conflict and rivalry must be managed as well. And as the family grows in size, the potential for new conflict increases progressively. Dealing with the resulting intergenerational and generational dynamics around succession and transition issues can become an extremely draining experience both for the people running the business and for the business itself.

   Stressful or not, these issues demand attention, as the dismal statistics that characterize entrepreneurial and family firms testify. Only three out of ten family businesses survive into the second generation, while only one out of ten survives into the third. The average lifespan of these firms (after a successful start-up) is twenty-four years, which coincides with the average time the founder is associated with the enterprise (Beckhard and Dyer, 1983a, 1983b). Obviously, entrepreneurial and family enterprises can be highly unstable, given the complex issues and the potential for problems. Many owners of such enterprises need help, often in the form of outside intervention, to break existing stalemates. Given the unique qualities of family businesses, innovative diagnostic methods have to be found to make these interventions more effective.

THE CLINICAL PARADIGM

Unfortunately, too many students of organizations (entrepreneurial and family businesses included) take a "neutron bomb" approach to their studies, giving their attention to structures and systems instead of to the people involved. Even when people are taken into consideration, however, the theories of individual motivation, decision making, and group behavior that are applied to them are oversimplified. Such mechanistic theories of human functioning are rather insulting: they make the people who run these organizations look one-dimensional. Most often, differences in personality are ignored (Kets de Vries, 1989; Kets de Vries and Perzow, 1991), and very little attention is given to the unique aspects of an individual's character: a person's specific motives, needs, defenses, fantasies, symptoms, fears, and anxieties.

   An increasing number of students of organizations have come to realize, however, that there are limitations to logical decision making and that extrarational forces can strongly influence leadership, group functioning, organizational strategy and structure, and corporate culture. This book will take that realization into account, applying the clinical paradigm to bring the human being back into the organization.

The complex psychological forces that make up the personality of the various actors are the real keys to understanding the psychodynamics of the family firm. Consequently, this book will explore the role of unconscious motivation, the effect of intrapsychic reality, and the impact of childhood experiences on adult behavior. In deciphering these psychological dimensions by using the clinical paradigm, I will draw on concepts and theories taken from psychoanalytic psychology (particularly object relations theory, self-psychology, and ego psychology), dynamic psychiatry, child development theory, personality theory, cognition, and family systems theory.

This clinical approach to organizational diagnosis and intervention is ideally suited to the kind of complex situations that entrepreneurial and family businesses present (Kets de Vries and Miller, 1984b; Kets de Vries et al., 1991). After all, business leaders (certainly founders and owners of business enterprises fall into that category) are not necessarily rational, logical, sensible, and dependable human beings. And many leaders of entrepreneurial and family businesses are especially prone to irrational behavior (Zaleznik and Kets de Vries, 1975; Kets de Vries, 1984; Kets de Vries and Associates, 1991). Clinical investigation has demonstrated that many organizational problems originate in the private, inner world of the organization's senior executives – in how they act out their deepest conflicts, desires, and fantasies and in how they use their personal defense systems in a business setting (Levinson, 1972, 1981, 1984; Zaleznik, 1966, 1989; Hirschhorn, 1988; Kets de Vries, 1995, 1996).

Recognizing cognitive and affective distortions in decision making will help us to identify the extent to which unconscious fantasies and out-of-awareness behavior affect management practices within organizations. Thus, rather than looking simply at the surface consequences of the behavior of individuals in family businesses, I will, for the purpose of diagnosis and intervention, look at "deep" structure: the inner motives, fantasies, drives, and resistances of the principle actors. It is my hope that using a clinical orientation in studying problems unique to entrepreneurial and family enterprises will contribute to a better understanding of these kinds of businesses.

In developing a clinical paradigm for understanding entrepreneurial and family businesses, I will make use of approaches, techniques, and vocabulary that are more often used in psychology and psychoanalysis than in discussions of management issues. I will describe these briefly here before further developing the paradigm itself.

In terms of the overall clinical paradigm used in the case studies and analyses included in this book, I first make the major assumption that the investigator cannot avoid being affected by the subject of investigation. As a matter of fact, the idea of doing research without being influenced by personal and professional biases is an illusion. There is always something happening between the researcher and his or her subject (Glaser and Strauss, 1967; Devereux, 1967; Turner, 1974; Edelson, 1984; Schein, 1987). Thus, instead of ignoring such factors as personal emotions, researchers should recognize and welcome these, viewing them as important sources of data. Researchers should be prepared to engage in a process of self-reflection so as to turn these feelings to their advantage; they should constantly think about what is happening to them while doing the research they have undertaken.

Like it or not, the researcher is part of the social system being investigated. At some stage in the research or intervention process, the subject of the investigation starts "talking" to the researcher and evokes certain responses in him or her – that is, "countertransference reactions." Countertransference traditionally refers to the feelings that the patient arouses in the therapist (Epstein and Feiner, 1979); in this case, however, it applies to the feelings that the subject arouses in the researcher. While a patient or subject has transference reactions toward the therapist or researcher, the therapist or researcher has countertransference reactions toward the patient or subject.

Countertransference and transference processes are critical concepts in interpersonal understanding. They are processes whereby a confusion of person, place, and time occurs, due to a "reliving" of earlier relationships. They are a kind of repetition, resulting in persistent, stereotypical behavior patterns that originated in privileged relationships with early caretakers. Transference and countertransference are ubiquitous elements of the human condition – the way in which we process information and organize experience. They are organizing activities indicating the continuing influence of a person's early life experiences. These psychological processes – distortions of the whole context of one's relationships – are present in all meaningful human interactions, including those that take place in entrepreneurial and family businesses. When reactions appear unusually intense, irrational, out of place, or emotional, a transference reaction may be taking place. Careful evaluation of these transference and counter-transference reactions gives the therapist or researcher another source of information that can be used concurrently with more conventional data. Although countertransference reactions can be handicaps when researchers or consultants are unaware of them, an understanding of one's positive and negative biases toward a subject can be a great asset if used properly.

Another important clinical research concept is that of "text," by which is meant groupings of interrelated information and of all types of data containing messages and themes that can be systematized. In "decoding" family business texts, significance is extracted from interrelated factual, cognitive, and affective units constructed out of the researcher's experiences with the people in the business. Texts can include both the obvious, such as managerial statements, writings, and observable behavior, and the implicit, such as symbolic behavior, organizational myths, specific strategic decisions, particular interpersonal styles, and the type of organizational structure. All these give clues to what life in an organization is all about. Understanding these texts adds a further dimension to our analysis of organizational phenomena. If we are alert to underlying themes, to meanings behind metaphors used by the executives, to reasons for the selection of certain words, and to implications of certain activities, our knowledge of organizational life becomes much richer (Kets de Vries *et al.*, 1991).

A number of rules are helpful in decoding these texts. First, there is the rule of thematic unity. When we try to analyze an organizational story, we have to shape the different observations into an interconnected, cohesive unit. We have to make an effort to build up a "gestalt" or whole. Second, we are engaged in pattern matching, looking for structural parallels, for a "fit" between present-day events and earlier incidents in the history of an individual or organization; we are watching for revealing repetition (Geertz, 1973, 1983; Spence, 1982). Pattern matching is based on the tendency each of us has to become entangled in displacements in time. Instead of remembering the past, we may misunderstand the present in terms of the past and relive the past through present actions. Here the notion of transference returns to the fore. We often react to important individuals and situations *as if* these were figures or incidents from the past. But what might have been an appropriate reaction at one time now turns out to be transparently anachronistic; this is the case on occasions when certain reactions seem inappropriate or overly intense. On those occasions, it is time to pay attention.

Third, interpretations need to be guided by the rule of psychological urgency. The challenge is to identify the pervasive relationship patterns, the core conflictual relationship themes (Luborsky, 1984; Luborsky *et al.*, 1988). We need to tease out the "operational code" of a person's life (Leites, 1953; George, 1969). The assumption is that somewhere in the text it will always be possible to identify an individual's most pressing need or needs, intentions, or ways of acting. To understand what is going on, it is essential to identify constantly repeated patterns. There are always consistencies in an individual's relationships.

Fourth and finally, there is the rule of multiple function (Waelder, 1936). Depending on the psychological urgency of the matter at hand, a part of a text can have more than one meaning and can be looked at from many different points of view. Sometimes organizational resistances and defensive processes stand out. At other times, the key dynamics may be related to the way organizational participants manage aggression or affectionate bonds. Processes evolving around shame, guilt, envy, jealousy, and rivalry can also become important. To complicate matters even further, these issues may all play a concurrent role and can occur at the individual, interpersonal, group, intergroup, and organizational levels. It is thus necessary to seek out meanings at multiple levels and to determine the individual and organizational roots and consequences of actions and decisions.

In this case book, these ideas about textual analysis will be integrated with an existing body of literature on leadership, executive behavior, group dynamics, organizational stress, power and politics, organizational design, culture, strategy, and organizational consultation, all looked at from a clinical perspective. The application of rules derived from the clinical paradigm to the more traditional management literature will help to disclose patterns that can be woven into a unified gestalt, revealing a matrix that helps us to explain the psychodynamics of life in entrepreneurial and family businesses. In the process, the researcher becomes a sort of translator and cryptographer, transforming different levels of understanding.

AUDIENCE

I believe that a book with this perspective will be useful to a number of audiences. Having read this book, *students* of business administration will be better able to understand the problems associated with working for or running a family enterprise. *Management consultants* will find ways to improve their effectiveness in organizational diagnosis and intervention. The cases will be useful in dealing with the kind of interpersonal issues not often found in publicly owned businesses.

For the *academic*, this book will provide an in-depth understanding of human motivation and action in a family business setting. It will help in the development of more realistic models of organizational functioning. For the venture capitalist, investment banker, lawyer, accountant, estate planner, tax adviser, or other *professional*, this book will prove useful in judging the stability and potential of the entrepreneur and the business owner or manager (and their companies).

A fifth audience for this book consists of *entrepreneurs, family owners, family owner-managers*, and *executives* working for family firms who want to deepen their understanding of the particular problems associated with involvement in a family enterprise.

A ROADMAP

The best way to learn about entrepreneurship and family business is by dealing with the people in family-run organizations. To find oneself immersed in what can be very trying family dynamics, however, can be a trial by fire. The learning, the "a-ha!" experience, is there, but the sudden understanding of the various connections may come a bit too late. To prevent costly mistakes, there is something to be said for the case method, which enables students of all types to learn through identification. Rich case descriptions allow students to step into the shoes of the protagonists, trying to make sense of complex situations. Empathy, comparison, and identification then become ideal vehicles for learning.

Although this book includes a conceptual section, it is first and foremost a practical book. Granted, it presents a number of theoretical concepts, but it is not meant to be a book on the theory of entrepreneurship and family business. (Readers interested mainly in theory may refer to some of my other writings.) A considerable portion of this book consists of cases, most of which I have developed and taught myself. Although the cases make an attempt at factual narrative, I hope the reader realizes that they are full of human error and bias. For each of the cases, I give some of my reflections on what I think is happening – but those reflections represent only *my* perspective. The reader should examine the presented material carefully and draw his or her own conclusions, asking after each case, "What went wrong? What went right? What would *I* have done in that situation?"

In studying the cases, the reader should also guard against falling into a "decision trap." There is something to be said for a temporary suspension of disbelief. Readers who overcome the temptation to look for premature closure and instead mull over the material may discover that there is often more than one solution to a problem. Readers should be particularly careful of the quick fix: many problems are very deeply rooted, making solutions hard to find.

Many of the cases presented in this book are not happy tales, and some consist of mystifying problems that thwart easy answers. Their inclusion can be explained on pedagogical grounds: because much can be learned from situations that end up in failure, many of the cases are written to illustrate the range of things that can go wrong in running an entrepreneurial or family business. Some of the cases may even be unsolvable, the protagonists having embarked on a self-destructive journey. Often the cases are presented from the point of view of a consultant who is trying to solve an organization's knotty problems.

I hope that these cases, in spite of the difficulties they present in arriving at solutions, will set into motion a train of thought that will make future problem solving more successful for readers. If readers can acquire a certain amount of clinical insight, perhaps it will serve them when they find themselves in similar situations.

This book consists of two parts. Part I is devoted to the discussion of a number of issues pertaining to entrepreneurial and family enterprises. Part II is centered around the various case studies.

This introductory chapter is followed by Chapter 2, which is based on research involving over 300 interviews with owners, owner-managers, and managers working for family enterprises. It looks at the kinds of problems particularly applicable to family firms. Chapter 2 sets the stage for the subsequent chapters, where attention is given to the unique kind of psychodynamics pertaining to these firms. Chapter 3 looks at the intrapsychic world of entrepreneurs, examining some of the themes that preoccupy them and investigating how these affect their behavior on the job. Some of the difficulties in working with these people are also addressed.

Chapter 4 starts with a discussion of narcissistic development and its vicissitudes. Because a "reactive" form of narcissism is quite common among people in family businesses, its dynamics are explored. Attention is also given to the question of separation-individuation – the process of becoming a person and differentiating oneself from one's family. In this context, the role of transitional objects and transitional space is outlined. The chapter ends with a discussion of envy and the way this emotion colors generational and intergenerational dynamics. This sets the stage for an examination of sibling rivalry and Oedipal problems. Chapter 5 has a more interpersonal orientation. It examines the psychological pressures to which leaders of organizations are subject and provides some insights into the reasons why some leaders derail when they reach the top of their organization.

How certain types of family entanglements and "unholy" coalitions can affect the family business is the subject of review in Chapter 6. This chapter explores various dysfunctional family myths and ends with an examination of the psychodynamics of succession.

The second part of the book consists of a series of case studies taken from various countries, including the United States, Canada, France, Switzerland, Sweden, and the Netherlands. In a way, they are all variations on the same major themes in family firms: the personality of the founder, the transposition of leadership to the next generation, and the interaction between the family and the business systems. All the cases are true stories, although sometimes the names are changed to protect the identity of the protagonists. The Francine Gomez and Waterman case, Steinberg case, Anton Dreesmann case, and the Bonnier case, however, use the real names of the company and the people involved.

Each of the different cases allows us to explore one or more of the issues and dynamics pertinent to entrepreneurial and family firms. The cases are grouped under four major headings, though this division is slightly arbitrary. The organization of the material indicates a certain focus, but many of the cases spill over into other areas. Each case is followed by a commentary.

The first three cases are combined in a section titled "The Intrapsychic and Interpersonal Theater." "The razor is mightier than the pen: Francine Gomez and Waterman" is a very personal narrative – one presented by Gomez herself about her life and her tenure as president of Waterman, a French company that produces high-quality pens. She discusses frankly the problems she has faced on a personal level, juggling responsibilities as an executive, wife, and mother.

"Triumphing over women and witches: Hollywood in the Alps" is about a company based in Denmark and Switzerland that operates in the vocational training field. The company is experiencing both growth and succession problems. Most of these problems, however, are due to the irrational behavior of the founder of the company. Because a considerable amount of personal information is provided, the case offers the opportunity to examine how personal issues become externalized on a public stage.

In "Working with an entrepreneur: Life at the Chantel Corporation," a number of executives describe the experience of working for a volatile founder-entrepreneur running a Canadian lingerie business. The case provides an opportunity to study the behavioral patterns of an entrepreneur. It also highlights how difficult it can be for a consultant to be effective in such an environment.

Section B of Part II, titled "Symbolic Parricide," is about the intense and often destructive father–son relationship as found in the context of family firms. In "*Rashomon* in organizational life: The Fashion Shoe Company," a son, who becomes the new owner of an American shoe manufacturing company after the death of his father, symbolically tries to kill father figures by setting traps for older executives. Subsequently, a consultant is brought in with the implicit assignment of firing the president. The key issue in "Exorcising a ghost: The Dunor Corporation," about a French firm, is succession. The reader is asked to make some sense of the conflicting behavior of the group of executives running this organization – one in which executive meetings, among other things, are not working. Closer analysis reveals that the group is engaged in displaced parricide.

Other intense interpersonal and affect states frequently present on the family stage are "Envy, Spite, and Sibling Rivalry." In this third section, four cases that touch upon these problems are discussed. "Who is the leader? The Nadia Corporation" highlights a number of conflicts typical of family firms. Nadia, a European firm operating in the luggage business, is losing money; the principals running the firm are fighting with each other, and the company's leadership is dysfunctional. The case highlights some of these problems and suggests strategies for intervention.

"Alice in Wonderland: Roland and Stone Inc." is about a US manufacturer, wholesaler, and retailer of high-quality men's shoes. The company is deteriorating because of a lack of direction and the confused allocation of responsibility among its senior executives (due to rivalry between the principals). The case offers a good example of the long-lasting effects of sibling rivalry.

"The sins of the parents: Steinberg Inc." is the tragic tale of a chain of retail food stores that was once one of the most prominent family businesses in Canada. Looking at three generations of owners, the case demonstrates how the second generation, headed by Sam Steinberg, sowed the seeds of what later turned into a bitter family feud centering around succession.

"Medea revisited: Valtex Inc.," about a textile firm operating in the southern part of Holland, demonstrates the extent to which spite, vindictiveness, and envy can dominate people's lives and eventually rip apart both a family and a company.

The final section, titled "Multigenerational Issues," contains examples of the kind of difficulties one encounters whenever a family firm is expanding and/or exists for several generations. "Superman with feet of clay: Anton Dreesmann" describes the vicissitudes of one of the most prominent family firms in the Netherlands. Succession is a central theme in the case. The discussion centers around Anton Dreesmann, a flamboyant entrepreneurial owner who turned the company into a highly diversified conglomerate with interests all over the world. It highlights some of the psychological pressures on leaders and examines a succession process that failed.

The final case, "Managing for continuity: The Bonnier Group," ends on a more positive note and describes the history of the Bonnier family dynasty, one of the most influential family enterprises in Scandinavia, with particular interests in publishing and the media. The discussion centers on how the company has managed to survive through six generations and how it is preparing for the seventh generation of ownership.

The book finishes with concluding remarks about what family businesses can do to manage for survival. Particular attention is given to the process of generational transition and continuity.

Chapter 2

Challenges and hazards of running a family enterprise

In this chapter, I will look at how working in an entrepreneurial firm or family business differs from working in a publicly held corporation. Perhaps a good place to start in explaining the difference between these two settings is with a story.

Once upon a time, there was a potter who made the most beautiful pottery in the world. Everyone who saw his pottery immediately fell in love with it and wanted to buy it. As a result, the potter's shop flourished and became known far and wide. After some time, demand for his products became so great that the potter found it impossible to do all the work himself. He started a factory and hired helpers. As the years went by, he employed more and more workers. Eventually, the potter spent all day managing the factory. He no longer had time to make pottery himself. Sometimes he longed for the good old days when things seemed so much simpler and he did everything himself. He did not really like to be so dependent on others, since very few people could live up to his standards of excellence.

Fortunately, his children, who were now older and had begun giving him a hand, were becoming increasingly helpful in managing the business. Although the potter was reluctant to let go, he began to realize, as the years went by, that he really had no choice: his health and endurance were waning. But he wanted to keep the business in the family. Seeing the family name on the building gave him a sense of the continuity of life. For him, the business was a way of keeping the family together. After all, he had worked so hard primarily to create a better life for all of them.

When the potter died, he left the company to his two sons and only daughter. Under their guidance, the factory and the sales outlets continued to prosper. Indeed, more plants opened, and then more; the operation expanded across borders, and the business diversified into related products such as glass, crystal, and silverware.

When the children's children became older, they were also brought into the business. Unfortunately, with so many family members around, the original family cohesiveness began to unravel and things started to go downhill. There were periods when those who could remember times past thought nostalgically of the good old days – times when the old man was in control. Everything had seemed so much simpler then; everyone knew who was in charge!

The cousins and siblings began to argue about money, shares, power, and responsibilities: who got what and who made what. Envy reared its ugly head. Eventually, what had started as mere bickering degenerated into bitter feuding. The two brothers and the sister, along with their wives, husband, and children, spent all their time and energy fighting, while employees were forced to choose one of the many factions. Soon the most capable employees began to leave. Product quality decreased, and customers stopped buying.

In the end, the strife led to bankruptcy for the company and poverty for the family members. Thus ended the potter's dream. The family had gone from rags to riches to rags in only three generations.

The people in this fairy tale did not live happily ever after. Clearly, they made a mess of things. But when it comes to working at family businesses, we are talking about more than fairy tales. Stories like this are told all too often in the popular press. Examples of destructive family feuds are not hard to find.

Take, for example, Edward Wyllis Scripps, one of the most colorful pioneers in American newspaper history. Scripps was responsible for creating the country's first major chain of newspapers with his Penny papers, so named because they were sold at a cheaper price than the competition's. These papers became America's first popular press, and United Press (the media wire service) eventually grew out of Scripps's empire. During his lifetime, Scripps got along with almost nobody. He feuded for twenty years with his older brother – the person who had given him his start at the newspaper. His relationship with his oldest son, Jim (who contributed considerably to the success of the newspaper chain), was equally stormy. In 1921, Scripps threw Jim out of the business, and he continued his mean-spirited ways after Jim's death by disinheriting his widow and her children, an uncommon act of vindictiveness (Casserley, 1993).

Another example of numbing family strife is the saga of the three Horvitz brothers, heirs to one of America's largest fortunes: a $700 million newspaper, cable television, and real estate empire. After their father died, the fight over who would gain control of the business began in earnest. It reached an appalling crescendo when the mother, who had acted as peacemaker, died. Accusations and counter-accusations flew; fistfights became par for the course. Lawsuits on both sides led to years of legal wrangling. As a son of one of the brothers said, "Decisions were based on how the brothers felt when they were twelve" (Gubernick and King, 1987, p. 81).

Factional infighting can become extremely complex in firms that have survived a number of generations and are run by large families. Obviously, maintaining a cohesive family unit becomes more difficult as the generations spread out. Too much time may be spent on conspiratorial activities rather than on the substance of the business. The politics of succession may become a major diversion as emotion overpowers reason.

The statistics concerning the longevity of family firms are nothing to brag about, because family firms have a built-in Achilles' heel. The two systems that interact in these firms – the family and the business – are not necessarily compatible. On the contrary, they are often in conflict with each other.

From a systems perspective, identifying role and mood carryovers from one of these two systems to the other can be worthwhile (Rosenblatt *et al.*, 1985). The role relationships of parent and offspring or of husband and wife in the family system, for example, tend to be transferred to and repeated in the business system, complicating relationships in both. A spouse supervising a spouse, parents supervising children, a sibling supervising a sibling – all these are situations that can create an emotional burden for marital, family, and work relationships. It suggests that in a family the most infectious diseases tend to be psychological.

What are some of the issues for people – family members and non-family members alike – who work for family businesses? How do people describe the strengths and weaknesses of these companies? In this chapter, I will look at the proverbial tip of the iceberg, focusing on the more traditional family business issues from a management point of view.

THE GOOD NEWS

For family members, one of the obvious advantages of working for the family firm is the perception (illusory as it may be, as we will see later) of being in control of one's own destiny. Running something in which one has a personal stake certainly creates a feeling of independence. Moreover, the narcissistic pleasures inherent in such a situation are not to be underestimated. To have one's name on a building makes for a sense of immortality, and it has other beneficial side effects. As one family member of a media conglomerate said, "The name I have has certainly helped me to get access to top executives of companies – persons who under other circumstances would have kept their doors shut." Nor should we underestimate the possible financial benefits: there is always the chance of becoming really successful in the family firm.

The long-term perspective

Compared to publicly held companies, family firms generally tend to have a long-term view of their business. They are not fly-by-night operations, playing for short-term gains at the cost of long-term investments. Leaders of family businesses may have a different outlook vis-à-vis their employees, their customers, the community, and other important stakeholders – an outlook that can positively affect the quality of their product. Having their name on the building or a product makes these leaders more conscious of their standing in the community, prompting them to guard their reputation jealously.

In many instances, the company and its products affect the very identity of family members. To be associated with defective or inferior products becomes a reflection on the self. Thus a family might find it singularly unattractive to go for short-term financial gains if doing so would tarnish the company's standing. When a family has been producing wine for many generations, as has the house of Torres in Spain, or trading grain food, as has Cargill in the United States, members want to be proud of their products.

Moreover, compared to publicly held corporations, family firms are not the slaves of Wall Street, haunted by quarterly results. Because they are under less pressure and less public scrutiny, they experience greater independence of action. The fact that family firms do not have to divulge as much information as publicly held corporations can be a competitive advantage, because it is not as easy for competitors to know what they are up against. Competitors who have tried to get information about famous but secretive family corporations such as Mars (the candy manufacturer), Michelin (the tiremaker), or C&A (the department store chain) know what this means.

Furthermore, privately held companies worry less about takeover threats; as a result, they have less need to create elaborate schemes involving "white knights," "poison pills," and "golden parachutes." Executives can save their energy for other causes. Finally, family firms tend to be more resilient during hard times, given their greater willingness to plow profits back into the business.

The family culture

Family businesses often have greater certainty than publicly held companies about what kind of leadership will prevail in the firm. With effective succession planning (a subject I will discuss later), everyone knows who is next in line. With this peace of mind, there tends to be less infighting for position.

The family spirit determines the prevailing attitudes, norms, and values in the company, while the values that family members express create a common purpose for employees and help to establish a sense of identification and commitment. In well-run family firms, the employees feel like part of the family, and frequently the atmosphere is much more caring than that of publicly held corporations. In addition, because there is less bureaucracy (and decision making is therefore quicker and more effective), access to senior management comes easier.

For example, the kind of corporate culture that permeates furniture manufacturer Herman Miller Inc. has become legendary. This company has been repeatedly listed as one of the best-managed companies in America. D. J. De Pree founded the company in 1923 and was succeeded first by his son, Hugh, and then by Hugh's son Max. At Herman Miller Inc., we find a group of people strongly committed to the beliefs and ideas of the senior family members, particularly those of Max De Pree. Employees share the family's outlook toward customer service, quality, and productivity – a covenant that works both ways. Family members back up their strong belief in the potential of people with a set of rights that determine the psychological contract between workers and management. Included in the "ground rules" for working at Herman Miller Inc.

are the right to be needed, the right to be involved, the right to understand, the right to affect one's own destiny, the right to be accountable, and the right to appeal decisions perceived as arbitrary or unfair.

This focus on rights goes beyond mere talk; it affects everyone's wallet. The company has a long-standing Scanlon Plan entitling workers to a share of the financial gains resulting from their suggestions for improving design, customer service, quality, and productivity.

The atmosphere and management style established in this family company have remained intact ever since the company went public. A stock option plan grants stock to all regular employees who have worked in the firm for at least a year, and there are "silver parachutes" for *all* employees in the case of an unfriendly takeover (not just golden parachutes for top management). Herman Miller Inc. continues to function less bureaucratically than would a company that has always been publicly held. The family culture continues to make the firm much less impersonal. Encouraging employees to feel like part of the family facilitates access to senior management. Even the lowliest production worker has no difficulty knocking on Max De Pree's door. Such an atmosphere expedites decision making and leads to greater flexibility of procedure and action (De Pree, 1989; Labich, 1989).

The business expertise

Family members' extensive expertise can provide family businesses with another important competitive advantage. After all, these people have been in contact with the business from early childhood onward. Breakfasts, dinners, outings, family gatherings, after-school work, and summer jobs have all created opportunities to learn more about the business.

One executive recalled how as a child he would take long walks with his father, during which they would visit stores to look at competitors' products. Afterwards, his father would ask him which products he liked most, and this would lead to lengthy discussions about each product's quality. The son felt that the expertise he gained during those informal outings about customers and competition proved invaluable later in life.

In-depth business knowledge may give family members a head start over executives entering the business later on. Early training such as this helps to explain the sometimes puzzling appointments of very young family members to senior positions. Actually, such "age-inappropriate" appointments can have a beneficial effect, in that they may lead to a rejuvenation of an arteriosclerotic group of top executives.

THE BAD NEWS

Obviously, family businesses do not create and receive only good news, as the dismal statistics about the longevity of family firms indicate. On the debit side, there are the "technical" difficulties that dog family ownership; tax codes covering inheritance, for example, can create problems that threaten the continuation of a firm. In addition, family corporations usually have greater difficulty obtaining access to capital markets, with a resultant inhibition of growth. While technical issues such as these present challenges, they are not the main areas where most family firms falter.

Organizational issues are not the primary culprit either, although the organization of family firms frequently looks messy and confusing: authority and responsibility may not be clearly defined, jobs may overlap (with even executives holding a number of different jobs), and the decision-making hierarchy may exist only to be bypassed.

Despite these technical and organizational challenges, interviews with people in family firms reveal that the key problems facing these businesses are not structural but psychological, centering on issues such as the fit between the senior executive's leadership style and the company's stage of development, the overflow of family conflicts into the business, collusion among various family members (which detracts from the substance of the business), and the question of succession.

Any of these problems can turn into high drama. At times, corporate life veers between soap opera and the extremes of Greek tragedy. Cronos, King Laius, Jocasta, Medea, and Oedipus are regular guests at the family table. Because certain psychologically based problems recur again and again, often affecting management practices, they deserve closer examination. Let us start with the more obvious problems that family businesses face.

The question of nepotism

Family logic often overrules business reason in a family firm. Senior owner-managers often show a remarkable capacity for closing their eyes to the weaknesses of their beloved sons or daughters, welcoming family members regardless of their ability to contribute to the business.

Working under a person who is clearly incompetent places a non-family member in a highly undesirable position. When there is a blatant imbalance between contribution and credit, employees cannot feel that they are in an equitable situation. This absence of fair play undermines one of the pillars of corporate culture: trust. Lack of trust in turn influences job satisfaction, motivation, and performance.

This situation is particularly ironic if, as is often the case in family firms, family members demand a high level of commitment from non-family members. Such demands are acceptable if management gives non-family members due credit for work well done; they are unacceptable, however, if the existing incentive system is heavily biased toward non-contributing family members. In such a case, it becomes difficult to attract capable managers, endangering the company's future. The people who are willing to stick around under such circumstances may not be the ones the company needs most.

Consider the example of a well-known firm in the clothing business.[1] The president of this company, Jack Lang, was completely blind to the incompetence of his only son, Tom. Having survived a severe coronary attack, Jack (encouraged by his wife) placed Tom, who had been busy flunking out of every school he had been sent to, in a senior position. Tom's behavior quickly soured the atmosphere in the company. His worst habits included laying the blame on others for forgetting appointments, failing to follow up on clients, and allocating resources poorly; nothing was ever his fault. Eventually, many of the more competent employees could take it no longer and left the company. When Tom, against all advice, acquired a firm with outdated product lines and obsolete machinery, the whole company went into the red. This finally opened the father-president's eyes: Jack Lang realized what had been going on and reasserted his control.

The Spoiled Kid Syndrome

In the typical family business scenario, the principal protagonist is a hard-working entrepreneur completely obsessed by his business. He (it is usually a man) works day and night, thinking about nothing else. Obviously, this lifestyle leaves him very little time to devote to his family. Although he is aware of what he is doing, he cannot help himself: he perceives the demands of the business as too overwhelming. He rationalizes his behavior by saying that he is working so commitedly in the best interests of the family, cherishing the notion that, because of his efforts, everyone will be better off later on. He fails to realize, however, that he may be cannibalizing that very future. There may be no "later on," because he is not spending any effort on one of his most important tasks: educating his children to become responsible human beings. Often these men gradually become estranged from their children as well as their wives.

A man who gets caught in this kind of behavior trap often develops feelings of guilt. To deal with such feelings, he begins bribing the family members, paying them off for not being available emotionally or otherwise. The payoff may start with a big teddy bear when the children are young; later, it may take the form of sports cars, jewelry, expensive vacations, or condominiums. Unfortunately, these gifts will never replace the attention the children missed during childhood.

Often the seeming generosity of the gift-giving father serves another purpose: the possessions he lavishes on his children are a way of making up not only for his absence but also for hardships that he himself experienced. He is giving to his children what he once longed for himself. In trying to create a better life for his offspring, he is full of good intentions. But his behavior creates more problems than it solves. Possessions – rather than a set of well-internalized values, feelings of affection, and mutual respect – become the overriding reward for the children.

A family firm famous for its consumer products offers a prime example of the spoiled kid syndrome. After the death of the founder, the children battled for control of the business. In talking to some of the people in the know, I learned that the children had been spoiled rotten in terms of material possessions as they grew up. One of these people said of this entrepreneur, "When it came to his children, John's pockets were deep; there was nothing they couldn't have. They were never to know the kind of life he had had, growing up in poverty. Proven accomplishments that applied to all the other people working for John didn't apply to them."

From interviews with people involved in the company, it became clear that John and his wife had paid very little attention to the intangible needs of their children. They seemed to have given little value to education, business training, and social responsibility and to have rejected the notion that with authority comes responsibility. After John's death, his children wielded enormous power as the company's major shareholders, and their poor understanding of the business had catastrophic consequences. The rivalry between the children, suppressed while their father was alive (but unconsciously encouraged by his behavior), made the situation far worse and led eventually to the company's breakup.

The ghost of the padrone

Another difficulty inherent in family firms is the tendency toward autocracy. Many founder-entrepreneurs have rather autocratic, domineering personalities; after all, without their dominance and persistence, the company would never have taken off. But the corollary of autocratic rule is paternalism. What started off as "well-meaning" behavior may end up as a stifling or even perverted imposition of the founder's personal style.

A good example of paternalism carried to the point of moral caricature is found in the house of Krupp, the 400-year-old dynasty that armed Germany during four major wars. For generations, members were guided by Alfred Krupp's *Generalregulativ*, the company constitution laid down in 1872. This document detailed the absolute obligations of the *Kruppianer* (Krupp employees). It said, among other things, that the house of Krupp was entitled to receive from its workers full and undivided energy, punctuality, loyalty, and love of good order. Furthermore, a *Kruppianer* who ran up debt would be sacked; anyone arriving five minutes late would lose an hour's wage; troublemakers would be dismissed.

Despite these punitive rules, Krupp's social welfare policy made it hard for the *Kruppianer* to leave. The employees were entitled to health services, an emergency relief fund, pension schemes, low-cost housing, non-profit retail outlets, and homes for the aged – all welfare policies undoubtedly ahead of their time. The company's paternalistic attitude became a grotesque travesty during the Second World War, however, when Krupp, despite its enlightened policies, willingly used almost 100,000 prisoners of war and concentration camp inmates as slave laborers (Manchester, 1970).

While the Krupp dynasty may be an extreme example of paternalistic, autocratic rule, lesser examples are not hard to find. One can hypothesize that people willing to work under such conditions are likely to possess many of the characteristics of the dependent personality (Millon, 1981). If this hypothesis is true, these companies attract "yea-sayers" – hardly the kind of people to move the company forward. A company haunted by the "ghost of the *padrone*" can, then, be secretive, conservative, and traditional. Consequently, it may become too inward-looking, ignoring developments in the environment. Naturally, such an attitude does not foster change and can seriously threaten the firm's continuity and survival.

Milking the business

Another problem arises when companies are turned into a kind of "summer camp" for family members. The logic runs as follows: the new generation should be kept busy, but since these individuals have not acquired many useful skills, they need to be given something to "play" with. What better playground than the company? That viewpoint, however, can lead to costly mistakes. When a number of family-member employees add little or no value, the company risks turning into a welfare institution that gives family members "something to do" without actually engaging them in any productive work. Most companies cannot afford to have many of these people around for long. Apart from the financial strain, unproductive hangers-on can lead to serious morale problems: hard-working employees who have to pull the weight of others become increasingly resentful. Furthermore, these hangers-on, as owners, can have an unholy influence on strategic decision making, self-assuredly making recommendations regarding issues they know nothing about.

In one consumer products company, three of the five family-member employees drew large salaries, used company-chauffeured cars and planes, and lived in company financed luxury apartments. Furthermore, they spent most of their time at a fishing camp or on the golf course, participating courtesy of company memberships. However, the occasional hours they spent at the office did more harm than good. When the economy turned sour and the company went into the red, these individuals refused to accept the new reality, in spite of warnings by a company adviser. In due course, the company went bankrupt.

I have addressed in this chapter some of the obvious complications of life in family-controlled businesses (see Figure 2.1 for a summary). While under certain circumstances these enterprises can have major business advantages over publicly held firms, their problems can be serious symptoms of dangerous conflicts having to do with the relationships between family members. To understand these underlying dynamics, we have to delve much deeper, taking a look at some important psychodynamic themes. A starting point for that exploration is the inner world of the person who is the creator of the family firm: the entrepreneur – the subject of Chapter 3.

ADVANTAGES	DISADVANTAGES
Long-term orientation	Limited access to capital markets
Independence of action • Little (or no) pressure from stock market • Little (or no) takeover risk	Confusing organizations • Messy structure • Lack of clear division of tasks
Family culture as a source of pride • Stability • Strong identification/commitment/ motivation • Continuity in leadership	Nepotism • Dominance of family reasons over business logic • Tolerance of inept family members • Inequitable reward systems • Difficulties in attracting professional management
Resilience in hard times • Willingness to plow back profits	Spoiled kid syndrome
Limited bureaucracy and impersonalism • Flexibility	Internecine strife • Quick decision making • Family disputes that overflow into business
Financial benefits • Possibility of great success	Paternalistic/autocratic rule • Resistance to change • Secrecy • Attraction of dependent personalities
Knowledge of the business • Early training for family members	Financial strain • Family members milking the business • Disequilibrium between contribution and compensation
	Succession dramas

Figure 2.1 Family-controlled firms

Note

1 All names in this book are disguised except in references to business people who are in the public domain.

Chapter 3

The intrapsychic world of the entrepreneur

As we saw in the fairy tale told in the previous chapter, every family firm starts somewhere, usually with a founder-entrepreneur who has not only a business concept but also the will and persistence to bring that concept to fruition. Many people have ideas, but very few have the stamina to turn their ideas into action; and as some aspiring entrepreneurs have discovered the hard way, a vision without action is nothing more than an hallucination. To be successful, entrepreneurs must have *both* vision and drive. Even entrepreneurs who possess those attributes have to overcome many odds, however. And successful entrepreneurs do: they are the kind of people who will go to great lengths to turn their fantasies into reality.

As the number of failed start-ups indicates, many things can go wrong along the way. One frequent problem is the entrepreneurial disposition: most entrepreneurs are not easy people to work with. Far from it, as many executives who have had dealings with entrepreneurs can testify, including those who have acquired entrepreneurial firms and tried to co-opt the previous owners into their own organization.

James Henderson, president and CEO of an established company in the office equipment industry, is a good example of that latter sort of executive. He had the opportunity to acquire a small electronics components business whose founder had no successor. Since the company's products were a valuable addition to his office equipment line, Henderson was eager to pursue the matter. He was not sure what kind of arrangement he should make with the company's founder and owner, Tom Freeman, however. During their discussions of the buyout, Freeman indicated that he was prepared to stay on for some time after selling his company. Although Henderson recognized Freeman's contribution to making the company a big success, he wondered how a continuing association would work out. Once before he had tried to take an entrepreneur on board, and he still remembered that period as a major headache. In fact, the relationship turned into such a big mess that it had to be settled in court. Now Henderson was asking himself if this situation would be any different. Would Freeman's personal style be in tune with Henderson's organization? Were there any aspects of Freeman's personality that he should watch out for? What would be the indicators of dysfunctional behavior? Would Freeman accept being in a subordinate position and having Henderson as his boss?

James Henderson's concerns are not outlandish. Many entrepreneurs find it hard to accept another company's way of doing things and can create a working atmosphere that makes adaptation difficult. On the other hand, obstructive behavior is not always the norm; quite a few entrepreneurs are well equipped to deal with different company environments.

This little case vignette brings us to the question of what entrepreneurs who found family businesses are like. What distinguishes them from other businesspeople? Although as a group they are not easy to describe, some characteristics seem to be common to all of them.

Generally, founder-entrepreneurs are achievement-oriented, they like taking responsibility for decisions, and they dislike repetitive, routine work. Creative entrepreneurs possess high levels of energy and great degrees of perseverance and imagination; this combination, along with a willingness to take calculated risks, enables them to transform what may have begun as a very simple, ill-defined idea into something concrete. Furthermore, entrepreneurs can instill highly contagious enthusiasm in an organization (Kent, *et al.*, 1982; Sexton and Smilor, 1986; Dyer, 1992). By conveying a sense of purpose, they convince others that they are where the action is. Whatever it is – seductiveness, gamesmanship, or charisma – entrepreneurs somehow know how to lead an organization and give it momentum.

Despite their mystique, however, these founders of business enterprises can have personality quirks that make them tough people to work with. Their personal development may have something to do with it: quite a few aspiring entrepreneurs had to deal with many hardships while growing up. For some of them, dislocation, poverty, death, illness, and desertion were major themes of childhood (Collins and Moore, 1970; Kets de Vries, 1977, 1996), and these experiences color their outlook on the world later in life.

Some of the other difficulties entrepreneurs can create in their own firms stem from their bias toward action, which makes them respond quickly rather than thoughtfully at times; this tendency can have dire consequences for an organization. Additionally, some entrepreneurs – especially those who found it hard to follow orders as employees – have great difficulty taking direction from experts whose help they need in running their own business. Most important, many of them have difficulties with authority figures and structured situations, which leads them to conclude that they had better take charge of everything themselves.

As Derek du Toit, an entrepreneur himself, admits, "The entrepreneur who starts his own business generally does so because he is a difficult employee. He does not take kindly to suggestions or orders from other people and aspires most of all to run his own shop. . . . His idiosyncrasies do not hurt anybody so long as the business is small, but once the business gets larger, requiring the support and active cooperation of more people, he is at risk if he does not change his approach. It has been correctly stated that the biggest burden a growing company faces is having a full-blooded entrepreneur as its owner!" (1980, p. 44).

Du Toit raises questions about what you should look out for if you deal with one of these founder-entrepreneurs. What can cause problems? Are there pitfalls to avoid? If so, what are the options in difficult situations? What provisions can you make to accommodate the typical entrepreneur? Do founder-entrepreneurs have more personal problems than other people? In short, what is the dark side of entrepreneurship?

DECIPHERING THE INTRAPSYCHIC THEATER

In addressing these questions, let us keep in mind that entrepreneurs are not a homogeneous group. They come in all shapes and sizes, each with his or her own characteristics. Those I discuss here are founder-entrepreneurs I have studied and worked with whose personalities were responsible for their own or their companies' failures (Kets de Vries, 1977, 1996). To make these people more understandable, I will try to decode some of the themes prevalent in their intrapsychic theater.

The need for control

A significant theme in the life and personality of many founder-entrepreneurs I have known is their need for control. Occasionally, that need affects entrepreneurs' ability to take or give direction appropriately and has serious implications for how they get along with others. Some entrepreneurs are strikingly ambivalent when an issue of control surfaces: they are filled with fantasies of grandiosity, influence, power, and authority, yet they also feel helpless. They seem to fear that their grandiose desires will get out of control and place them ultimately at the mercy of others.

Consequently, some of the founder-entrepreneurs I have studied have serious difficulty addressing issues of dominance and submission and are suspicious of authority. This attitude contrasts greatly with that of hired business executives. While executives seem able to identify in a positive and constructive way with authority figures, using them as role models, many of the entrepreneurs I have observed lack the executive's fluidity in changing from the role of superior to that of subordinate. Instead, they often experience structure as stifling. They find it very difficult to work with others in structured situations – unless, of course, *they* create the structure and the work is done on *their* terms.

This attitude may originate in a family constellation in which the child does not properly identify with parental authority and does not perceive dealing with authority figures as a positive experience. In these situations, authority figures are perceived as dangerous: they are inconsistent, unpredictable, and over-controlling. Consequently, the child (and later the adult) turns into a rebel. Every authority figure (real or fantasized) triggers misplaced transference reactions, creating an irresistible urge to fight authority and thereby complicating relationships.

Larry Malcolm, a successful founder-entrepreneur in the sporting goods industry, is a typical example of this kind of personality. In my discussions with him, he talked about the fights he used to have with his father. He explained that he had run away from home a number of times. Only the efforts of his uncle, with whom he often sought refuge, made him return home. He had great problems when he had to work for other people, always getting into arguments with the person in charge. After he dropped out of college, Malcolm started work as a sporting goods salesperson for a department store. He liked the experience (sports had always been his great passion), but a fight with the department head over the "right" way of displaying merchandise prematurely ended his stay. He then found a clerical position in an apparel company that manufactured active wear. Although he managed to stay on longer at this job, he disliked the working environment, felt stifled, and finally quit.

In his third job, Malcolm did not fare much better, but by this time, he had begun to realize that working for others was not his forte. Not knowing what to do and wanting time to think about the future, he took his savings and made an extensive trip to Europe. At a sporting goods fair in Germany, he met a designer whose work he liked. Returning to the United States with some of the man's designs, Malcolm managed to get a few orders from a department store and a number of small retail operations. All of a sudden, he found himself running his own business.

Larry Malcolm's story is not unusual. Not only are many founder-entrepreneurs allergic to authority figures and organizational rules; they also seem to be driven by a "magnificent obsession" – some idea, concept, or theme that haunts them and eventually determines what kind of business they choose to be in. Malcolm's great passion was sports, for example, and that passion extended to everything related to sports. This partially explains his talent for finding designs that were both functional and attractive.

Many founder-entrepreneurs are, in effect, misfits who need to create their own environment. Offering the deference a subordinate usually owes a superior often suffocates this type of person. Many of the entrepreneurs I have studied are preoccupied with the threat of subjection to some external control or infringement on their will. When such people are suddenly placed in a subordinate position, power conflicts are inevitable. They then tell themselves that they do not want to be at the mercy of others. Even when they move away from old controlling influences, these concerns linger on.

There is another aspect to the superior-subordinate relationship that affects entrepreneurs. People who are overly concerned about being in control generally have little tolerance for subordinates who think for themselves. As a result, they are not likely to delegate. In entrepreneurial organizations, this desire for control can lead to extreme behavior; a founder-entrepreneur might ask, for example, to be kept informed about even the most minute operational details. One entrepreneur I studied – a man responsible for a $20 million consumer products operation – opened not only his own personal mail every morning but also all mail directed to the company. In addition, he had to approve all requisitions, no matter how small. He justified his actions by saying that they gave him a feel for the overall functioning of the organization.

That once may have been the case, when his company was small. But a concern with that level of detail, while sometimes appropriate in the start-up phase, increasingly becomes a burden to the organization: it stifles the information flow, hampers decision making, and inhibits the attraction and retention of capable managers. In this entrepreneur's situation, although his subordinates admired many of his qualities, they deeply resented being infantilized. Good performers did not stay. Moreover, because true account-ability was lacking, information needed for decision making did not circulate. As a result, sales and profits plateaued, and the future growth of the enterprise was endangered. Buyers of entrepreneurial companies started by such people should be prepared to inherit a mediocre management group.

The sense of distrust

Among many entrepreneurs, a proclivity toward suspicion of others is closely related to the need for control. What makes some of these founder-entrepreneurs stand out as extreme examples is their distrust of the world around them. Perhaps because some of them had the experience of being victimized while growing up, they live in fear of being victimized again. That childhood experience left them with a paranoid streak: they are always on guard against authority figures, always ready should disaster strike. Paradoxically, quite a few of these people feel at their best when their fortunes are at their lowest. There is a cyclical nature to their behavior. When they are at the top of the success wave, they imagine themselves incurring the envy of others, a legacy of dysfunctional parental or sibling relationships. So as not to tempt the wrath of the gods, when people ask them how things are, they respond by saying that business is "only so-so" or "not too bad." But if their fortunes turn and they are close to bankruptcy, it is as if they have paid the price, done their penance for having been successful. Because it produces a sense of relief, their predicament can have a positive effect on them. With the alleviation of anxiety, they have the energy to start anew, which they do with enthusiasm and a sense of purpose.

People who are dysfunctional in this way are continually scanning the environment for something to confirm their suspicions. This behavior pattern does, of course, have its constructive side: it makes these people alert to competitor, supplier, customer, or government moves that affect the industry. But while anticipating the actions of others protects these entrepreneurs from being taken unaware, such vigilance can also lead them to lose all sense of proportion. Focusing on certain trouble spots and ignoring others, founder-entrepreneurs burdened by this proclivity may blow up trivial things and lose sight of the reality of their situation.

When a strong sense of distrust, assisted by a need for control, takes over, the consequences for the organization are serious: sycophants set the tone, people stop acting independently, and political gamesmanship becomes rampant. In these situations, the troubled founder-entrepreneur can interpret harmless acts as threats to his or her control and see those acts as warranting destructive counter-action.

Sometimes these threats are seen as coming from competitors. In one case I studied, an entrepreneur hired a consultant to help him assess his company's profitability by product line and then to develop and implement a strategic marketing plan. When the consultant arrived, the entrepreneur would not let him look at the financial statements, however, on the grounds that the consultant might use the information to help the competition. At another time, when his machines were idle and he had to lay off employees, this same person refused to sell goods-in-process to a non-competing business because he had once been burned when a competitor used his goods-in-process to manufacture a line of products that competed with his own, and he was not going to let that happen again.

In other cases, threats are perceived as coming from within. One entrepreneur had television cameras monitoring the front and back entries of both his plant and his office building. To allay his fears that employees were stealing from him, he kept two split-screen consoles on his desk and watched them constantly.

It can be difficult to counter such distorted forms of reasoning and action, because *some* reality always lies behind fears and suspicions. If one looks hard enough, there is always some confirmation of the founder-entrepreneur's suspicions – someone stealing something, for example. Unfortunately, the entrepreneur who manages this way forgets the price the company pays when employees are exposed to constant distrust: deteriorating morale, low employee satisfaction, and declining productivity.

The desire for applause

The classic heroic myth begins with the story of the hero's humble birth, describes his rapid rise to prominence and power, and then tells of his conquest of the forces of evil, his vulnerability to the sin of pride, and finally his fall through betrayal or heroic sacrifice. The basic themes – birth, conquest, pride, betrayal, and death – are relevant to all of us. And with the symbolic Greek chorus of the employees – consultants and other outsiders in the background – applauding the entrepreneur's achievements but warning him about pride, these themes are particularly important to some founder-entrepreneurs as they act out a heroic myth in a theatrical event that leads many of them to live with a great deal of tension.

The origin of the need to play a particular mythological role may have something to do with a lack of recognition while the entrepreneur was growing up. Perhaps the entrepreneur's parents were not sufficiently encouraging to the developing child; perhaps something else did not go right when he or she was developing as a person. Future entrepreneurs lack a secure sense of self-esteem and are left with a strong need to show the world that they have to be taken into account, that they matter. Consequently, besides feeling that they are living on the edge, that their success will not last, many of these people also have an overriding concern to be heard and recognized, to be seen as heroes. They need to show others that they amount to something, that they cannot be ignored.

A very gifted founder of one enterprise was experiencing great stress while working out how fast to expand his business. During this time of stress, he repeatedly had a dream in which he was standing on a balcony, looking down to see a group of women smiling admiringly up at him. This scene would soon fade, and the admirers would turn into harpies. Feeling suffocated, he would wake up screaming. He also recalled dreams of himself as a swaggering cowboy climbing an ever-narrowing trail leading to the top of a mountain. But below the top, a gate blocked the road. To move past it, he had to risk sliding back down the mountainside he had worked so hard to scale.

Symbolically, these two dreams demonstrate, albeit in a simplified way, both wishes and fears. One of the more noticeable characteristics of both dreams is their grandiosity; they involve high positions – balconies and mountains – and the way to both is viewed by the actor in the dream as fraught with many dangers. We want to ask, "Why does he want to go there at all? Who is he trying to impress? What are the dangers? How do women figure in all of it? What makes him scream, and what causes the feelings of suffocation? What is behind his hyperactivity?"

As I have indicated, one way of looking at such a person's need for applause is as a reaction against feeling insignificant, of being a nothing. Some founder-entrepreneurs I have known hear an inner voice that tells them they will never amount to anything. But regardless of who put this idea into their minds, these people are not retiring types who take such rebuke passively; they are the defiant ones who deal with it creatively through action. They possess enough inner strength to prove the voice wrong and show the world that they *do* amount to something. They fight their way to the top in spite of all the dangers; they get the applause; they find a way to master their fears.

A manifestation of this need for applause is seen in entrepreneurs who feel compelled to build monuments as symbols of their achievements. The term "edifice complex" is sometimes used to describe such people. The monument may be an imposing office building or production facility; sometimes it is a product that takes on symbolic significance. For example, because he wanted to show people in the section of town where he grew up that he had amounted to something, one entrepreneur built an imposing head office and new factory. The contrast between his building and the decrepit surroundings was striking. That this action jeopardized the company's financial position – it was during a period of economic decline, and all his advisers advocated offshore production – made the decision even more bizarre.

Given these strong needs, it is reasonable to ask if it is possible to harness them. Can such entrepreneurs relinquish their need to invest in certain organizational symbols? Can they live under the constraints of corporate budgets, expense controls, and long-range plans? Can they adapt their leadership style?

DEFENSIVE STRUCTURES

People's personalities are largely determined by the way they balance their intrapsychic view of the world with external reality. Character consists of the enduring, pervasive behavior patterns that complex, deeply embedded psychological characteristics create (Kets de Vries and Perzow, 1991). Although each of us may behave differently, one thing we all have in common are defenses that help us deal with the stresses and strains of daily life. The relationships we develop with others are colored by the kinds of defenses we use.

People who are in trouble psychologically (who have difficulty balancing their internal and external worlds) often resort to "splitting" as a way of coping. Splitting, as I noted in Chapter 1, is the tendency to see everything as either ideal (all good) or persecutory (all bad). This splitting extends to the way these people see both themselves and others; their perspective becomes so dramatically oversimplified that they fail to appreciate the complexity and ambiguity inherent in human relationships. Instead, they tend to see other people and themselves in extremes, idealizing some people and vilifying others. Their attitudinal pendulum shifts all too easily.

Let us look at an example. One founder-entrepreneur I studied made a point of hiring young MBAs just out of school. He would marvel at their mastery of the latest management techniques and hold the new executives up as examples for his other employees, telling them that these were the kinds of executives they needed to ensure the future of the firm. Inevitably, his lavish praise would stir up enormous resentment among the rest of the employees (with predictable spiteful consequences). But also, just as inevitably, the president's infatuation with his latest recruits would soon exhaust itself, and disappointment would set in. No new recruit could live up to his exaggerated expectations, and eventually the latest MBA, like others before, would leave or be asked to go.

We all have a tendency to externalize internal problems: we "project" our discomforts and fears onto others. When we attribute to someone or some event a threat we feel, that threat becomes more manageable; but if this tendency becomes exaggerated and serves as the predominant reaction to stressful circumstances, it can be problematic. Such scapegoating is a method that people commonly adopt in an effort to see themselves as blameless: they project on the outside world what they fear in themselves. If used to the extreme, though, this way of managing stress becomes a dysfunctional personality characteristic.

People endowed with this characteristic experience little sense of personal responsibility. They distance themselves from problems and deny and rationalize away whatever responsibility they have. They refuse to see what they do not want to see and instead blame others. In an organization, this kind of thinking contributes to political infighting, denial of responsibility, insularity, and the creation of warring factions.

One founder-entrepreneur I know refused to accept reports that sales were dropping rapidly and that a number of creditors were ready to pull the plug. Instead of recognizing that the downturn resulted from mismanagement on his own factory floor and in his own design department, he denied responsibility in the matter and blamed adverse indications on the government and on customer malice. He also kept arguing that the new product line had miraculous potential, and nobody in the company was bold enough to contradict his statements. Instead, his subordinates continually reassured each other that the president's opinion must be correct. The banks eventually intervened and declared bankruptcy.

Finally, quite a few founder-entrepreneurs I have worked with are inclined to deal with the difficulty they experience controlling impulses and managing anxiety and depression by turning the passive into the active. Such entrepreneurs defend against their anxiety, which is evidenced by their restlessness and irritability, by turning to action as an antidote.

As these founder-entrepreneurs try to steer between their fear of success and their fear of failure – as they wonder, often unconsciously, whether success will last or whether they will suffer the dreaded fate of the mythical hero – they finally cannot stand the tension. Their fears heighten their anxiety until they flee into action, even impulsive and thoughtless action. It is not so much that waiting out events has no attraction for them as that they fear that being passive will make them overdependent, ultimately controlled by others. The only option they finally see is to act counter-dependently.

Most of us work continually to keep a balance between dependency needs and the wish to do things on our own, to be independent. Some founder-entrepreneurs seem to have a particularly rough time maintaining this balance and preserving a stable image of themselves; they teeter, prone to deep mood swings. There is a cyclothymic quality to their behavior (American Psychiatric Association, 1994; Kets de Vries, 1996). When things are going well, everything is terrific. But when the bubble bursts and something goes wrong, the pendulum shifts completely in the other direction. Then everything is terrible, the situation is hopeless, and bankruptcy is just around the corner.

One founder-entrepreneur I got to know compared himself at one point to the mythological King Midas, implying that everything he touched turned to gold. He would describe at great length the fantastic success and profitability of his company. In this state of mind, letting himself see only what he wanted to see and using all the defensive patterns I have just described, he did not bother to read sales and financial reports. If anyone questioned him about that lack, he would say that his reporting system was just fine; everything was terrific. Only news from the head office controller pointing out that the company had suffered a loss during the previous quarter roused him from his self-deceptive state. Needless to say, he did not take the report with equanimity; his mood plunged. He feared that he was in over his head and that his operation was finished. It took him some time to pull himself together.

TURNING ON THE LIGHT

I have described some of the darker sides of the behavior of founder-entrepreneurs in this chapter. The cases I have outlined here are extreme; not all entrepreneurs self-destruct. Entrepreneurs do not necessarily have more personal problems than other people, nor do they inevitably have personality disorders. What we can extract from the previous descriptions of their inner theater, however, is that entrepreneurs often have unique ways of dealing with the stresses and strains of daily life. In certain instances they will be swept away by those stresses, while in other situations they manage to maintain their balance. Naturally, the influence of certain countervailing forces (such as the government, banks, labor unions, the press, and a person's health and good judgment) may help in preventing excesses.

People dealing with entrepreneurs should keep in mind that the personality quirks in evidence may be responsible for entrepreneurs' drive and energy, important factors in making them successful. Thus instead of fighting these idiosyncrasies, we should regard working with and around them as a challenge.

There are many entrepreneurs who seem to know how to manage and prepare their companies for continuity. Often their sense of reality prevents things from getting out of hand. But the boundaries between creative and aberrant behavior can be blurry; normal and irrational behavior are not discrete categories on a scale. It is generally the mix of creative and irrational that makes entrepreneurs tick and accounts for their many positive contributions in creating new industries and jobs that stimulate the economy.

Chapter 4

The psychodynamics of family firms

For every executive – as for every individual, whether in business or not – the original model of an organization is the family. As a result, how people design and manage organizations reflects how their own families operated. But in entrepreneurial and family businesses, family imagery plays an especially large role in organizational structure and function; indeed, the world of business and the world of the family become inevitably and often confusingly intertwined.

We have already examined some of the personal characteristics that affect the business environment that entrepreneurs create. In addition, we have looked at some of the issues with which family businesses struggle. In this chapter, we will look at the etiology of the intrapersonal, interpersonal, and group processes that people in entrepreneurial and family businesses have to face. What lies at the origin of all these intertwined family dynamics? The best place to begin this process of inquiry is with a discussion of narcissism.

NARCISSISTIC DEVELOPMENT

An individual's personality begins to be shaped early in life, particularly during the first three years of childhood. These are the years during which the core patterns of a person's character are developed, when we emerge as individuals with a sense of our own body, gender identity, name, mind, and personal history. The foundations are laid for the kind of person we are going to become (and are likely to remain for the rest of our life). Of course, this does not mean that later life experiences are of no importance, but these tend not to have the same impact as those of our earliest years.

The clinical term for the changes that take place during these early years of life is "narcissistic development." To many people, the word *narcissism* carries a negative connotation, evoking associations of egotism, self-centeredness, and exaggerated self-love. The Greek myth of Narcissus tells of a youth who fell in love with his own reflection in a pond and wasted away pining for his love, who was no other than himself.

While we may be amused by Oscar Wilde's comment that "to love oneself is the beginning of a lifelong romance," it is important to realize that a healthy dose of narcissism is essential for human functioning and that it helps constitute the basis of self-esteem and personal identity. But narcissism is a strange thing, a double-edged sword. Having either too much or too little of it can throw a person off balance, and when equilibrium is lost, instability may develop in the core of an individual's personality.

Narcissism (when we go beyond the everyday usage of the word) refers to a stage of infantile development we all have to pass through, a stage during which the growing child derives pleasure from his own body and its functions. This early stage is an extremely delicate time in the child's life. The kind of treatment he or she receives will very much color his or her view of the world right through adulthood.

The role of parents and carers in the development of narcissism is obviously very important. Are these people supportive and consistent or rejecting and inconsistent? Are family circumstances such that the child is subjected to a number of traumatic experiences? Does the child receive a sufficient quantity of narcissistic "supplies"? Support and care are a sine qua non for establishing the foundation of a secure sense of identity and positive self-regard. But of course no parent is perfect, and becoming a person is not at all like that comfortable period of intrauterine existence when everything was auto-matically taken care of. While growing up cannot take place without a certain degree of frustration, normal development requires that frustration occurs in tolerable doses.

In an attempt to deal with the frustration of not receiving perfect care – that is, having every wish taken care of instantly – children try to retain their original impression of the perfection and bliss of the early years by creating both a grandiose, exhibitionistic image of themselves and an all-powerful, idealized image of their parents, with the latter taking on the roles of saviors and protectors. Psychoanalysts call these two narcissistic configurations the "grandiose self" and the "idealized parent image" (Kohut, 1971, 1977; Kohut and Wolf, 1978). Over time, if children receive what can be described as "good enough" care, the two configurations that make up the bipolar self are tamed by the forces of reality. Parents, siblings, and other important figures modify children's exhibitionistic displays, channeling grandiose fantasies of power and glory in proper directions and laying the foundation for realistic ambitions, stable values, well-defined career interests, and a secure sense of self-esteem and identity.

People who grow up with an opportunity to experience healthy narcissism become "constructive narcissists." They are well balanced and have both a positive self-regard and a secure sense of self-esteem (Kets de Vries and Miller, 1984a; Kets de Vries, 1989, 1993). In addition, they have the capacity for introspection, radiate a sense of positive vitality, and are capable of empathetic feelings. Narcissists of this type can become excellent leaders.

But not everyone is lucky enough to establish a special caring bond within the family or to receive age-appropriate frustration. Many things can go wrong in the process of growing up. Prolonged disappointment due to parental over-stimulation, understimulation, or highly inconsistent, arbitrary behavior, for example, can lead to problems of a narcissistic nature. And if violence and abuse are the norm in the family, the stage is set for an inner theater peopled with malevolent players.

Children who have been exposed to dysfunctional parenting may come to believe that they cannot depend on anyone's love or loyalty. As adults, they then act according to that conviction. These are people who, despite their claims to self-sufficiency, are troubled in the depth of their being by a sense of deprivation, anger, and emptiness. In order to cope with these feelings, and perhaps as a cover for their insecurity, some people allow their narcissistic needs to turn into obsessions; they become fixated on issues of power, beauty, status, prestige, and superiority. They have a grandiose sense of self-importance (exaggerating their achievements and talents), require excessive admiration, have an unrealistic sense of entitlement, can be interpersonally exploitative, and are unable to recognize or identify with the feelings of others. Furthermore, they can come across as arrogant as they try to maneuver others into strengthening their shaky sense of self-esteem (American Psychiatric Association, 1994). To add to this rather negative picture, people with narcissistic disorders are preoccupied with thoughts of getting even for the injuries (real or imagined) that they experienced while growing up, and they can be extremely envious. In the case of public figures, all these negative and destructive ways of relating to the world are acted out on a much larger stage later in life.

Reactive narcissism

Many people in leadership positions reach the top because they can perceive and seize a "historic moment": they are the right people with the right ideas at the right time. But clinical studies of leaders have also shown that a considerable percentage of these people have become what they are for negative reasons. For some, including many entrepreneurs, the driving force is a desire to compensate or get even for past hurts, real or imagined. Due to the hardships these people encountered in childhood, they are driven to prove the world wrong. Having felt belittled and mistreated when young, they are determined to show everyone that they are to be reckoned with.

Pierre Cardin, the French clothing designer, seems to be an example of this sort of person – a "reactive" narcissist. Growing up as an Italian youngster in France, Cardin was teased by other children, disparaged with names such as "macaroni." Cardin's family had lost most of their possessions during the war, and this had affected his father very badly (Morais, 1991). As a result, his father drifted from job to job, adding to the sense of disarray in the family. The young Cardin was kept going, in spite of all the turmoil around him, by the strong support of his mother. (This brings to mind Freud's famous statement that the child who has been the "mother's undisputed darling [will] retain throughout life the triumphant feeling, the confidence in success, which not seldom brings actual success with it" [Freud, 1917, p. 156].) We can speculate, however, that these narcissistic injuries left Cardin with a feeling of bitterness, a sense of having to get back at his tormentors by showing that he could amount to something, a drive to become the redeemer of the family. And he certainly accomplished these things in a rather nice way. Ironically, perhaps because once people had looked down on him and his family, he became a specialist in leveling. He democratized fashion and brought haute couture to the common man and woman. At present, sales under his name amount to over a billion dollars. Almost 200,000 people work for his label through more than 840 licensing arrangements in 125 countries. He has put his name on everything. He even thumbed his nose at the French upper classes by buying the famous restaurant Maxim, once their favorite watering hole. But no longer: Maxim has been democratized. You can now eat there with sales representatives from Cleveland.

While many reactive narcissists continually try to boost a defective sense of self-esteem and are preoccupied with emotions such as envy, spite, revenge, and vindictive triumph over others, Pierre Cardin's example illustrates that it is entirely possible for a person with a narcissistic disposition to channel it in a positive way. Cardin's striking need to boast about all his achievements, however, remains indicative of the fragility of his psychic equilibrium.

Although some reactive narcissists eventually overcome their feelings of bitterness and are later motivated by "reparation" – that is, trying to prevent others from suffering as they have – true reactive narcissists tend never to reach this stage; they retain their grandiose sense of self-importance, habitually take advantage of others in order to achieve their own ends, remain addicted to compliments, and continue to live under the illusion that their problems are unique. These people can never lose the feeling that they deserve favorable treatment and that the rules set for others do not apply to them. Both their envy of others and their rage when prevented from getting their own way can be formidable (Kernberg, 1975).

Managerial implications of dysfunctional narcissism

Reactive narcissism is probably the most salient indicator of defective leadership. It is at the center of a host of character problems, such as paranoid, schizoid, passive-aggressive, antisocial, abrasive, histrionic, and compulsive behavior patterns and "neurotic styles" (Kets de Vries and Perzow, 1991). And as we have seen in the previous chapters, what is bad enough in an individual can, when played out in an organizational context, have serious repercussions.

As a matter of fact, parallels can be drawn between individual pathology – excessive use of one neurotic style (such as reactive narcissism), for example – and organizational pathology, which results in poorly functioning organizations, or what I have elsewhere called "neurotic organizations" (Kets de Vries and

Miller, 1984b). "Irrational" personality characteristics exhibited by the principal decision makers in an organization can seriously affect the overall management process. To quote a Spanish proverb, "Fish start to stink at the head." At the top of a "neurotic organization" (especially one in which power is highly centralized, as usually is the case in entrepreneurial and family businesses), one is likely to find a top executive whose rigid neurotic style is strongly mirrored in the inappropriate strategies, structures, and organizational culture of his or her firm. If this situation continues for too long, the leader's actions may sow the seeds for the organization's decline or even self-destruction. In many entrepreneurial and family businesses, the peculiarities of the person in charge are very much reflected in the company's corporate culture.

Two destructive leadership styles – the "dramatic" and the "suspicious" – frequently surface in entrepreneurial and family firms. The "dramatic" organization is one run by a leader who needs constant attention, excitement, activity, and stimulation and who has a tendency toward extremes. Such leaders can be highly impulsive and dangerously uninhibited in their ventures, while subordinates attracted to dramatic organizations tend to be of the dependent type and thus have limited influence on policy making. Leaders who favor the dramatic style hoard power. Consequently, their organizations tend to be overcentralized; structure and information systems are often too primitive for the firm's many products and broad markets.

In the "suspicious" organization, leaders are guided by the belief that a menacing force is out to get them. And they act accordingly: they are vigilantly prepared to counter any and all attacks and personal threats; they are suspicious and distrustful of others and consequently tend to be secretive. In extreme situations, they may even transform a company into a kind of police state, setting up elaborate information systems to keep informed of all internal and external trends.

Naturally, the impact of these kinds of leadership on an organization can be devastating. Leaders prone to reactive narcissism, for example, do not create mature, innovative, learning organizations. On the contrary, they force their personality on their subordinates in such a way that relationships become enmeshed, true differentiation unacceptable, and uniformity the norm. Anyone who wants to remain his or her own person leaves the company, while those who decide to hang on often regress to infantile, dependent behavior patterns. For someone to be an individual in his or her own right is difficult in such organizations.

THE CHALLENGE OF BECOMING ONE'S OWN PERSON

As the previous discussion of narcissism pointed out, a major challenge in the child's developmental process is to realize a sense of differentiation, to develop as a person in one's own right. This "separation-individuation" refers to a process that takes place quite early in life (Mahler *et al.*, 1975) – one whereby the child acquires a sense of separateness, the perception that he or she is a discrete entity, a creature apart from the mother. Thus separation-individuation refers to the child's emergence as a person with a name, a body, a mind, and a personal history.

To become a whole person, to attain a coherent sense of identity, is not easy. First the child needs to attain the capacity for intrapsychic separateness, the ability to feel adequate in the absence of the other person.

The paradox of transitional space

To understand the process by which a child becomes an individual, it is important to realize that we all are in contact with two worlds: the everyday world (with all its readily identifiable demands) and an intrapsychic world (a world of inner reality, where drives, wishes, and needs rule). Early in life, it is hard to separate these two worlds; but eventually, when a person's reality testing becomes more sophisticated, the outer and inner worlds become truly separate and distinguishable. Before this happens, however, the child also has access to an important third world: a space of fantasy and illusion, a place where connections can be drawn between the other two spheres. This imaginary world is a "transitional place," an intermediate area of experience, a play area between reality and fantasy (Winnicott, 1971, 1975).

This is the world occupied by such "transitional objects" as strings, blankets, and that ultimate paradigm of transitional objects, the teddy bear. At one time these objects may be an almost inseparable part of the child, but they can also be viewed as the first not-me possessions. These familiar objects help a child link his or her outer and inner realities. When the mother is absent, transitional objects prolong the soothing and calming experiences she originally provided. Over time, the infant is able to stop using such objects by developing the capacity to internalize the soothing functions of the mother.

The capacity to explore and investigate, the development of an inner sense of cohesion and an external sense of reality, has its beginnings in the illusory transitional space of childhood. This transitional world is also the incubator for creative thought. This is where such processes as symbolization, make-believe, illusion, daydreaming, playfulness, curiosity, imagination, and wonder all begin.

Transitional objects and transitional space play a major role in our development in a very basic way: they serve to help us establish who we are. For most of us, the transitional world is part of the process of resolving the developmental tasks of childhood so that we can arrive at adulthood and maturity with a unique sense of self.

One way of looking at a family business is to see it as an intermediate area of development, as a kind of transitional object. In many instances, the family business provides family members with transitional space, a stage between the comforts of family life and the realities of the harsh outside world. This space becomes a safe haven from possibly painful experiences. The business as a transitional object may help the person take on the challenge of going from dependence and symbiotic attachment to individuation and autonomy.

Positive as this may sound, the family firm can also represent a barrier to healthy individuation. This is one of the paradoxes of the family firm: it offers enormous opportunity for taking up responsibilities at an early age; at the same time, it can become a block to further personal development. If the early environment of the child was not secure, if parents failed to provide the conditions for the attainment of true separateness, then the child may develop a shaky sense of identity in moving into adulthood – and the need for a transitional object continues. Soon that need becomes incompatible with the person's life trajectory. Like it or not, a family business is not a teddy bear. To hang on to the company as a symbolic teddy bear does not make for successful business practices. When the family business is used as a transitional object, dysfunctional processes from the family are transferred to the business and old behavior patterns perpetuate themselves in a never-ending circle. In this sense, family firms actually enhance the risk of arrested psychological development; in other words, the level of proximity and familiarity they provide adds to dysfunctional behavior. In certain family businesses, people may get stuck, never attaining a true sense of separateness.

Entangled relationships

As I have indicated, the goal of adulthood is to go from dependence to independence. In a dysfunctional family, however, this is an illusory goal. In a family where independence is not truly possible, the most that can be hoped for is a willingness to accept a state of interdependence. And if such a family runs a family firm – particularly if the firm becomes too much of a transitional object – it is quite likely that entangled family relationships will repeat themselves in the business setting. In the most extreme case, the firm will be structured in such a way that an effort is made to control the children even beyond the grave, creating in the next generation a continuing state of helplessness.

In some families that do not permit true differentiation, strong pressure is wielded to make everyone be and feel alike. People who want to go their own way are given a hard time. Criticism of "deviant" behavior is continuous until the wayward individual capitulates. Such a family is characterized by strict rules and regulations – spoken or unspoken – governing how to behave; if this family runs a family business, those behavior patterns are echoed in the culture of the company.

"Enmeshment" is another way of describing these undifferentiated relationships (Bowen, 1978; Minuchin, 1974). In the case of enmeshment, family members function as if they were part of each other. The differentiation between each member is not respected; there is no sense of specific boundaries, and relationships are symbiotic. At the other end of the scale, we find families with complete "disengagement," meaning that family members behave as if they had nothing to do with each other. Extremes of either enmeshment or disengagement make for different forms of alliances within families and may lead to collusive arrangements.

Healthy development implies adaptability: the possibility of moving back and forth between the two extremes of close involvement and aloneness. Healthy people achieve a balance between their needs for autonomy and individuality and their needs for intimacy, dependency, and belonging. People with high levels of differentiation are able to function effectively, making their own judgments and decisions independent of their family of origin. They are aware of their own strengths and weaknesses and are able to assess those of others. They clearly identify how they are different from other people. People with low levels of differentiation, however, are unable to separate their thoughts and feelings from those of their family.

The inability to attain true differentiation creates serious problems later in life. The adult will still be, in some ways, the child who has trouble standing on his or her own two feet. The situation improves for many people when they move out of the house to enter a larger circle, however; this gives them the opportunity to continue what may have been arrested development and offers them a new chance to disentangle themselves.

Children remaining in a family business have a handicap in their development. Because these children remain within a web of family relationships, true separation is much more difficult for them. Even though they are adults, their parents may treat them as if they had not yet grown up, both generations remaining locked in early family dynamics. The business itself becomes a transitional object that can never be given up, and the negative feelings of the "perpetual children" remain unresolved, often with destructive repercussions for the enterprise.

THE IMPACT OF ENVY, JEALOUSY, SPITE, AND VINDICTIVENESS

For children growing up, early experiences (both painful and pleasurable) have a great deal to do with how their future family entanglements unfold. To understand the destructive consequences of these entanglements, we have to understand their emotional origins, which often include envy. Interestingly enough, the high dramas of adult life often have deceptively innocent beginnings.

On March 27, 1995, the world was shocked to hear that Maurizio Gucci, former chairman of the Gucci luxury leather goods and fashion dynasty, had been shot in broad daylight while entering his office in central Milan – a miserable end to the career of one of the scions of the Gucci family. Maurizio Gucci's career had been marked by family feuding as he struggled with other family members for control of the company. Trials and tribulations of the family firm were a veritable soap opera: family members sued each other for breach of contract, misconduct, and even assault and battery.

Founded in 1922 by Maurizio's grandfather, Guccio, the company initially grew slowly. Post-Second World War prosperity, however, led to a period of rapid growth. In 1953, the year that saw the death of the company's founder, Gucci opened its first store in the United States. Guccio left the business to his three sons, Aldo, Vasco, and Rodolfo. Aldo, the most entrepreneurial among the brothers, was made president of worldwide operations. Vasco ran the factory, while Rodolfo was more interested in pursuing an acting career.

As the company expanded and was passed to yet another generation, it became more difficult to hold together. While the three brothers were no strangers to sibling rivalry, the fight really started when Guccio's grandchildren became involved. A true civil war began in 1980, when Rodolfo managed to get the board to fire his brother Aldo's son Paolo. Paolo then set up a new, separate venture selling similar products under the Gucci name and soon became embroiled in litigation with the relatives. Lawsuit was piled upon lawsuit. Eventually Paolo, out of spite, provided documentation showing that millions of dollars in taxable US revenue had been removed to offshore accounts in return for fictitious services. This evidence was used in court in the United States and resulted in the conviction of his father, the president of the company, on charges of tax evasion. Aldo Gucci, who eventually pleaded guilty to the US tax authorities, was fined $7.4 million in back taxes. Other lawsuits followed. Accusations of fraud and forgery became the order of the day. In 1983, when Maurizio's father, Rodolfo, died, Maurizio was accused by his relatives of forging his father's signature to evade inheritance tax. In November 1988, having been convicted of that crime, Maurizio was sentenced by a Milan court: he received a fine and a one-year suspended jail sentence (which was later overturned). In 1988, two of Maurizio's cousins sold their share in the company to an investment firm; in 1993, Maurizio followed suit, selling his share.

Newspaper accounts of the fights between Guccio's grandchildren reveal only the surface of this multigenerational drama – a drama whose origins lay with its founder (McKnight, 1987). Guccio made a habit of playing his three sons against each other, stirring up intense feelings of envy and rivalry. These emotions then echoed among *their* children as the fathers used their sons as proxies to resolve long-ago battles, trying to spite one another. Like spoiled children, the family members became obsessed by greed and devoted themselves to seeking ways to double-cross each other until their vengeful activities resulted in self-destruction.

What is envy, this emotion that can create so many difficulties for generations of family members? At its heart is an unpleasant feeling caused by the desire to possess what someone else has – perhaps wealth, power, status, love, or beauty. This feeling may then give rise to further feelings of frustration, anger, self-pity, greed, rivalry, and vindictiveness.

The first component of envy is clearly the wish to equal, imitate, or surpass the envied individual. The second component seems to be a narcissistic wound – a sense of lacking something – connected with feelings of inferiority, inadequacy, and injured self-esteem. Someone consumed by envy engages in self-devaluation while longing for a desired possession. He or she develops a feeling of anger at the possessor, which may be expressed either mildly (as chagrin or discontent), moderately (as resentment or ill will), or severely (as impulses to spoil or destroy or actions that are malicious and spiteful).

Envy is one of the most primitive and fundamental emotions. It begins to evolve as soon as the infant sees the mother's breast as the source of all gratification and good experiences. The baby wants complete possession, wants to have access to this wonderful thing all the time. But soon the infant realizes that he or she is not in full control of the object: it comes and goes. Often, just as the child is coming to terms with all this, a new baby arrives, aggravating this situation and stirring up envious feelings (Klein, 1975). The older child begins to see that love is like a zero-sum game where there are winners and losers: when the new baby gets more of the mother's attention, the older child gets less. With this realization, envious feelings become intensified in the older child. The arrival of a third person – the younger child – into the original mother–child dyad transforms the older child's rather simple envy into jealousy. Jealousy characterizes itself by the wish to hold on. It is a protest against a loss of a loved one. Unlike envy, jealousy never pertains to a two-person situation. It refers to a complex group process involving three or more people. Envy consists of the need to *have*; it is the destructive feeling that someone else possesses something desirable, that leads to the wish to spoil and take away whatever the other person has. Due to the effect of envy, rivalrous feelings build up and lead the older child to compare his or her own qualities with those of the baby. The result: a sense of competitiveness and rivalry that can extend far beyond childhood.

Because of the narcissistic injury that accompanies envy – that is, the deflation of the older child's self-image – the wish to return injury for injury may become central. Vindictive triumph – the satisfaction that comes with restoring injured pride – becomes for some people the only thing worth living for.

People who make this vindictive triumph the governing passion of their lives seem to suffer from what has been called the "Monte Cristo complex" (Castelnuovo-Tedesco, 1974). This pattern of behavior is named after the hero of Alexandre Dumas's romantic story of suffering and vindication. Victim of an injustice that led to the loss of everything dear to him and to prolonged incarceration, the hero single-mindedly spends the rest of his life tracking down his enemies and taking revenge. In the Count of Monte Cristo, as in many entrepreneurs, envy is the underlying force that fuels reactive narcissism.

The intensity of envy a child feels is very much determined by the environment provided by his or her parents. The parents' skill at providing nurturance affects the child's relationships to his or her siblings and to other people later in life. Given the difficulties many parents have in managing their own emotional lives, however, it is no wonder that they sometimes have trouble handling their children's emotions well.

One of the great challenges in parenting is to minimize the occurrence of sibling rivalry. That necessitates a considerable amount of maturity on the part of the parents: they must have a certain tolerance if they are to neutralize possible conflict in and among their children. Furthermore, parents should be able to make their children feel that their treatment of them is fair. But parents differ greatly in their ability to contain their children's envious feelings (Schoeck, 1969; Davies, 1980; Kets de Vries, 1992). In the children of those who are less successful at that task, complicated emotional entanglements leading to destructive rivalries may continue throughout their whole life, with possible disastrous effects on their business dealings.

The Wars of the Roses

Another factor that can influence how children develop and handle envy and rivalry is their parents' emotional availability. If parents are too preoccupied with themselves, the children may start fighting for whatever little quality time is available. Sibling rivalry and competitiveness then become the dominant patterns in the family. Children in households so characterized soon become expert judges in who has preference in the "love equation." When children's early feelings of envy and jealousy are not resolved, their dysfunctional entanglements are likely to linger throughout life, like a chronic disease that continues to remain troublesome.

In normal circumstances, siblings eventually separate and choose their own course in life. With time and geographical distance, residual childhood irritants and resentments are less likely to flare up; vindictive triumph becomes less of a burning passion. Joining the family firm, however, makes this resolution more difficult. Continuing closeness aggravates the situation, while the presence of the parents in the business may rub additional salt in never-healed wounds. Old feelings of envy and jealousy cannot be put to rest because all the actors in the play are still present. The family members may end up in a vicious circle of endlessly repeating conflicts – a continuation of the old emotional "games" of childhood.

Furthermore, the web of unresolved childhood entanglements becomes more dense in adulthood as other generations and in-laws join the family drama. When love has been a scarce commodity and an object of competition during the developmental years, the stage is set for later internecine strife. Because family and business disputes tend to become confused, decisions in family firms corroded by envy may be made on an emotional basis only, rather than according to sound business sense. Since these disputes have their origin in early childhood, they can become extremely messy – far more difficult to disentangle than would be the case in publicly held corporations.

This factional infighting can become extremely byzantine in family firms that have survived a number of generations and are run by large families. Obviously, maintaining a cohesive family unit becomes more difficult as the generations spread out and entanglements become progressively complex. As the Gucci case indicates, the danger is that too much time and attention will be spent on conspiratorial activities and not enough on the substance of the business.

King Laius revisited

Sibling envy and jealousy are not the only factors that contribute to dysfunctional entanglements in family businesses. Even the most basic relationships, such as those between parents and children, can be the source of problems. From a normal developmental point of view, father–son relationships are always fraught with a considerable amount of ambivalence. As Freud (1933) indicated, sons identify with their fathers and want to be like them; at the same time, every son competes with the father for the mother's attention. Fathers or mothers may become jealous of their children, given the attention they receive – attention that the spouses reserved for one another in the prechildren years. In other words, envy of and rivalry with the children may arise on the part of the parents themselves. Parents may deprive their children of certain privileges and pleasures out of envy and then hide their motivation behind an attitude of moral righteousness.

In normal circumstances, the children leave the house and these emotions fade. If the child remains in the family business, however, problems may be compounded, with parents setting traps for the younger generation, causing their grown-up children to fail or keeping them in a subservient position. Under the slogan "One day it will all be yours," they hold on to their power and keep their children down.

It can be very difficult to live in the shadow of a captain of industry, and the eldest son (women have a different relationship) bears the brunt of the father's vindictiveness. Experience has shown that children born later, as well as children of second marriages, tend to have a much easier time, perhaps because the aging entrepreneur perceives them less as a threat to his power base and more as a symbol of his potency and vitality.

In his autobiography, *Father, Son, & Co.: My Life in IBM and Beyond* (1990), Thomas Watson, Jr., describes his conflicts with his father. Watson, who was not much of a student, would come home from school in tears saying that he could not do it, referring not only to the schoolwork but also to the general expectation that he, as the oldest son, would take over the business from his father, Thomas Watson, Sr. (Although the senior Watson had a minority position at IBM, the company was run like a family enterprise.) Tom Jr. always found it difficult to live up to his father's expectations. He saw his father as a "giant of a man" who made him feel inconsequential. He was convinced that he was lacking in some way and always felt a deep uncertainty about his ability to meet the expectations of his father and of the world.

The younger Watson experienced bouts of depression as a child, often accompanied by asthma attacks. These bouts worsened after he noticed how people bowed and scraped and ingratiated themselves in his father's presence.

He saw his father as a blanket, smothering everything. Once he reached adulthood, the two men had terrible fights that frequently led to the brink of estrangement. Later on, as president of IBM, Tom Jr. performed an annual ritual on the anniversary of his father's death: he would take stock of what the company had accomplished in the past twelve months and tell his wife that he had managed yet another year alone.

Many male entrepreneurs, even those whose relationship with their father was strained, had a strong relationship with their mother as they grew up. Some of these men seemingly experienced an "Oedipal victory" by gaining the major portion of their mother's love and affection, thus bettering their father. But often these men do not allow their own sons a similar triumph. They do not let their sons shut them out as they shut out their own father. Instead, some entrepreneurs go to great lengths to belittle their sons, continually cutting them down to size. Consequently, their sons may give up, do poorly at school, and behave irresponsibly in an effort to become the antithesis of their father, either temporarily or permanently. Of course, these psychodynamic processes do not necessarily happen consciously; but whether conscious or unconscious, the experience remains emotionally devastating for the sons.

The first Henry Ford and his son, Edsel, had a particularly destructive relationship (Jardim, 1970). Henry Ford was in the habit of building his son up at times, then going out of his way to humiliate him. One of Edsel's major frustrations came from his father's continuous rejection of his well-thought-out plans to improve products and conditions in the company. Henry preferred to listen to people who were brutalizing the work environment. Edsel never found the nerve to stand up to his father, who portrayed his son as weak, incompetent, and "too fond of cocktails and decadent East Side Living" (Lacey, 1986, p. 395). The strain of this relationship led to medical problems for Edsel, probably contributing to his stomach ulcer and premature death. According to the biographer Lacey, in his book *Ford: The Men and the Machine* (1986), when Edsel died, his wife, in a fit of anger, told her father-in-law that he had killed his own son.

The Watsons and the Fords are not unique. Although most father–son relationships do not come to a tragic ending, they can complicate the puzzle of family businesses. In comparison to the father–son relationship, father–daughter, mother–daughter, and mother–son relationships are more complex from a clinical point of view. While these relationships seem to be less prone to conflict in a business context, there are so few female company presidents that it may be wise to suspend judgment regarding the family business ramifications of these relationships for the time being.

In this chapter, we have seen that the driving forces of narcissism, sibling rivalry, and envy can be very powerful indeed. If these are not properly harnessed early in life and given constructive outlets, dysfunctional entanglements may occur, with devastating results – particularly if the people in question are running a business enterprise together.

Chapter 5

The interpersonal world of business leaders

While entrepreneurs and family business owner-managers have no monopoly on dysfunctional behavior, their quirks and problems become more noticeable because they are at the top of the organization. At that level, dysfunctional behavior can have serious repercussions, impacting organizational structure and strategy and creating a company culture that mirrors the personality defects of the man or woman at the top (Kets de Vries and Miller, 1984b, 1987).

In organizations, the leader, more than other participants, has the ability to make his or her fantasies a reality. However, there is a price: this ability can cause people to lose a sense of their boundaries and can lead to all kinds of inappropriate behavior. Given the power that entrepreneurs and family business owners wield, they are particularly prone to this pitfall of leadership. When they are ruled by the darker side of their personalities, their behavior can have devastating consequences for the organization.

THE PSYCHOLOGICAL PRESSURES OF LEADERSHIP

Why do some people derail when they reach the top? What is the nature of the psychological forces that affect some entrepreneurs and family business owner-managers? Why does an individual who seems bright, likeable, and well-adjusted suddenly resort to strange behavior when he or she becomes the person in charge? There are no simple answers to these questions. In order to address them, we must deepen our understanding of the psychodynamics of leadership and the vicissitudes of power.

The case of Robert Clark

Before Robert Clark took over the family business from his father, he had always been well liked. Other employees had been impressed by his capacity for work, his helpful attitude, his dedication, and his imaginative methods for solving problems. Although there were other candidates in the family who had expressed interest in the top position, everyone had always expected Robert eventually to run the family firm. In the period immediately after Clark took over, he received many accolades for taking a number of long overdue steps. Gradually, however, many of the older employees concluded that Clark was undergoing a change of personality. He became less accessible, and his once widely acclaimed open-door policy and advocacy of participative management disappeared. He became increasingly authoritarian, impatient, and careless about the feelings of others.

The organizational effects of Clark's transformation were quickly forth-coming. The company atmosphere became increasingly politicized: because of their apprehension, the subordinates tried to please Clark in every way. Nobody took a critical stand against wrong decisions; instead, executives jostled for Clark's attention, wasting time and energy on power games and intracompany squabbles. Company morale sank to an all-time low, and the financial results were predictably dismal.

What happened to Clark – and why? Certain psychological forces – his own and those of his followers – came into play, creating a multitude of problems. Let us consider three factors that may have contributed:

- Being in charge of a company is necessarily isolating. Separated from others (who now directly report to him or her), the person at the top is left without peers. As a result, the leader's normal dependency needs for contact, support, and reassurance rise up and overwhelm him or her. In addition, the new leader of a family firm may feel a certain us-against-them mentality – himself (as a representative of the family) versus the employees.
- Whether consciously or unconsciously, employees expect their leader to have reached a high degree of perfection – perhaps even to be gifted to some degree with "magical" powers. If the founder-entrepreneur was a highly energetic and charismatic individual who built the organization based on his or her unique vision, employees may expect the same characteristics from a second-generation leader. These expectations put a lot of pressure on the person at the top.
- Troubled by guilt feelings about their success and fearful that it may not last, some leaders unconsciously cause themselves to fail. For some, failure may come as a release; at least these leaders are free to disentangle themselves from the family web and do something else with their lives.

To some degree, every human being is susceptible to these reactions and feelings. History provides innumerable examples, ranging from political leaders such as King Saul, Caligula, Nero, Hitler, Qaddafi, and Saddam Hussein to business leaders such as Howard Hughes and Robert Maxwell. This is not to say that every founder-entrepreneur or leader of a family firm will resort to pathological behavior upon reaching the top of the organization. What differentiates those who "crash" from those who do not is the latter's ability to stay in touch with reality and to deal with psychological pressures. Many leaders are very good at handling the pressures that leadership brings; indeed, some individuals who may previously have been rather colorless turn into great leaders when they attain positions of power and influence. However, some individuals who create or run a family business cannot tolerate the pressures; the regressive pulls simply become too strong. Since we are all susceptible to these psychological forces, I will discuss their dynamics in detail.

Isolation from reality

The term "loneliness of command" has been used frequently in the context of leadership. The inability to test one's perceptions, the tendency to lose touch with reality because one occupies a top position, can endanger anyone in a leadership post.

The case of Peter Noro

When the family council of the Noro Corporation made Peter Noro its new president and CEO, he thought that his personal and professional life would continue more or less as it had before. The appointment had been very routine; as one of the senior vice presidents of the company and the son of one of the owners, he had been the logical choice for the job.

In reality, however, Noro had to deal with a host of lifestyle changes. Soon after he assumed the presidency, he realized that in spite of his efforts to maintain his previous amicable working style, he was creating more distance between himself and his employees. The interpersonal dimension had changed. Although he tried for a while to be "one of the boys," he discovered that this was no longer possible. In short, Noro now had difficulty balancing the need to socialize with an employee, on one hand, while making tough career decisions about the same person, on the other; life seemed much simpler if he maintained some distance. He also discovered that friendliness to an employee was quickly interpreted by others as favoritism, while attempts at closeness by an employee were viewed as a lobbying effort.

Although Noro simplified matters by keeping his distance, this too had a price. While still working his way up the management ladder, he had always felt that others were apprehensive when dealing with him because he was the son of one of the owners. He knew and they knew that he had privileged access to the top. Still, he was able to build up relationships. As the president, however, he increasingly experienced a sense of isolation, a loss of intimacy. He could talk to his wife, but that did not seem to be enough. He wanted to confide in someone more familiar with what happened in the business, someone who could be a sparring partner.

Sometimes he thought nostalgically of the time before he became president. Occasionally, he found himself longing for a way to resurrect the broken network of relationships, searching for a way of sharing, but this had become impossible. As a side effect, he felt increasingly irritated about having got himself into the top position; it was not what he had expected. What is more, he began to wonder if his increasing aloofness was affecting his ability to make decisions.

This example shows us one of the pitfalls of assuming the position of CEO; for some, it is a mixed blessing. The organization's leaders are supposed to take care of the company's existing strategic and structural needs; they are expected to articulate a vision of the future, show others how to achieve it, and set performance expectations. But there are a number of other, subtler aspects to leadership; one of these is taking care of the dependency needs of the employees. Given the universal nature of these needs, however, one must ask: Who is then left to take care of the dependency needs of the leader himself?

Employees of a family firm always view the sons and daughters of the owners as different. This wariness is accentuated when a son or daughter becomes the top executive. The network of complex mutual dependencies the new leader built up over the years is now changed forever. Some family business executives can overcome this loss and find other forms of gratification; others may even enjoy a certain degree of detachment. However, many become upset at finding themselves in a solitary situation and react accordingly, feeling frustrated and angry or even wanting, irrationally, to get even with those who do not fulfill their dependency needs. The resulting scapegoating behavior can create a politicized organization torn apart by interdepartmental rivalry.

The aggression these new leaders sometimes direct toward subordinates can also be turned inward, leading to depression and/or alcohol and drug abuse. Obviously, if these extreme responses are unchecked, they can have dire consequences for the organization.

The dangers of transference

Another factor that can lead founder-entrepreneurs and family business owner-managers into difficulty has to do with transference, a concept I described in Chapter 1. Leaders of companies, as authority symbols, are prime targets for transference reactions – reactions that some entrepreneurs and family business owner-managers are poorly equipped to handle.

In addition to acting as catalysts in the achievement of the organization's objectives, top executives frequently become the embodiment of employees' ideals, wishes, feelings, and fantasies. Attempting to transform their subjective fantasies into objective reality, employees may imbue leaders with mystical qualities despite the leaders' attempts to resist this idealization. When transference kicks in, the boundaries between the past and present may disappear, and previously unresolved conflicts with significant figures from the past may be triggered. Employees then may endow their leaders with the same omniscience (and faults) that they attributed in childhood to parents or other significant figures. This "transference factor" may be acted out in several ways and can affect both leaders and their employees (Kohut, 1971, 1977; Langs, 1976; Kets de Vries, 1989, 1993).

Sometimes employees idealize their leaders in an attempt to recreate the sense of security and importance they felt in childhood, when they were cared for by apparently omnipotent and perfect parents. Because leaders, as authority figures, fall easily into employees' subconscious definition of the "parent" role, employees may endow their leaders with unrealistic powers and attributes; this in turn can inflate the leaders' self-esteem. During periods of organizational upheaval (such as cutbacks or expansions), when employees are particularly anxious to believe in their leadership as a way of maintaining their own sense of security and identity, employees will go a long way to please or charm their leaders – including giving in to extravagant whims. Thus in times of organizational crisis, leaders may be surrounded by yea-sayers. If leaders are hampered by an excessive love of self-display and a desire to get attention from others, this "mirroring process" (and the resultant lack of critical opinion) can obviously have dire consequences for their companies, leading to rapid deterioration in the quality of decision making.

If leaders get too much uncritical admiration from their employees, they may begin to believe that they really are as perfect, intelligent, or powerful as others think. Losing one's grasp on reality in this way is a common human failing, but it can be particularly dangerous for entrepreneurs and presidents of family firms, because they often have the power to act on their delusions of grandeur.

When dealing with parents and their grown children in family firms, we cannot really talk about transference problems. We cannot say that the new CEO acted *as if* the founder-entrepreneur were a parental figure, for example, when the founder really *is* the father. Thus the concept of transference truly applies only to the non-related employees. However, some narcissistically inclined founder-entrepreneurs may be able to convince those of their children who are working in the firm that their abusive behavior is for their own good. In many instances, these adult children give in, believing in the supposed wisdom of the parent. Given the strength of unresolved problems of childhood, these children may never make a break with the fantasized parental figure of the past to develop a mature adult perception of their parent as a human being like themselves, with normal strengths and weaknesses.

The opposite may be true as well: sons and daughters in family firms may continue their childhood rebellion against a parent's authority. Sometimes they do so in a passive-resistant manner, unconsciously undermining the parent in subtle ways. Their rebellion sometimes breaks out in the open, however, resulting in symbolic parricide (as we shall see in more than one of the case studies in this book).

Although leaders of family firms may find it hard to accept, all interpersonal exchanges involve both realistic and transference reactions. Leaders in family firms are particularly likely to be subject to confusion in this area. After all, the original parent–child relationship that is the model for later transference reactions is very much operative, given the presence of family members in the company.

Leaders who fall victim to grandiose delusions favor highly dependent employees – those who are in search of an all-knowing, all-powerful leader.

However, such leaders can be very callous about employees' needs; they may exploit employees and then drop them when they no longer serve their purposes. Some employees react with legitimate anger to this type of behavior in a leader. Others, though, subconsciously blame the leader for failing to live up to their own exaggerated expectations. Especially if their anger is aggravated by callous, exploitative behavior on the part of the leader, these employees may quickly turn from admiration to hostility and rebellion. Like children, dependent employees tend to divide all experiences, perceptions, and feelings into unambiguously good and bad categories. Thus the new CEO of a family firm who is initially welcomed as a messiah may be surprised to find out how suddenly the employees' mood can shift. After one setback, employees may view the leader as responsible for all the company's problems – even problems that developed long before his or her arrival.

Faced with this transition in employee attitudes from admiration to rebellion and anger, leaders may become irritated and even develop feelings of persecution. They may be tempted to retaliate – possibly by firing their critics – if they do not receive the expected dose of admiration. They may fly into rages, creating a climate of fear. As we saw in Chapter 3, "splitting" may become a dominant behavior pattern among both leaders and their followers.

Thus there is a group of leaders who tend mentally to divide their employees into those who are "with" them and those who are "against" them. Such an outlook is liable to breed an organizational culture of fear and suspicion. Employees who are "with" their leaders share their views and support them even if they engage in unrealistic, grandiose schemes or imagine the existence of malicious plots, sabotage, and enemies. Effective leaders, however, know how to contain their excessive emotional reactions and avoid being caught up in groundless fears.

The case of Ted Howell

The following case study illustrates how these psychological forces can affect the leader of a family firm. After the unexpected death of his father, Ted Howell was appointed president of the Larix Corporation, an electronics equipment company. Howell had been working in a related business in another part of the country. Soon after his arrival, Larix's senior executives saw signs that Howell was having difficulty dealing with the pressures of the job: he made a number of rash, ill-advised decisions in his first week at the office. The company recovered nicely from these mistakes, however – at least initially – because of a couple of favorable events. First, one of the company's main competitors went out of business, freeing up an important segment of the market. Then a Larix employee came up with an excellent marketing idea that Howell quickly adopted (and that proved successful). While some executives were disturbed because Howell, rather than their colleague, received credit for the marketing idea, they were nevertheless pleased that these two factors helped to get Larix back into the black.

Unfortunately, his early success went to Howell's head. After the turnaround, he embarked on a dramatic expansion program, ignoring cautionary remarks from his employees, consultants, and bankers. Howell relocated the company's headquarters to "more suitable surroundings" and acquired an expensive company plane. These two expenditures put a heavy strain on the company's finances. Those executives who expressed disagreement or concern about the new moves were fired; consultants who suggested that Howell change course suffered the same fate. In the end, only sycophants who were willing to share his grandiose ideas and accept his aggressive outbursts were left.

As could have been expected, the unrealistic plans and high expenditures put the company into the red. Howell was unwilling to admit his role in the débâcle, however. When questioned by members of the family who were also shareholders, he became defensive and denied any responsibility for the losses; instead, he blamed them on vindictive actions by fired executives and on unexpected developments in the industry. In his opinion, a turnaround was just around the corner. While an increasing number of board members found Howell's behavior unacceptable, they did not know how to deal with him. Unfortunately, the board's reluctance to take decisive action enabled Howell to bankrupt the family firm.

As in the case of Robert Clark, this was an individual who was apparently well adjusted and who had previously performed well. When he was subjected to the pressures of taking his father's place, however, he began to behave irrationally.

The excessively high expectations that Howell's employees had for him as his father's son seemed to contribute to Howell's problems. Overwhelmed by the attention that he was suddenly receiving, he allowed his sense of reality to become marred. Unable to withstand the psychological pressures, he may have assumed that some of the qualities ascribed to him were actually true, and thus he behaved accordingly. When his grandiose actions backfired and he could not deliver, his employees reacted with anger. Howell then began to show signs of paranoid behavior and retaliated by putting the blame on others. This kind of distorting reaction pattern is typical of the irrational behavior we sometimes find in people at the top.

The fear of success

It has been said that there are two tragedies in life: failure and success. In our success-oriented society, failure is looked upon as a catastrophe, something we all fear. But while fear of failure is understandable, fear of success is more of a puzzle. Sigmund Freud tried to demystify some of the dynamics behind this fear in an article entitled "Those Wrecked by Success" (1916), noting that some people become sick when a deeply rooted and longed-for desire comes to fulfillment. He gave an example of a professor who cherished a wish to succeed his teacher – a wish to "overthrow" an authority figure who reminded him of unresolved childhood conflicts with his father. When his wish eventually came true, the professor was plagued by feelings of depression and self-deprecation and found that he was unable to work.

The case of George Nolan

Sometimes we can see how entrepreneurs or owners of family firms fall victim to the fear of success. Reflecting on his career, George Nolan recalled being surprised when the family council of his multigenerational family firm asked him to succeed his uncle, who had had a stroke. He had assumed that his uncle's oldest son would become the next president, but when he himself was offered the role of president, he accepted.

When he began his new work, however, Nolan noticed that he felt slightly ill at ease, a feeling that persisted. He began to have difficulty sleeping at night: he tossed and turned, tormenting himself by wondering whether his previous day's actions had been correct. He often felt like an impostor, someone who had been "lucky" to get the job. He found it increasingly difficult to concentrate and make decisions at work. To make matters worse, he also developed a full-fledged drinking problem. He wondered how many of his problems in handling the top job were noticed by his employees and his relatives. When were they going to realize that they had made a mistake, that he was really an incompetent fake?

However, as Nolan said himself, he was fortunate. His wife was a great support to him. Because of the changes in his behavior, she encouraged him to see a psychotherapist. As he explored the underlying causes of his anxiety, Nolan began to realize that he had always been anxious in positions of responsibility; previously, however, he had been able to cope better because there were others in a similar situation with whom he could talk. This time, however, he was on his own.

With the psychotherapist's help, Nolan explored the relationship between his past and his present feelings. In reviewing his life, he realized how successful he had been, having done much better than his siblings and his father, who had been unsuccessful in the various jobs given to him in the family firm. He also recognized that with this success had come feelings of guilt and betrayal, that "Oedipal victories" do not come without a price. His surpassing his father resulted in irrational fears of retaliation. He explored these feelings with his psychotherapist and succeeded in becoming more objective by integrating the feelings of fear with his current situation. Being able to see the connections with his past and working through insights about those connections brought him greater peace of mind. What is more, he came to see that he was doing a fairly good job in his new position.

Nolan's experience exemplifies the belief – sometimes conscious, sometimes not – that success can be attained only by displacing someone else. People who think this way, especially those with unresolved sibling rivalry, see success as a symbolic victory over their parents or siblings. Gaining success and tangible accomplishments in adulthood can be a Pyrrhic victory for such people. Success becomes symbolically equated with betrayal – a provocative, hostile act that not only leads to feelings of guilt but also invites retribution (because it arouses the envy and resentment of others). People in the grip of these beliefs fear their "competitors," and their unresolved competitive feelings become confused with present-day reality. Because success is seen as an invitation to negative consequences, these successful individuals downgrade their accomplishments or view themselves as impostors rather than as people who achieved success through their own abilities.

In management situations, these irrational thoughts and behavior patterns may not become evident as long as the executives experiencing them are in a society of equals; here their problems may be subdued. But as soon as these executives reach a leadership position, they are likely to become anxious, deprecate their accomplishments, and even engage in self-defeating behavior.

STAYING ON COURSE

Leadership is part of a complex mosaic of interactive patterns that depend both on the personality and background of the leader and on the nature of the relationship between leader and employee. This mosaic takes shape within a specific situational context. Here entrepreneurial and family firms pose special challenges.

Entrepreneurs and family business owner-managers need to be aware of the psychological forces discussed in this chapter and able to identify potential signs of trouble. They should engage in a regular process of critical self-evaluation. The following questions can be helpful in this process, both for the leaders themselves and for those who work with them.

- Does the leader exercise a form of parental authority by hoarding all decision-making power?
- Does the leader have a short-term, fire-fighting mentality? In other words, does he or she feel that the company should act according to his or her whims? Are priorities unclear? Is there a lack of long-term planning?
- Is the leader resistant to change, believing that as the chosen representative of the family, he or she must know best?
- Is morale deteriorating in the company, as evidenced by politicking and infighting? Is there a lack of trust?
- Is the leader equally accessible to family members and non-family members?
- How does the leader react to bad news or criticism?
- Does the leader think of employees in terms of those who are "with" and those who are "against" him or her? Do only yea-sayers survive?
- How realistic is the leader's vision of the company's future? Does the company exist primarily to provide employment for family members? Is there a large discrepancy between the leader's own and others' points of view?
- Is the leader willing to accept responsibility if things go wrong, or does he or she blame others?

- Is the leader quick to take offense and prone to feel unfairly treated?
- Is the leader's relationship with individual family members the overriding factor in the way the business is run?
- Does the leader have a great need to blow his or her own horn?
- Does the leader feel anxious and guilty when successful and have difficulty believing that professional success is caused by his or her own accomplishments rather than by sheer luck?
- Is there any planning for succession?

These questions are crucial, because entrepreneurs and family business owner-managers have the ability to change some of their fantasies into reality. This ability, which can be like the mythological siren's call, can (and often does) cause an individual to change as soon as he or she attains a leadership position. The potential for losing touch with reality and behaving irrationally is dormant in all of us.

Paranoid reactions and visionary experiences feed very well into certain types of situations. Indeed, many successful political and religious leaders have acted in precisely the ways described in these pages. (Consider Joseph Stalin or the Reverend Jim Jones, for example.) But while it is sometimes this very irrational quality that makes leaders effective, those who evoke regressive tendencies in others and provoke aggression set in motion forces that may be impossible to stop.

Publicly held companies tend to have a number of safeguards that help prevent excessive dysfunctional behavior. Leaders in many large organizations are constrained by an organizational structure based on checks and balances. For example, in the instance of key policy decisions, a number of individuals and agencies such as the government, unions, banks, and other stakeholders, often take on the role of a countervailing power, helping to keep leaders in touch with reality. Moreover, organizational processes in large publicly held companies find their own momentum and are resistant to dramatic change. These processes have their own way of providing a "safety net" for individuals through their inherent structure. Unfortunately, entrepreneurial and family firms do not necessarily have the same kind of safeguards, because of their concentration of ownership. Consequently, these firms have to develop a keen awareness of what can go wrong and must be vigilant in identifying signs of decay.

Founder-entrepreneurs and owners of family firms and their employees are like partners in a dance: the experience can be very exhilarating, but the dancers sometimes fall over each other's feet. Both parties carry a heavy responsibility for making the interchange work. They must be willing to listen to and respect each other's points of view. This requires both a certain amount of self-knowledge and a preparedness to reflect on one's actions. Empathetic listening on the part of both parties is also essential to a genuine understanding of the leader–employee dialogue. Only by establishing a psychological contract based on relationships of mutual support, respect, fairness, honesty, consistency, and trust can the organization ensure a frank interchange between leaders and employees. Such a contract constitutes the strongest force in preventing regressive behavior in leadership. And given the nature of power in organizations, making the leader-employee relationship work – making the organizational "dance" graceful – is the real challenge for all concerned.

Chapter 6

Games family business members play

As the business dramas presented in the previous chapters indicate, families operate in a multiperson forcefield that structures relationships, often across many generations (Böszörményi-Nagy and Spark, 1973). Among the forces at work in these relationships, transference reactions, narcissism, and envy can play major roles. Eventually, particularly in dysfunctional families, some of these forces will rigidify, thereafter influencing the future course of family relationships. Subsequently, an intricate set of family myths and rituals becomes part of daily life, and the family's social organization is shaped by this subculture of coalitions, myths, rituals, and ideologies – all of which frequently stress the danger of subversion if anyone deviates from his or her fixed family role.

In well-functioning families, alliances are relatively flexible, depending on the issue at hand. Alliances come and go; they do not turn into rigidly defined roles. In contrast, in dysfunctional families, as family members side against each other, relationships harden. Other people (both insiders and outsiders) are frequently drawn into these conflicts (Selvini Palazzoli *et al.*, 1978; Bowen, 1978; Hoffman, 1981). Family activities turn into plays in which everyone has well-defined scripts but the drama never ends.

UNHOLY TRIADS

An article in the *Wall Street Journal Europe* entitled "Daddy Dearest" (Cohen, 1994) described the feud engaged in by the members of the dysfunctional Posner clan over the spoils of their large family business. A decade ago, Victor Posner, an entrepreneur who built up a business empire that grossed as much as $26 billion in annual sales, was one of the United States' most feared corporate raiders. Although he seemed more adept at acquiring than running companies and mismanaged many of his companies into bankruptcy, Posner left, at his death, at least $400 million in cash, stock, and real estate in Florida and Maryland. Even while Posner lay critically ill in the hospital, his fighting relatives began accusing him of incest, wife abuse, and destruction of their inheritance. Some of these accusations may have been true: Posner seemed to excel at both destroying his various businesses and harming his family. The feud following his death has been fueled by multiple divorces, legal troubles, internecine fighting over who will inherit what, and various allegations of incest and sexual molestation committed by Posner against his two daughters (from two different marriages) and a granddaughter. The article mentions that his second wife referred to her exhusband as a "freak of nature" and a "total beast."

During his lifetime, Posner acquired a whole string of companies, starting with DWG Corporation, a Detroit cigar company that he used as a vehicle for many of his acquisitions. His management style was extremely dictatorial and intimidating. Attending a board meeting was like attending an old-fashioned camp meeting: all directors were supposed to say amen to each of his statements, no matter how outrageous they were. On many occasions, Posner yelled at his oldest son, Steven, calling him a moron and telling him to shut up. Predictably, soon after each of his acquisitions, some of the best executives left. Eventually, because of mismanagement and asset stripping, many of the companies that Posner controlled filed for bankruptcy.

By the mid 1980s, Posner's legal problems were mounting. Posner and his son Steven were charged by the SEC with conspiring (with Michael Milken and Ivan Boesky) to "park" shares to gain control of the Fischbach Corporation. In 1990, the two men were sued by other shareholders for plundering DWG. Victor Posner settled the suit by selling half his shares. In 1993, a New York federal district judge banned Posner and his son from any further involvement with public companies. They were ordered to give up control of the companies they still managed and to repay the ill-won gains. After the trial, Posner blamed his son Steven for all the legal problems.

Steven, meanwhile, had problems of his own. When he was unable to pay his share of the penalty in the Fischbach case, his father refused to help him, saying that he had already paid enough money to his son. Cut off by the judge's ruling from money coming from companies previously controlled by the family, Steven fell deeper and deeper into debt. Now he is facing more than eighty lawsuits brought by his creditors. The *Wall Street Journal Europe* noted that he even had to give up his Bentley and his Ferrari Testarossa! To add insult to injury, Steven is now being sued by his half-sister, who accuses him of mismanaging her share of a trust.

According to some acquaintances, although Posner could be harsh and punitive, when it came to material possessions his children and grandchildren were totally indulged in their early years. The disastrous results of this type of upbringing were predictable. At the age of twenty, Posner's younger son, Troy, was arrested on (and pleaded guilty to) felony drug possession charges and entered a rehabilitation center to avoid prison. A few years later, Troy got into a fight with his father's bodyguards, ransacked Posner's office, and threatened to kill him because he believed that his father owed him $100,000 from a business deal. Posner did not speak to Troy for a decade after that episode.

Posner's relationship with one of his daughters was not much better. He cooled considerably toward his daughter from his second marriage, Tracy, after she decided to get married. According to Tracy, he offered her future husband $10 million to leave her, an offer that was refused. Posner did not attend the wedding. Later he tried to persuade Tracy to move back to Florida, where he lived, to work for him for a $15 million annual salary. He also offered her husband a job that would require him to travel the greater part of each week. When the couple rejected the offer, Posner threatened to cut them out of his will (Cohen, 1994).

There is probably much more to the Posner story – both good and bad – than is disclosed here, but even this brief tale illustrates a range of extremely dysfunctional family entanglements that not only had calamitous consequences for the members of the family but also negatively affected the family business.

The Posner case, with its dysfunctional behavior patterns, is a good example of how *not* to manage a family. One can only surmise what Posner's relationship with his two wives must have been like: to be accused of incest and called a beast and a freak of nature does not indicate a well-functioning marital relationship.

In the best of all worlds, parents relate well to each other, and tension is minimal in the family. But as the Posner case dramatically illustrates, the reality of the situation is often quite different. If tension between parents cannot be contained, it spills over to the other members of the family system. Third parties are drawn into the fray. Children in particular are used for obscuring or deflecting parental difficulties. And because children thus involved are consequently less differentiated, they are highly vulnerable. These children become "triangulated" in their parents' efforts to reduce tension. The children then start to act in destructive ways, and so the drama expands.

Characteristically, such triangles have two insiders (one or both of whom are attempting to settle a troublesome emotional problem) and one outsider. Jealous feelings toward a third party are frequently at the heart of the problem, with at least one of the insiders trying to get even for whatever wrong is perceived to have been done to them. Not surprisingly, when one or both insiders begin to move against an outsider, the outsider is likely to retaliate. The result is an escalating situation that often creates a very unpleasant legacy for all the battling parties.

When people get involved in collusions within the family, the normal boundaries between parents and children are crossed. Sons line up with mothers against fathers; fathers line up with daughters against mothers; parents line up against their children – there are many unhappy combinations and permutations. Naturally, crossing traditional family boundaries (as defined by society) comes at a high emotional price. The usual consequences of such actions are anger, resentment, guilt, and depression.

An interesting classification of collusive family arrangements comes from family therapist Salvatore Minuchin (Minuchin *et al.*, 1978), who describes a number of dysfunctional parent–child triads. According to Minuchin, *triangulation* refers to a situation in which each of the parents involved in overt or covert conflict – parents unable to respond to each other's needs for

companionship, support, and affection, and unable to resolve their differences –
tries to enlist the child's support and sympathy against the other parent.
Obviously, when these parents get their children involved in their problems, they
create an intense conflict of loyalty. The obvious victims in such conflict are the
children, dependent as they are on their parents, but the horizon can easily be
expanded to members of the extended family (and even non-family members).

Minuchin outlines two specific types of triangulation. In the case of the
parent–child coalition, described above, the coalition itself is out in the open:
one parent overtly sides with the child against the other partner. The intense
closeness of the child with only one parent can have serious repercussions. Such
triangles may result in gender problems and may prevent true separation-
individuation.

Minuchin also discusses the *detouring coalition*. Here the parents scapegoat
the child as a way of displacing their own problems: scapegoating becomes the
parents' way of diffusing the stress between them. This maneuver allows the
parents to avoid looking at themselves as they bond together to control the child;
they often succeed in putting the legacy of badness on the child instead of on
themselves. Another permutation of this detouring triad is parents who brand an
essentially normal child as "sick" and devote their attention to the child's care.
While at one level this is a strategy of overprotection, it also serves as a way of
bringing the parents closer together at the cost of a healthy relationship with the
child.

Obviously, a child who gets involved in any of these processes will experience
difficulties in becoming a person in his or her own right; real differentiation will
be hard to achieve. Other family members may well thwart any attempt by the
child to escape from an unholy triangle. While such an escape might save the
child, it would be an intolerable threat to the family's equilibrium.

When families run businesses, these unholy triads have a tendency to shift
from the family system to the business environment, with dysfunctional
relationships reenacted in the business setting. Given the impact of top
management on the corporate culture of the firm, the consequences can be quite
destructive.

Coalitions and collusions are part and parcel of organizational life, to be sure.
They make up an inevitable political dimension. Anyone with leadership
ambition has little choice but to learn how to live with such alliances. As one
politician put it, "If you can't stand the heat, get out of the kitchen." However,
while getting out of the kitchen is relatively easy in a publicly held organization,
in a family business it is a different matter altogether, given the kind of
entanglements exemplified by unholy family alliances.

GAMES FAMILIES PLAY: THE ROLE OF FAMILY MYTHS

Over time, unholy alliances may become hardened into family myths. These
myths – a set of beliefs that are shared by the family members and offer a

rationale for individuals' behavior – can take on a powerful, navigating function. These myths usually include mutually agreed upon roles and rigidly prescribed appropriate behavior, all of which help determine how family members function together. Just as with cultural myths, they give structure to the family's experiences, create continuity between past and present, serve as a guide for future actions, contribute to equilibrium in the family, and serve as a buffer against the forces of change. As we have seen, generational envy, jealousy, and sibling rivalry play a major role in the genesis of the family myths, while certain traumatic life events (such as death, birth, desertion, and illness) may also contribute to their eventual makeup.

Myths play important defensive and protective roles in families (Wynne *et al.*, 1958; Ferreira, 1963; Kepner, 1991). They can help people cope with stress and anxiety and, by prescribing ritualistic behavior patterns, enable the family to establish a common front against the outside world. Although they can be useful, family myths often enable a family to cover up unpleasant real-life situations with idealized self-images. In this sense, the myths can be considered a kind of family compromise: because the myths the family propagates must be endorsed by everyone in the family, all the family members must take each member's needs, wishes, and defenses into consideration. This not necessarily healthy "cooperation" can also deteriorate further into a kind of collusion whereby unwanted parts of one family member's behavior are repudiated, split off, and transferred to another family member. Eventually, perceptions of this transferred behavior harden over time until the original reality of who really does what is permanently distorted.

Family myths become a blueprint for family action, but as such they can also turn into a straitjacket, reducing a family's flexibility and capacity to respond to new situations. If the family is also involved in a family business, the impact of these myths can become quite considerable, hampering the company's ability to deal with changes in the environment.

Family myths often become mobilized in times of crisis. Family members start to operate on automatic pilot; the defensive system is activated. To use the words of Ferreira, "The family myth is to the relationship what the defense is to the individual" (1963, p. 60). These myths create a defensive posture that is not challenged within the family in spite of their reality distortions. The power of these myths can be enhanced by the fact that the rules that govern each family myth are not necessarily explicitly defined. Much of what makes up a family myth takes place deep beneath the surface. Thus, while family myths offer a rationale for the behavior in the family, they conceal the true issues, problems, and conflicts.

Because these myths can be so important to a family, it is not surprising that they have a serious impact on the corporate culture of the family firm. Family myths orchestrate the unspoken dos and don'ts within a company, and structure company behavior. They have an influence on the kind of people who are taken into the company, the kind of people who are identified as having high potential, and the kind of socialization methods used in developing these individuals. Family myths also determine taboo issues within the organization, and because they are such good social defense mechanisms (with their unspoken objective of keeping the family together), they are not easily challenged. In corporate culture, the employee questions the myths at his or her own peril.

Certain myths develop regularly across the spectrum of family firms (Stierlin, 1973; Pillari, 1986). One common myth is the fantasy of togetherness: the myth of *harmony*. In spite of all the evidence to the contrary, and notwithstanding the fact that there is an enormous amount of conflict and tension within the family, the principal members of the family business may buy into the myth of harmony, ignoring the reality of the situation through denial and idealization. The company functions in a state of "pseudomutuality," trying to exclude any evidence of non-complementarity from open recognition. While the various family members wish intensely for mutual relatedness, that wish excludes the tolerance of differences. The illusion of pseudomutuality is what keeps the family together. Children are therefore caught in a dilemma: every attempt to differentiate, to find their own way, disturbs this carefully established equilibrium and can lead to disaster (Wynne *et al.*, 1958). Thus facts are ignored and history is rewritten. This method of dealing with reality – or rather, *not* dealing with it – originates in the belief that the world is basically a dangerous place. Families governed by that philosophy believe that it is safer to stick together, to avoid rocking the boat. Naturally, such an unrealistic outlook does not augur well for the future of the family-run enterprise.

Another common myth is that of *stereotyping*, in which everyone in the family has a specific assigned role. Stereotyping is based on the expectation that if certain behavioral boundaries are crossed, catastrophe will follow. That expectation dictates that there be no flexibility, no possibility of trying something new. Preconceptions dating from childhood predetermine adult opportunities: for example, Johnny, who was a sickly child, is not put in charge of sales, even though he might be rather good at it. According to the myth, he is not strong and should not travel. More recent preconceptions are also factored in: Father should be spared certain types of information since he has a weak heart. And so the story can go on and on. These ill-advised role definitions hamper organizational creativity and adaptability, leading to possibly dire consequences.

Another common myth is that of *martyrdom*. Martyrs create their identity around the idea that they must constantly do things against their will. Despite the power they hold, they maintain that they have no choice or control. A good example of this is the owner of a company who protests that he does not really like working long hours but is obliged to do so in order to provide for his family; he will not admit that there are other ways to go about his work, that he does not have to put in such long hours, that he could delegate more. People who subscribe to this myth cannot acknowledge the fact that they act the way they do simply because they *enjoy* it. They *like* to be at the office, exerting control. As

Sam Steinberg, the late owner-manager of what was once the largest grocery store chain in Canada, used to say, "I don't have ulcers; I give ulcers." The martyrdom myth, like the others, leads various members of the company to engage in a sham, corroding candor in the company.

In the myth of the *scapegoat*, the blame for all the problems in the company is put on a single family member rather than on an outsider. The argument goes something like this: "If only Jane knew how to behave, how to pull her own weight, everything would be all right." The real source of the problem and the responsibility others should take for it are not recognized. As with other myths, scapegoating originates with certain tensions in the family that need an outlet. Rather than addressing those tensions appropriately, the myth-driven family finds an appropriate family member – a vulnerable victim – and assigns him or her the scapegoat role. But the choice of a scapegoat is not a random process; specific factors determine why a particular person is chosen. Often the shortcomings of the scapegoat symbolize certain weaknesses of other family members. For example, if there is a conflict in the family because of the family business leader's lack of success, a child who is a poor student at school may become a natural scapegoat, allowing the father's failure to remain unacknowledged. The mother who cannot expose her dissatisfaction with her husband's lack of success can blame the child instead. The child then becomes the appointed incompetent, the black sheep, the klutz. And to keep the family harmony, everyone in the family, *including the scapegoat*, obliges and institutionalizes that role.

Unfortunately, a scapegoated child finds it hard to change roles later in life. He or she – often designated the "problem child" – remains the bearer of all the family's ills. Eventually, problem children no longer merely tolerate but actively play the part, as long as it serves the purpose of reducing tension in the family. Unconsciously, these children may even realize the critical importance of their role in keeping the family together. And these kinds of attributions flow over to the family business. Thus the same black sheep is blamed over and over again for all that is going wrong in the family business, while others' blunders are repeatedly overlooked.

Finally, there is the myth of the *messiah*, the notion that redemption and salvation will come from an omnipotent source. The unfortunate person anointed as the messiah walks into an environment overburdened with expectations. He or she is supposed to make right everything that is wrong in the organization. Usually, messiahs are outsiders coming into the family firm to set things right. The messiah can be a consultant, a newly hired senior executive providing much-needed skills, or a highly praised, recently arrived (non-family) president, for example.

The messiah myth is grounded in the expectation that finally there is someone who can change the course of events, someone who will transform the dreadful situation the company finds itself in. Of course, no one can live up to such grandiose expectations; the messiah figure is bound to fail. Indeed, failure is covertly expected; as a matter of fact, tripping up the messiah strengthens the family's belief that they were right after all, that they do not really have to change. Lining up against the messiah does good things for family cohesion, creating a sense of belonging and a feeling of righteousness. The messiah may have different feelings, however, as he or she recognizes the trap. The high turnover in family firms among both consultants and much-praised, newly hired senior executives is symptomatic of this process in action.

THE SUCCESSION CONUNDRUM

The creation of family myths can be compared to unconscious "conspiracies" – conspiracies that can dramatically affect organizational life. Of all the conspiracies in entrepreneurial and family businesses, however, one is paramount: the conspiracy of succession (Lansberg, 1988; Kets de Vries and Miller 1988; Handler, 1994). All too many companies seem to suffer from "corporoeuthanasia" – the process of willfully killing a business that has been built up carefully simply by failing to provide for continuity (Danco, 1982, p. 110).

To many entrepreneurs or business owner-managers, letting go of the business feels like signing their own death warrant. Many people faced with the issue of relinquishing the power that comes with the job seem addicted to their job's tangible and intangible benefits; they try to hang on as long as possible. Think only of Serge Dassault of Dassault Enterprises, the French airplane builder, who was sixty-one before his father gave him the chairmanship of the family company. Thomas Watson, Sr., of IBM handed over control to his son only when the father was eighty-two years old. The late Armand Hammer of Occidental Petroleum and William Paley of CBS are other notorious examples of entrepreneurs who seem to have experienced great difficulty in grooming crown princes. It seems that many entrepreneurs or leaders of family businesses are Shakespearean scholars; they are well aware of what happened to King Lear.

Entrepreneurs have a hard time accepting their own mortality, confronting that ultimate narcissistic injury: the disintegration of the body. Some presidents of family firms, particularly founder-entrepreneurs, act as if death were something that would happen to everyone except themselves. Other family members begin to respect the taboo and strenuously avoid talking about the possibility that the president eventually might die. Raising that topic would be a hostile act, one potentially interpreted by the man in charge as a wish to have him dead. (Although children, in moments of anger, often have this wish, the strong feelings of guilt they experience as a result lead them as adults to suppress or even repress such thoughts altogether.)

This conspiracy of silence within the family can be augmented by the fear of abandonment. The children may wonder whether they will be able to cope without their parents around. Given the kind of dynamics we have seen in many of these families, those fears may be all too real: the children may indeed have become overdependent, unable to stand on their own two feet.

If there are several children, they may worry about who is going to be the *primus inter pares*. Parents like to maintain the illusion that their children are equal, because singling somebody out as the successor may lead to discord. Of course, the assertion that everybody is equal is really a lie: relationships with children, like any other relationships, are always differential. But this is often one of the best-kept family secrets. In other cases, the children may fear, often for good reason, that there will be open conflict when the parents are no longer there to act as arbiters. All these issues may mean that everyone prefers to let matters slip rather than face succession problems head on.

The symbolic role of the company as perceived by its leader also aggravates succession problems. As we have seen, for many founder-entrepreneurs, the enterprise becomes part of their core identity. The company is very much a part of their inner world, a symbol of who they are. Not only do they have an enormous emotional investment in the business; in addition, they have come to depend on the company to calibrate their self-esteem. Moreover, some owner-managers equate losing control and retirement with a change in their privileged position in the family, a serious weakening of their power base. They may also be concerned about whether their successors will respect their legacy or destroy what they have built up so carefully. How will their successors treat the "family jewels"? Since these leaders have come to feel indispensable, they cannot trust anyone to be as committed to the business as they are.

Generational envy – the envy parents feel toward the emerging abilities of their children – should not be underestimated either. Many business owners display high artistry in finding reasons for crushing or humiliating their children. At the heart of this process is their concern about their own waning powers, physical and otherwise. To hand over power to the next generation is a singularly unattractive prospect.

When founder-entrepreneurs do eventually manage to select their successors, they often, in a kind of unconscious conspiracy, choose people who are bound to fail (Levinson, 1971; Sonnenfeld, 1988). Many entrepreneurs do not, in their heart of hearts, really want their successors to succeed. They want to see successors fail to prove that they themselves are indispensable. So some entrepreneurs may set successors up for a fall, hoping that they will be asked to return as the savior.

The inverse of this situation is the frequent reluctance of anointed successors to take the position finally offered to them. Many possible successors may be aware of the entrepreneur's unconscious conspiracy and legitimately fear that they are being asked to step into a trap. Others have the courage to recognize that they do not have what it takes to do the job, often because they have not had the proper training from the ambivalent founder-entrepreneur.

Some potential successors are reluctant to take on the challenge for other reasons. They may want to have a life of their own, not one that is programmed for them by others. They may fear that their life is being planned out for them, that they will be forced to become identical to their grandparents or parents. They anticipate no free choice: everything is predetermined, right down to a place reserved for their portrait in the family boardroom. Successors-elect haunted by such a *nemesis feeling* may choose to rebel, to break free, to be individuals in their own right. To go into the family business – much less to head it – is an ambivalent temptation at best.

The poet John Betjeman (1960, pp. 11, 16, 21), a person who must have struggled intensely with the feeling that the family business was his nemesis, presents this conflict very well in his autobiography:

> . . . Most of all
> I think my father loved me when we went
> In early-morning pipe-smoke on the tram
> Down to the Angel, visiting the Works,
> "Fourth generation – yes, this is the boy,"
> "Well now, my boy, I want your solemn word
> To carry on the firm when I am gone:
> Fourth generation John – they'll look to you."
> I was a poet. That was why I failed.
> My faith in this chimera brought an end
> To all my father's hopes. In later years,
> Now old and ill, he asked me once again
> To carry on the firm, I still refused.
> And now when I behold, fresh-published, new,
> A further volume of my verse, I see
> His kind eyes look woundedly at mine,
> I see his workmen seeking other jobs,
> And that red granite obelisk that marks
> The family grave in Highgate Cemetery
> Points an accusing finger to the sky.

As if the conflicts about succession within owner-entrepreneurs themselves were not enough, spouses (having grown accustomed to the perks and the vicarious recognition that come with the job) may also have problems letting go. Consequently, they may put pressure on retirement-age entrepreneurs to hang on. Some of them, especially women who have chosen to be homemakers, may also be apprehensive about what it would mean to have a retired spouse at home. How would they relate to each other? Would they drive each other crazy?

Succession issues in family firms vary by the gender of the parties involved. Father–son succession is complicated by the conflict that often characterizes the relationship that male entrepreneurs experience with their sons (particularly the oldest). Their tangled issues of identification and competitiveness may not be easily reconciled. In firms in which a woman is the founder-entrepreneur, the configuration is somewhat different. As with male entrepreneurs, a major theme in female entrepreneurs' internal theater is the wish to be in charge of their own lives, to be independent. For women, however, some clinical evidence suggests that this has to be seen in the context of a reaction against an unreliable father (toward whom the daughter may nevertheless maintain a feeling of special relationship) and a submissive mother (who may have been used as a doormat by the father). Coco Chanel came from this sort of background. She vowed that she would never find herself in her mother's situation; she was not going to be dependent on anybody. Sometimes, though, the scenario is positive: a family in which the father strongly supports his daughter (because he secretly wished for a son) and encourages her to be a tomboy, or a family in which there are a number of strong female role models. Unfortunately, there are not yet enough female entrepreneurs for any clear models of their attitudes toward succession to emerge.

Sometimes fathers consider their daughters rather than their sons as possible successors. Interestingly, in business, father–daughter associations usually work out rather better than father–son relationships. However, although male entrepreneurs may find it easier to relate to their daughters, many of them have a rather traditional view of the role of women and do not consider or prepare their daughters as possible successors. Perhaps they are trying to protect their daughters from the kind of hardships that running a family firm usually implies; fathers generally see sons as able to endure these hardships, but they look at their daughters quite differently. These attitudes are changing, however, and we can expect a greater number of female presidents in family enterprises in the future as more and more women take up entrepreneurial challenges. Whether these successors will become embroiled in the same kind of soap opera as their brothers remains to be seen.

Given the difficulty that most people have in coming to grips with their own mortality, succession is never going to be an easy issue to deal with. To paraphrase Dylan Thomas, many entrepreneurs and family business owner-managers clearly do not go gentle into that good night.

But if immortality is really a major concern for many of these people, they would do well to *prepare* for succession: all evidence indicates that the companies that provide for this issue are those that achieve continuity. Those that do not plan for succession – those that risk becoming victims of dysfunctional family dynamics – are the ones that go into the dark night of failure and bankruptcy. Perhaps the cases that follow will caution readers associated with family businesses not to follow this route.

Part II
Cases and commentaries

A. THE INTRAPSYCHIC AND INTERPERSONAL THEATER

The razor is mightier than the pen
Francine Gomez and Waterman

In 1988, the American company Gillette bought the Waterman pen company. Waterman France had been handed down through three generations of an aristocratic French family, and in each generation, the company had been headed by the family matriarch. Francine Gomez became CEO of the floundering company in 1969, after her mother stepped down from that position. Gomez turned Waterman around, gaining a 65 percent share of the French market in non-disposable pens; and for the next fifteen years, Waterman remained solidly in the black, becoming one of France's most prestigious companies.

Gomez undoubtedly would have stayed at the head of Waterman into her eighties, as her mother and grandmother had before her, but for a 1986 change in the French inheritance tax law – a change that meant she would eventually lose majority control of the company even as its head. Given that uncertain future, when Boston-based Gillette approached her with an offer for the company, she was willing to consider it. At about this time, Revlon launched a takeover bid for Gillette, forcing Gillette to buy back its shares on the open market. Despite the debt that it had incurred, Gillette went ahead with its purchase of Waterman in 1988.

Francine Gomez's tenure as CEO after the buyout was rocky. "I thought I had a beau [in Gillette] who was strong and handsome and rich," she said at the time. "In the beginning I was naïve; I thought we had a partnership."[1] The sentiment seemed to be mutual. Jean Veillon, Waterman's managing director in 1988, said about Gomez, "She is our queen – every company needs a queen."[2] She was soon to be disillusioned.

The Francine Gomez case study that unfolds below – based on an interview, conducted in English, that I had with Gomez in 1989 – begins at the point when Gillette had just bought out Waterman. In our interview, she spoke frankly about her past, her career at Waterman, and her personal life. Her stream-of-consciousness comments appear here as they were spoken; I edited only as needed to give the material some structure. Consequently, this is the most personal case in the book. It is a privileged look at the inner world of the woman who, in the late 1980s, was the most visible businesswoman in France. It is a reflection of a personal myth. By looking at Gomez's background, as well as her later life experiences, we can discern the mosaic of characteristics that make up this complex woman.

This case is particularly interesting in that it provides a number of insights into the issues faced by women business leaders. What kind of person is Francine Gomez? What are the themes that dominate her life? What are some of the factors that led to her taking over the family firm? Gomez admits that it was difficult for her to balance her career and her private life. Where did she go wrong? Are the problems that arose typical of women in executive positions? Given the increasing number of women at the head of family firms, there are salient lessons to be drawn from her example.

This case study can be supplemented with a twenty-five minute video, which is an edited film of the interview that I conducted with Francine Gomez.[3] The visual material is helpful in that it provides other kinds of information: it makes it possible to study Gomez's emotional reactions to questions and her non-verbal behavior patterns. However, all the major themes that seem to have had a determining effect on her life can be found in the written material.

FRANCINE GOMEZ

My family is unmistakably bourgeois, my father's side being Jewish intellectuals and my mother's Swedish-Scottish industrialists. Their marriage was very unpopular, as the Jewish intellectuals didn't want to give their son to the daughter of a rich industrialist, and the rich industrialists refused to give their daughter to the son of Jewish intellectuals. But it was a beautiful, romantic story, and they married regardless of their families' opinions. In 1932, three years later, I was born.

My unfading childhood memories are of an idyllic life. My earliest recollections are of the countryside, which has given me a passion for grass, the wind, and animals.

In 1938, my maternal grandmother, who had remarkable intuition and an understanding of her family, bought a charming little chateau in the Touraine region, close to Chinon. When war was declared in 1939, she packed up everything she loved and sent it all to this chateau. That included myself, my sister, my two older cousins (both boys), and five dogs. There I spent the happiest years of my life. I was the rich little girl who lived surrounded by old furniture and rare objects.

I was a model child, a very pretty little girl – prettier than children usually are – and so I was given a lot of attention and admiration. My sister, Jacqueline, who was three years younger than I, had a hard time. Not only did I keep hitting her, but she was not as pretty as I was and so did not exist in the eyes of the family. It was only when I reached puberty and began to eat too much and became fat that she was noticed. At my grandmother's house, I behaved like a boy because I was brought up with my two cousins. They fought with me all the time, upsetting my games and teasing me. They were horrible sometimes, putting stones in snowballs so that they really hurt. I was always covered with bruises. But we were never permitted to complain. Even if my cousins had beaten me to death, I would never have told my grandmother. The greater offense was to tell tales after the event. It was just not done. Jacqueline had devised an effective defense, which was to start wailing before I had even touched her, summoning grown-up protection.

Everyone was terrified of my grandmother – everyone except me. She was very authoritarian. All those who remember her – my mother, my sister, and others – tell me I am just like her. She was the head of our family and the first woman president of the family business, Waterman.

She came to be president by accident. My grandfather, who owned the company, died suddenly while he was still quite young. In fact, he died the year I was born. Rather than selling, my grandmother decided to run the business herself, which she did until she was eighty-four. This was not funny really, because she was the sort of person who wouldn't stop, who wouldn't give up. She owned Waterman, and there was no way she was going to let anyone else take over. She never retired, although she did have a general manager and eventually didn't do much except be there. However, she was the only person who could sign the checks. As she grew older, she couldn't see the problems that the company faced, and things began to slow down. When she died in 1964, my mother took over. My mother was hopeless. She couldn't even organize her own larder, let alone a factory. That's when the problems really started. By 1969, Waterman [France] was nearly bankrupt.

In my youth, I had no interest in the family business. My father had spent part of the war in a German prisoner-of-war camp as the surgeon of the *maquis* of la Creuse.[4] The declaration of peace came in 1945, and with it the reuniting of my family and our return to Paris. At first, I hated the noise of the traffic and the confinement of the first-floor apartment and sulked about the injunction never to go out alone. But soon the pretty little girl had disappeared, and with the onset of adolescence, I became demanding and disobedient. My father, I think, wanted me to become a surgeon like himself, but I went through a bad phase with my studies. All I wanted to do was to put on nail polish and listen to jazz.

My mother was not a strong woman, and as a teenager I was terrible. I was insolent and always answered back. I could never let a matter rest and was constantly starting arguments. I was terribly aggressive. My mother slapped my face right up until I was married. My father, on the other hand, had a great influence on me. Everything I did well was to please him, and if I did something wrong, I was afraid of what he would think. He died of cancer when he was fifty. I was twenty and just starting to have my own children. When he died, that was that. He was completely out of my life.

I have two daughters: Valerie, who was born in 1954, and Marion, who was born in 1956. I've been married many times. I consider it useless to continue to live with someone I don't love anymore. The most traumatic of my marriages was with the father of my children. I usually say he was my first husband, but he was in fact my second. He had a passion for horses and so, while he worked, I decided to use my time competing in horse shows. My time was divided between prams and stables, between two small infants who demanded to be fed yogurt every four hours and three horses that needed exercising come rain or shine. I took my duties seriously; with anything I undertake, I do it wholeheartedly. But the horses hadn't been bought with me in mind, and they were huge. What with them and the children, all my time and energy was absorbed. I never had a moment to myself. Eventually, exhausted and fed up, I left my husband, took the kids and my two dogs back to my mother, and filed for a divorce. It was granted in 1958, and my exhusband departed for Brazil.

After my horse period, I had my bridge period. (I think life is made up of "periods.") I played bridge all day and all night. I don't play bridge anymore; perhaps I'll come back to it when I retire. Throughout this period, I was being supported by my family, and I was what they call "difficult to live with." Then, in 1961, I inherited a small sum of money, sufficient to permit me to buy an antique shop in Saint-Germain-en-Laye. The furniture and fine objects were familiar reminders of my childhood, and suddenly I felt "at home." After six years of serious devotion to my career, I was able to claim financial independence from my relatives. It was a good feeling.

I wasn't taken seriously as a woman until I was over thirty. I had had my children and had ridden horses, played bridge, and passed the time in a nice way. Now I was making money from my shop and wasn't at all interested in becoming involved in the family business. It was full of old people who all wanted to tell me what to do.

Then I met and (in spite of having two children) married Alain Gomez in 1967. Alain worked for Saint Gobain and was an *inspecteur des finances*.[5] He attended Harvard from 1968 to 1969. At last my family approved of my behavior. Under the steadying influence of Alain, my conduct improved and my level-headedness grew. Before I knew it, I stood on the doorstep of Waterman.

Alain was a very brilliant man; he still is. Now he's president of the Thomson Group.[6] Anyway, it was with his encouragement and support that I agreed to help my mother, who was by this time facing financial collapse.

When I joined Waterman on December 1, 1969, my sole objective was a small 3,000-franc salary check at the end of each month. But it soon became clear to me why the company had lost 3 million francs in the previous year. The executives were far too old and had been inappropriately selected; the products were out of fashion and unreliable; manufacturing was unable to deal with seasonal fluctuations in demand; there was total ignorance of costs; and an expensive and badly planned decentralization program had begun. Everyone was terrified by what could happen. Some of the more senior staff members decided to retire once they became aware of the vulnerable situation of the company. The main labor force was too frightened to even dare move. So from very early on, I was free to act as I considered necessary.

I don't think that being a woman was any particular advantage or handicap. It didn't make much difference (except that perhaps if I had been a man I would have had more experience). On the other hand, [as a man] at thirty-seven perhaps I would have been tired and not so enthusiastic. I was completely fresh and new. My lack of previous experience wasn't a disadvantage either, because my head wasn't filled with "principles." It was a time when business principles were falling apart; they were no longer effective. I wasn't afraid to tell someone thirty years my senior that he was no good anymore. Perhaps if I had been in a company for years or had been to a business school, I wouldn't have dared to speak that way to those people. Because I wasn't indoctrinated, I think I could see things clearly. Being a family company, Waterman had no shareholders to account to – just my mother and aunt, who were absent most of the time. They were virtually non-existent, just there to sign papers when necessary. It was an extraordinary feeling not to need anyone's permission to spend money, decide upon a new product, or hire someone.

Waterman became my passion, and I became blind to everything else. It was like a marriage, and for fifteen years I hardly thought of anything else. I knew every little detail of the business and everything that was happening. I was thrilled with each step of progress and worried over each setback. Any success, I felt, was my success, and any failure was mine too. I didn't want to relinquish any of my responsibilities to anyone. I did everything myself. By 1972, I had been named president-director general of Waterman. I had all the power, and that felt quite good to me.

In 1969, we suffered a pretax loss of 2.8 million francs. My reaction was unhampered by sentimentality. First, I downsized the workforce. I had to fire people. I hated doing it, but I was the only one who could. Then I cut down on overhead, replacing, for example, the resplendent, 200-person central Paris office with a smaller (and some would say shabbier) 50-person office in the less expensive seventeenth *arrondissement*. (We are still there today.) Finally, I turned my attention to the products: the pens themselves. I have a good eye for design and color; it's only a small step from antiques and fine art to top-quality fountain pens. When I retire, I hope they will say of me, "It's a pity Francine's gone, because the collection was much better when she did it."

Anyway, my strategies were effective almost immediately, and in 1972 we were in a good position to purchase the remaining Waterman pen companies. Waterman was founded by an American, Lewis E. Waterman, who invented the first fountain pen and set up a factory in the United States to manufacture it. He sold the right to manufacture the pen to firms in Canada, England, and France (which also had the rights for the Far Eastern countries). In 1971, the American company was bankrupt and the owner, Baron Bich of Bic pen and razor fame, willingly sold it to me. He didn't see it as likely to come to much, especially with a woman chief executive officer. I bought the Canadian company at the same time, and a year later I purchased the British rights from Royal Sovereign Pencils. By 1974, our pretax profit was 14.5 million francs – up 50 percent – with a sales turnover of 70 million francs, a 23 percent increase over the previous year. The following year, I put my most ambitious plan into motion by floating one quarter of the family's share of holdings on the Paris Bourse. In June 1975, the shares were offered on the French stock market at an initial price of 180 francs each, with a price earnings ratio of 11.5 and a yield of 1.5 percent. By 1986, the share price had risen to 700 francs.

But it was not all successful. You can't, in my opinion, be a good mother and have a successful career. You can't succeed at both. This opinion has made me unpopular in some French business schools, because I've told the women that they have to make a choice. You may have children and a [healthy] family life, but you'll never be a good professional; or you may be a good professional, but you'll never be a good mother. I just don't think it's possible.

My marriage with Alain Gomez ended in 1982. It's a great exception for people to succeed on the same level in business at the same time. We had little time at our disposal for each other. Waterman took up most of my time, even weekends. When Alain became head of Thomson, our time together almost completely disappeared. The separation was inevitable. Waterman cost me my marriage!

It was also difficult for my daughters. When I started with Waterman, one was nine, the other eleven. I can't tell you the problems I had to face. The younger one started lying and fighting with me all the time. The older girl became a hippie and a little like Pinocchio. If someone told her, "You have to put your money in a hole and water it each day, and then it will grow," she would believe that person, yet she is far from dumb.

I can't have been a very tender mother. I don't really like babies, and I certainly don't like kissing and caressing them. From what I've read in books, though, I understand children like to be kissed. My grandmother and mother were undemonstrative like me. I was really brought up by an old maid, a nanny, and didn't much care for caresses myself. Despite all this, we all live together; both my daughters have houses in my garden. It's marvelous for the grandchildren, because they're all together and their mothers help each other. If [my daughters] get cross and don't want to speak to each other, they just shut their windows. We have plenty of space: my garden is one hectare of parkland. It's like a dream, the "Gomez Village."

In leadership terms, I'm like my grandmother: head of the family, which still includes my mother and aunt, now old ladies of eighty-four and eighty-two. Anything could happen to them almost any day now. That's one of the reasons I decided to sell Waterman to Gillette. With inheritance tax currently standing at 40 percent, I would have lost control of the company if both of them had died. I also wanted to enter the American market, for which I needed support. You can't succeed on the American market if you don't have the means: the big money and the big name. It struck me that this was a good time to form an association with someone who had the financial backing to launch us in the States, and Gillette seemed to be the people to do this.

Another consideration was that three years ago, in 1984, I started my political career. I was elected to the *conseil regional* for le Gard in southern France.[7] I have a holiday home there, where I've been going for the past twenty years. I'm president of the Export Commission for the region.

When I made the deal with Gillette, I was hoping to have some responsibility in the government, and so I began to prepare things. I hired a general manager. I negotiated a contract with Gillette to retain the presidency for the next ten years, with the option to take time off when my political obligations required it and to quit in five minutes if I wished. I also arranged that if I left Waterman, I could come back as a consultant on a five-day-a-month basis and earn the same amount as I do now.

My experience in public relations for Waterman has helped to prepare me for politics – lots of handshaking and constantly being in the news. Journalists are lazy people, and whenever they want an example of a successful business-woman, they think of me. I have no successor in this role at the moment, curiously enough. I think that's because none of my younger contemporaries are media-minded. I've always been open to journalists, and I'm invited to make a lot of after-dinner speeches and attend conferences in schools. I think this is tremendously important, so I go – no matter what the size or situation of the school. If you don't capture the interest of the younger generation, you won't exist politically.

Politicians, on the other hand, are an entirely different thing. They really don't want me – first because I'm a woman, and also because I don't need to be paid. In politics, men have to be elected, because if they aren't elected they have no means of earning their keep. In France, politicians don't have jobs, and as a consequence, they know nothing about anything. I have knowledge of how to run a company. I'm used to negotiating with unions. I wanted a chance to influence the central government, to share my experience, but politicians aren't interested. They tell me, "My dear, you do look nice today, charming! Come and sit by me!" It was never like that in business – I was taken seriously very quickly – but in politics, no! They can't forget that I'm female.

Now Gillette holds 95 percent of the Waterman shares. There are still a few shares left on the Paris stock exchange. I remain chief executive and president, but I'm no longer in complete control. Gillette knew it would be hard for me, but I don't think they imagined it would be this hard.

Originally, when I struck the deal with Gillette, it was a healthy company that seemed to have few problems. But when Revlon tried to stage a public takeover, Gillette was forced to buy back its own shares on the American stock market. As a result, they now need to recoup the money from their subsidiaries. Waterman is a profitable company with a magnificent net income. We're as careful as possible with regard to employment, hiring extra help only when it's absolutely necessary. So when Gillette sent instructions to fire 7 percent of my staff, I said, "We won't do it." I wrote to the chairman of the board, saying, "We aren't involved in your problems with Revlon. We sold you Waterman to develop it, not to impose restraints on it."

Well, they didn't like that, I can tell you! I was summoned to London to see my boss. "I feel you don't like us," he said. "What can I do to make you change your mind?" So I said, "Accept my budget: that's all." And he did. But then a week later, I received a telex from Boston informing me that they were completely restructuring the main organization and that my boss was no longer my boss.

All this happened during the first six months after Waterman was sold to Gillette. I think things will be much better now, because we've reorganized into product divisions (rather than geographical divisions, as was previously the case). I report to the vice president for stationery products, a splendid person from Brooklyn. He reports to the president, who's competing with someone else for the succession to the chairmanship of the board of directors. The present chairman is due to retire in two or three years. I get a bit confused about all that, but I think this arrangement should work well. My vice president is completely open-minded and understands the product line and its marketing problems. I feel I can explain things to him much more easily.

However, there have been other headaches concerning our acquisition by Gillette. They wanted us to change our reporting system, to go back to IBM, which we left ten years ago. My people were tearing their hair out. I've just hired someone to transform our normal reporting practices to suit Gillette, where they like to consolidate everything nearly every day.

Then there's the business of going to America for executive meetings. Normally, Gillette executives are permitted to travel business class if the flight is over seven hours long. I take the Concorde. I'll go to America only if I can travel by Concorde. I think I'm the only person in the company who travels on the Concorde. I never give in.

Leadership, for me, is all about recognition of competence and managing people, enabling them to accept some idea or fact that they wouldn't accept from someone else and persuading them to act on it. My style is very feminine: I'm not usually direct, but subtle, in my corrections. I think the French prefer it; no one loses face. When someone has done something wrong, I don't think you need to tell them directly; you only upset them.

I think women can do well in business. They have more feeling for hiring people and handling people. Men have their imaginations ruined by long periods of study. Their enthusiasm is dead by the time they start work. It might even help Gillette if they hired more women, but they would probably be American women and that's somehow different. The United States is a terrible country. People often think the American women are liberated, but it's not true at all. They're still considered a minority. I've met some American career women, and I've heard exactly how it is. I'm not so interested in the widows of successful men but in the young women of today – those who start in business aiming for the top. They're fresh and enthusiastic and don't want to be squashed by men. But there's no point in encouraging women to go into business unless they're prepared to fight all the way. Don't try unless you're prepared to sacrifice your children and your private life.

I don't like segregation, feminism, and the like. Females who stick together don't further the cause for other women. It's like putting blacks on one side and Jews on the other and females somewhere else. An American who was a distributor for Waterman in the States once told me, "I've tried working with black people, Indians, and women, and it doesn't work." That was ten, maybe fifteen years ago. But things are changing. There are many young men who take care of children now. Perhaps when these young men are older, they'll also accept without question a woman in a business role.

I've never looked for a man who would fight my battles for me, even among my husbands. I don't want someone to lean on. I have my problems, and no one can help. I'm perfectly willing to sell an idea, to prepare someone to accept my plans; but if I want to do something, no one can stop me. It's not so much my independence (I'm not as tough as that); it's those men who are always telling me what I should do. I can't stand that.

I also always sleep with the window open, and I don't think I could live with a man who snores. I like quiet men with whom I don't need to talk about my professional life and who enjoy the type of life I like.

I don't much care for Parisian life, but by necessity I have to live here during the week. I'm obliged to go out, attend dinners, and things like that. But I much prefer the country. I love peace and tranquillity. (I hate children screaming and splashing, so no one swims in my swimming pool when I'm at home.) My first happiness is in silence. I also take tremendous pleasure, for example, in the way the sunlight falls on a tree. Every time I cross the river Seine, for a few seconds while I'm on the bridge I feel magnificently happy. And I love hot baths, especially when it's cold outside. My main interest now is my garden. I would also like to improve my vineyard. I've planted two hectares and should have my first harvest in 1989 – 68 hectoliters, or something like that. I could expand up to 120 hectoliters. I would also like to take a course to learn how to make the wine myself. That would be marvelous.

I would like to have replaced my business career with politics, although at present I'm not as fed up as I was a year ago: there's a new challenge in this business with Gillette. I get bored when business is going too well or becomes too easy. I have two dreams: I would like to be *secrétaire d'état* or *ministre* – just once and not for very long, but just to have done it.[8]

I don't think that being successful has really changed me. I'm the same as I was when I was eleven. I don't think I've improved very much since then. When I was eleven, I was advanced for my age, and I don't think I understand much more now. I *know* more things, but I don't *understand* anything better than when I was eleven. I used to be shy, and the idea of having to speak to more than two people was horrible. The first time I had to make a speech to the executives of the factory was nerve-racking. There were thirty or forty of them – I can't remember now. But I got used to it. It's the same as riding a horse: the more you do it, the easier it becomes. Also, I never used to forgive people, nor could I understand their motives; but now, in my old age, I'm becoming much more tolerant.

I'm not a perfectionist, but I *am* impatient. I do like to get on with things. I give all my heart to a project and want to see it finished. I know my own limits, what I'm able to do and what I can hope for. I don't consider myself a superwoman. I have good health and I'm well balanced. Because I'm healthy, I have a lot of energy. I'll always be concerned with the basics. There's a French proverb that states that you must have a healthy mind in a healthy body and must resist manipulation by books or your environment. This is how I try to live.

Notes

1 P. Chutkow, "Her Nibs." *New York Times Magazine*, December 4, 1988, p. 35.
2 Ibid., p. 38.
3 Available through European Case Clearinghouse House, Institute of Technology, Cranfield, Bedford MK43OAL, England.
4 Maquis was the name given to members of the resistance movement during the Second World War.
5 These "inspectors" are the elite of the elite – those who graduated at the top of their class at the École Nationale d'Administration, the institute that trains people for leadership positions in France.
6 A large industrial holding in France.
7 The *conseil regional* is the local government responsible for the development of the region. Since 1981, as the French government has attempted to decentralize its power, these local governments have become increasingly important.
8 These positions – secretary of state and minister – are the top positions held in central government.

COMMENTARY

At first glance, it would be easy to dismiss Francine Gomez's success as due merely to her inheritance, her good fortune in having family wealth and circumstances. A closer inspection of Gomez's story, however reveals that her succession as the head of Waterman was not a foregone conclusion: she was not even in the running until she was over thirty years of age. In addition, she had competition from two candidates who had not only the same inherited claims she had but also the advantage of the right education and preparation for such responsibility. Gomez's rivals were her cousins, who, as men, would have been assumed to be the most suitable executives for the company.

Despite these hurdles, Francine Gomez took over Waterman with relatively little acknowledged business experience and not only won the confidence and respect of the personnel in a matter of two years but also staged a turnaround that saved Waterman from bankruptcy. By the late 1980s, she had become the most widely respected businesswoman in France. In recognition of her achievements, she was awarded the *Chevalier de la Légion d'Honneur* and *Chevalier de l'Ordre National du Mérite* – honors conferred by the French President.

The unique and dramatic story of Francine Gomez illustrates both the influence of personal characteristics on achievements and the influence of leadership style on organizational culture. The following analysis of Gomez's personality characteristics and leadership style offers a useful framework for examining these processes in more detail.

LEADERSHIP AND PERSONAL STYLE

Francine Gomez has the type of leadership style I described in Chapter 4 as *dramatic* (Kets de Vries and Miller, 1984b). She is outspoken and vivacious. She has been known to state her opinion in public without considering the consequences; seemingly innocent disclosures have resulted in very public personal and business rows. She seems to like attention. She has courted journalists and encouraged media interest in herself as a means to promote Waterman and her own political career. She likes activity and excitement; her interest in politics and the sellout to Gillette have provided her with adversaries, arguments, and conflict, all of which she finds stimulating.

Gomez's character contains a number of narcissistic themes (American Psychiatric Association, 1994). The following key features can be discerned in her behavior:

Grandiose sense of self

Francine Gomez describes herself as having been a model child, prettier than most, and used to being the focus of attention. As an adult in the business world, she sees herself as different from other women in her openness to journalists.

She seems to enjoy being different from everyone else in a variety of ways. For example, she mentions that she was the only person at Gillette to travel by Concorde, despite this being contrary company policy and the fact that she was president of a very small subsidiary.

The underlying theme throughout Gomez's story of success is her belief in her own worth: because she received very little formal education or business training, she is able to perform better than those whose heads are filled with business principles and whose imagination has been ruined by study. Her achievements have confirmed her belief in her own talent and have fostered her dreams.

Preoccupation with success and power

Some of Gomez's strongest and fondest memories of her reign at Waterman revolve around the power she had there before the company was bought by Gillette. She did not account to anyone during that time; there were no shareholders, and her mother and aunt were ineffectual or absent. Waterman was her passion, and any success was her success. "I had all the power, and that felt good to me," she recalls.

Gomez implies that she was drawn to politics partly because she gets bored when business is going too well or becomes too easy. She wishes to be *secrétaire d'état* not because she has a grand design to serve the citizens of France but "just to have done it." Having succeeded at Waterman without business schooling, Gomez feels that she has a better idea of what the government should be doing than those who have studied and trained to be politicians. There may be a grain of truth in this, but her dismissal of education and theoretical principles of management and organization appears premature.

Need for admiration

To maintain the admiration of others, Gomez makes a great effort to preserve her good looks, dainty figure, and stylish wardrobe. Traveling on the Concorde is part of her chic image, and even the giant Gillette could not interfere with that. Gomez captures the attention of the public with her outspoken and controversial views on motherhood versus career and with little gems of intrigue concerning the difficulties in her relationships. The effect of her presence in a room is invigorating: she has tremendous energy and a sense of fun, both of which are infectious, and she quickly becomes the focus of attention and interest.

During her years at the helm, Gomez's sense of the dramatic and her eye for style and esthetically pleasing impressions and images enabled her to produce fashionable pens that corresponded to market trends. She instinctively anticipated the symbols of the lifestyles to which the public aspired and built a corresponding corporate image – one that fostered Waterman's place as market leader. The sophisticated, clean, and uncluttered image of the Waterman pen corresponds well with Francine Gomez's own image.

Sense of entitlement

Francine Gomez's arrangement with Gillette appears to have been very one-sided. The assumption that she could leave her role as president of Waterman on short notice to take up a political career and then return at will as a fully salaried consultant implies that she felt that she was indispensable to both Waterman and Gillette. That arrangement did not take account of the people who stepped in to fill her shoes in her absence or of the dynamics of the organization's culture. The wisdom of this arrangement is questionable.

Subtle exploitation

Gomez's leadership style can be described as the gentle feminine manipulation of a seductress. She gives criticism obliquely, saving people's face but making quite clear what she does not like. Her gentle, playful image is made more powerful by the occasional swift, ruthless dismissal of those who fail to please. She is a perfect illustration of the proverbial iron fist in a velvet glove.

Lack of empathy

Gomez's many marriages indicate a certain lack of empathy. She does not easily accept male frailties. She experiences "being in love" but cannot sustain a loving relationship once the initial romance has died, as suggested by this statement: "I consider it useless to continue to live with someone I don't love anymore." Extrapolated into another context, we can infer from this statement that her relationship with Gillette was doomed from the start.

The most significant illustrations of Gomez's lack of empathic understanding are her description of motherhood and her dispassionate view of her own daughters. Because her need for affection as a small child was apparently denied, she seems to have shut off affectionate feelings at an early age and may, as a consequence, have been unable to identify or respond to them in her own babies. Perhaps she unwittingly inflicted on her own children an injury similar to the one she experienced.

Narcissistic reactions

By her own admission, Gomez is a bad loser. She does not like to be told what to do. She speaks of becoming more tolerant with age, but the facts belie her claim. In the face of frustration or defeat, she does not stay around to be humiliated but withdraws and bounces back somewhere else. Thus we have her succession of marriages, her stormy relationships with her daughters, and her growing sense of disappointment, frustration, and impasse with Gillette – an impasse that ultimately led to her resignation. Her intolerance of disappointment and defeat reveals a regression to reactive narcissistic patterns. Her management style has at times showed evidence of the envy, ruthlessness, arrogance, and dominance typically associated with the reactive narcissist. This style has occasionally aggravated breakdowns in communication and relationships. The origins of this type of behavior can be traced to her early childhood experiences.

FAMILY ORIGINS

Francine Gomez offers, in the quoted passage above, two important clues about her very early childhood (that is, before the age of seven). First, she describes her parents' marriage as a romantic relationship that met with strong family opposition; second, she notes that she was a model child, very pretty, special, and different from most.

The "perfect marriage" of Francine Gomez's parents would not have been easy to keep up. The young couple, having married against the wishes of their family, may have made it a matter of honor to ensure that their relationship was seen as idyllic. Both came from wealthy families and moved in a social circle characterized by opulence, gracious living, and refinement. A pretty baby confirmed the success of their marriage, but Gomez's mother was not interested in childrearing. In the interview, Gomez described her mother as a distant figure, undemonstrative and unaffectionate, but full of the social graces: "a beautiful image, a beautiful woman, but it stopped there." In her autobiography, *On ne bandine pas avec la politique* (One shouldn't joke about politics), Gomez briefly mentions her nanny, who was paid to care for her and who no doubt loved her in many ways. This woman may have been Gomez's first "good object," although Gomez gives the nanny no real acknowledgment or identity. It appears, then, that the first person to give Gomez unconditional acceptance and attention was a "nobody." The two people who were of greater importance to the child Francine (that is, her parents) continued their own lives with little interruption. This may have been the first narcissistic injury Gomez suffered.

In her attempts to deal with this sense of loss, she apparently discovered that by being a model child, she enhanced the myth of her parents' perfect marriage and was rewarded with their attention. By exploiting her dainty good looks and her (at first glance) innocent, charming, yet childish response to her environment, Francine Gomez established a pattern still apparent in her behavior today.

Gomez's infantile injury was reinforced by life circumstances. She was separated from her parents during the war and then later experienced the illness and death of her father as a major narcissistic injury: "When he died, that was that. He was completely out of my life." Yet given the central position of her father in her life, she never seems to have properly mourned him.

The underlying fear of not being considered as an individual in her own right (but instead being seen as just a pretty "object") can be traced throughout Gomez's history. Indeed, Gomez felt she was not taken seriously as a woman or as an adult until she was over thirty. She perceived her sister to be a victim of that fate as well: "She was not as pretty as I was and so did not exist in the eyes of the family." This concern has influenced Gomez's choice of business and political strategies through the years, especially her high public profile: "If you don't capture the interest of the younger generation [or others], you won't exist politically [or at all]."

The second underlying fantasy mentioned above – that of being a model child (with all that implies) – also pervades Francine Gomez's actions. Through her apparently open and unguarded spontaneity, she creates the impression of being naive, vulnerable, and defenseless. However, this impression is far from the truth. If anything, the soft and feminine exterior is both armor and camouflage. It hides a determination, resilience, and tenacity that, if displayed more openly, might invite aggressive attacks from competitors or colleagues.

"We were never permitted to complain," she reflects, noting that she would have honored that prohibition "even if my cousins had beaten me to death." The adults around her did not pay attention to her needs or offer to control or regulate behavior that they had not witnessed. The grown-ups in Gomez's life appear to have been content with here-and-now evidence of good manners, politeness, and social grace; they apparently paid attention to external impressions and behavior but did not inquire or care about internal, individual, or personal feelings. As long as the surface appearance was acceptable, what happened beneath did not matter.

Gomez seems to have "split" the three key people in her childhood into "good" and "bad" models. Gomez's father and grandmother formed her vision of perfection, and she sought to copy their lifestyles and attitudes. She is proud to be seen as being like her grandmother, on whom she has modeled herself (in preference to her mother, whom she looks upon as her antithesis, her negative identity).

From Gomez's description, her mother was not a strong character. In the child Francine's experience, she was a disappointing figure. She failed to maintain the family unit in the absence of her husband during the war, allowing her own mother to take control of the situation and remove her children. She continued to have a frivolous and social life in Paris in their absence (and after their return), failing to recognize or respond to the emotional needs of her children. She was a wealthy heiress, impractical, romantic, and self-absorbed, willingly led by her more domineering, pragmatic mother. It would appear that her strength lay in her beauty, sophistication, and compliance. She did not encourage her daughter's independence or self-expression; discounting internal feelings or ideas, she focused on the external characteristics of young Francine's behavior.

According to her description, Gomez's adolescence was unhappy, despite the reunion of her family. She gained weight; she found herself unable to satisfy her father's wishes and respect or agree with her mother. During this period, her mother came to represent all those things Gomez resented. Her insolence and defiance were more than just an adolescent phase, however. She fought her mother, answering back, rebelling against attempts to censor her own personality and raging against her mother as a parental failure, blaming her for the separation from her father and expressing all the pent-up anger of her childhood. Her rages were emotional explosions beyond reason or rational control; bordering on hysteria, they were halted only by physical punishment.

As a result of her anger at her mother's ineffective management of maternal responsibilities, Gomez chose to reject the soft and feminine role traditionally adopted by women – but not until she had tried it herself. Yet despite the younger Gomez's rejection, there is a distinct parallel between the two women. Both are beautiful, sophisticated, and socially adept, and both abandoned their children to follow their own interests.

In Gomez's claim that there is no point in living with someone once love is gone, there is a hint that her parents' marriage may not have remained the idyllic affair of their youth. The long separation during the war could not have helped the marriage. Perhaps reality – in the form of mundane life as well as the war – cut through the romance and idealization that had characterized the relationship and exposed the parents for what they were: human and imperfect.

We may conjecture that Gomez's relationship with her father was fraught with tension. As a child, Gomez may have felt anger and resentment at her father's leaving her alone and unprotected with her bullying cousins and unaffectionate grandmother. On another level, she may also have felt that he left her during the war not to protect and defend her but because she was unlovable. But to give vent to the anger she felt toward her father may have been too threatening. If she turned her anger on him, she might lose him; he might leave her again – this time forever.

Gomez sought her father's attention and approval by trying to please him. When she misbehaved, his displeasure was frightening because of the threat of rejection and abandonment. But in her attempts to please, Gomez was destined to disappoint. Her father wanted her to succeed at her studies and become a surgeon like himself, but his daughter's unconventional early schooling in the country had not prepared her for an academic career. She had not developed the personal discipline necessary to achieve entry to medical school, nor was she motivated by the idea (other than to please her father). Her father's ambition for her may have been short-sighted and constrictive, failing to take account of Gomez as an individual in her own right.

The special bond that existed between father and daughter (despite Gomez's fears of abandonment) may have been disruptive. Incorporating some aspects of her mother's style, Gomez learned how to be seductive and feminine, perhaps unconsciously becoming her mother's rival. In searching for warmth and affection, Gomez walked a dangerous path. Her efforts at a special relationship with her father must have added to her alienation from her mother.

Gomez needed an external "object" to love, whether her father or someone else. Her first marriage may have been both an act of rebellion and an escape of sorts – a safe way to find affection and intimacy without the Oedipal fantasy of having usurped her mother's special place in her father's affections. It would have made her sexuality socially acceptable while preventing further entanglements with her parents. It was, however, a costly experiment for Gomez herself.

Gomez's image of her father was shattered by his death. The slow deterioration of his health turned him into an invalid preoccupied with his bodily functions and weakness. Her anger and disappointment are evidenced in her initial reluctance to speak of him and in the suppression of her feelings with regard to their relationship.

Alain Gomez came close to Francine Gomez's ideal image of the "good father." Rather than expecting her to stay with her children, he encouraged and supported her in building her career. Even now, she retains a great deal of respect and affection for him. It would seem that she was close to resolving her distrust of and distance from men when Alain's career and ambition gained him a prestigious position in southern France. The frustration of lengthy periods of absence may have seemed like a repetition of her father's abandonment during the war, causing her fantasy of being unlovable and rejected to surface again and creating intolerable stress. When Gomez had to choose between Alain and Waterman, Waterman won.

Despite turmoil on many fronts, there is within Francine Gomez's inner theater a large area of stability, expressed in her appreciation of peace and tranquillity and her love of silence and nature. As a small girl, her comfort and solace appear to have come from time spent alone in the chateau and on its grounds, away from people. By the age of eleven, she had mastered the various arts of matching the aggression of her cousins, dominating her sister, pleasing the important and powerful grown-ups in her world (grandmother and father), and ignoring the ineffectual others (mother and housekeeper/teacher). This gave her free time to pursue her own interests and pleasures, and she found an equilibrium and an appreciation of herself and her place in the world. This became the measure by which she has monitored the rest of her life, as acknowledged in her statement "I'm the same as I was when I was eleven." That age remains her stage of paradise.

Such integration and maturation is the healthy side of Gomez's narcissistically-oriented character. The seeds of this positive development were sown through her relationship with her grandmother, whose influence during her childhood was both extensive and crucial. The old lady was a strict but constant figure in Gomez's life, someone who encouraged her to fight for her own interests, literally as well as symbolically. She praised independence and fortitude and offered a very different model of behavior from that of Gomez's mother. She also exhibited a dispassionate assessment of reality, as in her decision to send all her valued items – including furniture, fine art objects, her grandchildren, and her pets – away from the dangers of bombing in Paris. We may hypothesize that Francine Gomez was resentful of her grandmother for treating her as just another possession, but it is clear that she also admired and respected her (and perhaps obtained some reciprocal affection from her). This "good object" would appear to be Gomez's major psychological foundation.

Because of her strong identification with her grandmother and the assumption within the family that Francine was "just like her," Gomez was given an opening to express her previously unrecognized and unencouraged "other self" at a time when there was a gap in the leadership of both the family and the business. The legacy that her grandmother gave her was permission not only to be like her but to step into her shoes. Gomez's sudden and swift ascent to power was at one level unexpected, yet at another it offered no surprise. It confirmed Gomez's feeling that she had never really been understood or acknowledged as a child.

The family's neglect of Gomez's education and their early blindness to her potential makes her disparaging and critical of academics and formal business education. She relies strongly on intuition and the power of her femininity and charm to get her way. Her refusal to undertake a critical or objective appraisal of her leadership style and qualities is an expression of her vulnerability, her need to protect that part of herself that was neglected in childhood. However, this refusal in turn leaves her liable to reproduce in her environment fantasies that she has carried unchallenged from her infancy: that of being unacknowledged as a person with rights, ambitions, and potential of her own and that of not having her needs identified as important.

In conclusion, three factors in Gomez's background stand out as important in the making of an entrepreneurial woman. First, Gomez had a privileged relationship with her father – a relationship that must have given her a lot of strength – and his wish for her to be a professional must have given her a stimulus to succeed. At the same time – given the nature of their relationship – she realized that one cannot depend on men; they may not be there when needed. This gave her a strong belief in the need for self-sufficiency. Finally, Gomez had a negative role model in the form of her ineffective mother. Gomez probably told herself that she never wanted to become like her mother, choosing instead a positive role model of female business competence: her grandmother, who showed her that women did not have to be just pretty and pleasant but could also be tough and professionally astute.

PERSONAL STRENGTHS AND WEAKNESSES

Francine Gomez's strengths stem from the aspects of her narcissistic personality. Her exhibitionism and flamboyance give her a dramatic presence that encourages others' dependence and loyalty while energizing her surroundings. People like to be with her and like to please her. Her charming, unsophisticated energy and enthusiasm engender openness and frankness in others. She has been able to talk easily with her staff through the years, and they have been able to imagine themselves as her equal.

Gomez's internal sense of separateness and distance from others has enabled her to withstand the loneliness of being at the top. She does not desire intimacy; in fact, she avoids it. We may surmise that the existence of the protective mechanism of rejection of others as an attack against rejection *by* others gave her strength in the trauma of dismissing staff. After going through three divorces, Gomez had already well tested her resilience in the face of hostility, hurt, and disappointment. Her intolerance of frustration and failure also assisted her in retaining only the most able subordinates and eliminating any direct competitors who might have attempted to undermine her authority.

Similarly, the familiarity of a competitive and aggressive environment has enabled Gomez to feel energized and alive and to take on seemingly impossible situations and stage a turnaround. Her hunger for this kind of excitement is what gave her the ambition and drive to succeed; it then prompted her to change her interest from the business world to politics.

Francine Gomez has no qualms about using her femininity as a tool in business. On the contrary, she sees her gender as an advantage. Men assume that she is weaker than they and so offers no real competitive threat. She encourages this fantasy through her appearance, charm, and apparent innocence. An example of her pleasure in executing this kind of confidence trick is demonstrated in her Baron Bich reference.

However, all of these strengths are also in many ways Gomez's weaknesses. Her spontaneity and high level of personal disclosure lead her into public confrontations. Associates and colleagues are forced into loving her or hating her, and those who dislike her stay away. As a result, she risks being surrounded by sycophants and toadies. No one has been able to encourage her to understand herself; even the exercise of writing an autobiography failed to reveal to Gomez the dangers of her unrestrained approach.

Gomez's intuitive decisions are creative and energizing for those around her, but her lack of risk assessment and her limited foresight in planning take their toll. Consider, for example, the sellout to Gillette. Gomez did not really think through the consequences of being owned by Gillette. The trigger for the sale was allegedly the problem of potential inheritance taxes, but another reason may have been that she needed new stimuli and imagined that Gillette would provide a competitive and confrontational environment.

That search for new stimuli lay behind her move into politics as well. However, given her narcissistic disposition, she failed to anticipate what she would do if she were not elected. Furthermore, she underestimated her own reaction to the loss of power incurred in selling out. Just before the election of 1988, when Gomez was heavily involved in negotiating with Gillette about the budget allowances for Waterman, the election campaign became a nuisance. The outcome was not what she had hoped for on either front: she was not elected, and she found herself confronted with the millstone of the Gillette administration.

WATERMAN: AN OVERVIEW

What shape was Gillette in when it acquired Waterman? The company was in a depressive slump. It had overdiversified in an attempt to hold its own against competition. Power struggles between divisions, the succession battle for the chairmanship of the board, and an aging board of directors had all weakened Gillette's management. These problems, coupled with the company's size and excessive diversity, made it inwardly oriented as well as internally competitive and distrustful. Gillette's management depended on a massive organizational network that slowed down communication and decision making and restricted initiative. This led to dissatisfaction and bitterness among senior management and destroyed cooperation while at the same time promoting aggressive competitive moves against other divisions as well as market opponents.

The situation at Gillette presented Francine Gomez with a set of dynamics she had not previously encountered. Revlon's takeover attempts had unleashed paranoia at Gillette; control was tightened, and greater submission was demanded of subsidiaries. Gomez may have misread the situation in part because of cross-cultural differences resulting in a mutual lack of understanding of American-French business patterns.

Gomez found, once she was involved with Gillette, that her independence, initiative, and spontaneity were regarded as insolence and considered disruptive. Her non-conformist attitude irritated top management, increasing hostility and suspicion. Her creativity and individualism were not valued but rather were taken as a threat.

Thus it can be seen that the American-French acquisition was doomed from the start. Gillette did not respect Gomez's strengths, nor was she prepared to accept its authority. She was highly critical of Gillette's methods and decisions, challenging all her instructions and persisting with her own ideas and policies. The incidents she cites regarding her travel arrangements and Waterman's information system are small examples of her resistive stance. Yet Gillette was a Goliath greater than Gomez had expected.

It was therefore no surprise that on December 16, 1988, Francine Gomez announced her retirement from Waterman. The announcement was characteristically dramatic; but to those who had studied the situation, the decision was predetermined.

Case 2

Triumphing over women and witches
Hollywood in the Alps

For Robert Houtman, this assignment was one of the most challenging in his career as a consultant. He had been asked to advise Stephan Muller, founder and president of Vocatron, how he might break the impasse his company was in. After listening to Muller's story, Houtman felt that the actions to be taken were fairly obvious and straightforward, but his suggestions to Muller were met with an unexpectedly hostile reaction. Digging further, both to uncover alternative approaches and to discover the reason behind Muller's hostility, Houtman encountered some confusion about the capabilities of Muller's son, David. He seemed quite competent to Houtman, but others at Vocatron had a different opinion. Who was right? He also noted some puzzling human resource management practices in the firm, as well as the complicating factor of a large number of disgruntled employees.

Houtman quickly realized that the problem was far greater, and stranger, than he had thought. He was at a loss to explain some of the more irrational aspects of the organization – bonuses, for example, seemed to be determined by whim – until Muller described aspects of his childhood to the consultant over dinner one night. This information gave Houtman a better sense of what made Muller the person he was and proved to be a vital clue in developing an understanding of why the company functioned in such a strange way.

It is often necessary to be an organizational detective in order to make an effective diagnosis of and intervention into a company's situation. A couple of obvious questions need answers. First, is the stated problem the real problem? In many instances, a consultant will discover that the apparent problem is quite different from what really troubles the company. Second, what is the logic, the rationale, behind the behavior of the leader? Often it is only by putting these bits and pieces together that a consultant can catch a leader's attention and make effective recommendations.

HOLLYWOOD IN THE ALPS

The Vocatron Corporation was set up about fifteen years ago by Stephan Muller, who believed that there was a market niche for private vocational training programs, particularly for young people. His hunch proved to be right: over the years, the company expanded steadily. Muller branched out from his home base in Denmark and set up sales subsidiaries in most European countries, the United States, Canada, and Australia. Almost all of his fifty regional sales offices were run by women, most of them in their twenties or early thirties. Most of the selling took place by telephone and through home visits. For tax reasons, Muller had recently decided to move the head office from his home country to Switzerland.

Vocatron was now facing a couple of troubling problems. After a period of sustained, steady growth, profits were beginning to decline, and Stephan Muller could not determine why. Muller, now 57, had also begun to consider the question of his successor and wondered whether his son, who had been working for the company for two years, would eventually be able to take over from him. For advice, Muller turned to Robert Houtman, a consultant specializing in entrepreneurship and family business.

The company visit

Robert Houtman's initial visit to Vocatron was engraved in his memory. Vocatron's head office commanded a spectacular view of snowcapped mountains. The small parking lot in front of the building was full of expensive cars, all of which were completely upstaged by a splendid red Ferrari. Once Houtman was past the heavy security at the entrance, he discovered an opulent interior with white wall-to-wall carpeting and modern paintings and sculptures, including a Henry Moore. An attractive secretary pointed out a fitness center, complete with sauna, jacuzzi, and swimming pool. The whole complex was less than a year old.

Houtman had to wait for ten minutes before being greeted by Stephan Muller. The president was very well, if conservatively, dressed and seemed young for his age. His height, bushy eyebrows, and penetrating stare left a lasting impression. His manner of speaking was that of a man used to giving orders.

After showing Houtman into his spacious office, Muller explained that all was not well at Vocatron. After a period of rapid expansion, with sales doubling every three years, growth had leveled off and profits were falling. An explosive increase in the number of sales offices had come to a halt during the last year and a half. Muller attributed these new circumstances to the fact that his top executive group had become seriously overextended.

The president was clear about what he expected from Houtman: he wanted him to investigate how the company could continue to expand. Arrangements had already been made for Houtman to interview Vocatron's top management team and some of the more experienced subsidiary directors. Muller also wanted Houtman to assess his son, David. He mentioned as an aside that he had heard rumors that had sown doubts about his son's competence.

Houtman's interviews soon uncovered a number of problematic issues. The directors of the subsidiaries, who were flown in to talk with Houtman, turned out to be a deeply disgruntled group. These young people – almost all women – were unhappy about the way their careers were progressing. At first, working for Vocatron had seemed glamorous, because of the early responsibility, excitement, adventure, and travel. But as the years passed, the glamour was gradually wearing off.

Houtman was astonished to discover that none of the female directors had ever been to the new head office before. Most of their communication with headquarters took place by phone, fax, letter, or personal visits from senior management. Comparing the modest conditions under which she worked with the opulence of the head office, one of the sales directors exclaimed, "This place is unbelievable. It's like Hollywood in the Alps!" During her visit, this particular woman made several attempts to see the president. She was prevented from doing so by his secretary, who consistently maintained that he had gone off-site for a business meeting (although the sales director had heard that Muller had been seen on the premises). Houtman learned that Muller had made promises about this woman's future career that had come to nothing, although she had apparently been running the most profitable sales subsidiary in the company for the past ten years. Muller's previous attempt to pacify her by giving her a sports car as a bonus had obviously been only partially successful. In an angry attempt to get through the door to the president's office, this woman "accidentally" spilled a cup of black coffee on the immaculate white carpet, in Houtman's presence.

A complaint repeatedly made by the sales directors was that they felt stuck in their present positions. Most of them had joined the company enthusiastically in their early twenties. After all, there were very few companies offering such exciting and responsible opportunities to people with their relatively limited education and work experience. Setting up a sales office in a foreign country had been a great challenge. Over time, however, the long hours and average salaries had killed the spirit of adventure. Since most of the selling took place in the evening, and there was a lot of pressure to perform, everyone's social life had been seriously affected. Few of the sales directors were married or had stable long-term relationships. Indeed, the only relationships most appeared to have were with men from the head office who made regular visits to monitor their performance. Quite a few of the women complained of stress symptoms. Some had repeatedly been put on medication, and a few had even been hospitalized. Their major complaint was that career progress stopped with the position of director of a sales subsidiary. No woman had ever been promoted to the head office.

A close inner circle of all-male executives, many of them old school friends of Stephan Muller, ran the head office. Some of the sales directors compared this group to the KGB because of the control systems used to monitor sales performance. When Houtman asked the women why they did not leave the company, they seemed lost – not only unable to summon up a reply but literally not knowing where they could go. Many of them had left their home countries long ago and had a sense of rootlessness; their only feeling of belonging *anywhere* was grounded in the ambience of Vocatron. Whatever might be wrong with company policy, these employees hung on to the belief that people at the head office would look after them, under all circumstances.

During the interviews, some of these subsidiary directors talked about David Muller, the president's son. According to them, he was incompetent. Without his father's influence, they said, he would never have chosen a business career. They drew their conclusions from his behavior during internships at three of the sales subsidiaries and cited some rather vague incidents to illustrate what a failure he had been.

This view of David rather surprised Houtman. He was unconvinced by the subsidiary directors' comments. David Muller had come across as a rather thoughtful individual when Houtman interviewed him. He appeared to be reasonably well educated, having obtained a business degree. However, Houtman had discerned in him a certain amount of ambivalence toward his father, who, David said, "gives me impossible assignments, never praises me for work well done, keeps checking up on everything I do, and chastises me in front of everybody."

David Muller told Houtman that he had not been a good student, having been more interested in cafés and parties than studying. He explained that it had not been easy to grow up in his father's shadow. Only after leaving home and doing his military service (during which he had received a commission and become aide to a general who had taken a liking to him) had he become more sure of himself.

During an interview with Stephan Muller, Houtman asked him why, given his own assessment of the need for better top management talent in his company, he did not do the obvious: select the most capable subsidiary directors for promotion to the head office. Muller reacted with astonishing vehemence. He became agitated and then stiffened up, shouting, "Impossible! Women have only limited capabilities, and running a sales office is as far as they can go." According to Muller, having women in senior positions at the head office would seriously disrupt the general atmosphere. He then said, rather wistfully, "Wouldn't it be nice if I could get rid of all these older women in a pleasant way? They were all right when they were younger, but they turned into such bitches later on!"

In contrast to the female subsidiary directors, the six male executives who made up Muller's inner circle at the head office seemed to be quite happy working at Vocatron. They shared their boss's perception of women, believing that it would be very disruptive to have them at the head office in anything other than secretarial positions. In addition, they believed that the secretaries needed continuous surveillance; without it, they would begin to act irresponsibly. The men said jokingly, and with obvious sexual innuendo, that they knew how to keep their subordinates in line.

This group of executives claimed to be satisfied with the existing reward structure as well. Further prompting, however, revealed that Vocatron bonuses were given rather haphazardly. For example, one of the executives had once gone to Muller saying that he needed a sailing yacht. To the surprise of the executive and his colleagues alike, he had in due course received one.

Muller's personal background

During a subsequent dinner with the president, Houtman learned more about Stephan Muller's background. The wine seemed to have a relaxing influence on Muller, and he chatted openly. He was an only child who had been quite unhappy growing up, he said. His parents' divorce when he was only five years old was a key event in his childhood. After the divorce, his father had moved to another country and started a new family, never seeing Stephan again. What few early memories of family togetherness Muller had, he cherished.

Muller described his mother as an irresponsible, unreliable individual who went through an endless series of short-lived love affairs after the family's breakup. He felt that his father's departure had really changed her. She had become very moody, lashing out at her son and ordering him around. His tactic for survival after the divorce had been to minimize the amount of time he stayed at home, spending most of his free hours with a close circle of friends (some of whom now worked for him). The interest shown in him by an uncle who regularly took him on excursions had helped him to overcome his feelings of desertion by his father. This uncle had provided some stability, and Muller felt close to him.

Muller explained that his own marriage was not successful either. He and his wife had come to an arrangement: they still lived together for the children's sake, but each of them led a separate life. Although it had never been explicitly discussed, his wife was aware that he had had a number of mistresses.

When Houtman questioned Muller about stress symptoms, the president said that he sometimes had stomach problems. He also complained about recurring nightmares. When asked to say something more about the latter, he described a dream in which, with few variations, he was cornered by a horrible witch who jumped on his back and almost choked him. Whenever the dream reached that point, he would begin to scream, and that would wake him up.

Houtman was somewhat taken aback by Muller's confessions. He had to puzzle out the meaning behind them – and behind the serious problems at Vocatron. He knew that his task was now to sort out the different issues, offer Muller an analysis of the various problems, and present a set of recommendations.

COMMENTARY[1]

The information Muller gave Houtman over dinner put the irrational patterns prevailing in the company into perspective. An essential part of the "text" provided by Muller had to do with his relationships with women. From his intense reaction to Houtman's suggestion that women be promoted to positions of top management, it was clear that he had developed a mental block vis-à-vis women in response to the experiences he had had as a child. Based on his perception of his mother after the divorce, he saw women as dangerous, unreliable, and untrustworthy. In order to keep the upper hand with women, he had learned to play them off against each other: they had to be kept down; otherwise, chaos would prevail. By recreating his childhood situation within his organization, he and his small "band of brothers" could keep things in order and keep women subdued to prevent chaos. And certainly Muller knew all too well what chaos meant, given the disruption he had experienced while growing up.

In his company, Muller created a *folie à deux* situation, blatantly encouraging his key executives to share his misogynistic feelings (Kets de Vries and Miller, 1987). As a matter of fact, his colleagues did not have much choice: if they thought differently than Muller on the subject of women, they would be asked to leave. Muller had made it clear that women would never become part of the inner circle and that any kind of behavior was permitted to keep them in line – including, it seemed, sexual manipulation.

The organizational consequences of the president's behavior were predictable. A strong paranoid streak ran through the firm; a fight-flight culture prevailed. Not only was there a "war" going on with the competition; another "war" was taking place within the company, and the adversaries were the women. They were hired for the sole purpose of being continuously put down (although Muller was probably not consciously aware of his purpose). For Muller, it was not good enough to subjugate the women once; it had to be done over and over again in a futile attempt to overcome his feeling of insecurity.

This attitude toward women obviously fostered a lack of trust between the inner circle and the sales directors and a considerable amount of secrecy within each group. Information was a much sought-after commodity, with the sales subsidiaries usually kept in the dark. Amazingly – in spite of the irrational nature of Muller's actions – this formula seemed to have worked for many years. Only now, because of the company's growth, had it begun to crack at the seams.

As might be expected, discriminatory management practices were causing tremendous anger and bitterness on the part of the women in the company. In spite of the perks they still enjoyed, these women eventually came to feel that they had given the best years of their life to Vocatron. They had been molded into workaholics by an employer who gave no consideration to their private lives. And they had finally realized that what could have been a major "pacifier" – a top job at the head office – would never be offered to them. The accumulated result of the irrational practices at Vocatron was an unmotivated group of sales directors, overextended head office executives, stagnation in sales, and a decline in profits.

How did this state of affairs affect the president's son, David? When he was sent to the subsidiaries to learn the rules of the trade, he became the victim of displacement activities, serving as a scapegoat for the disgruntled group of directors who were trying to "kill" the father through the son. Did David ever really have a chance of joining the "band of brothers" that surrounded his father? Would those men – his father included – ever have been willing to accept an interloper? Apart from the directors' "displaced parricide," we should not rule out a problematic father–son relationship. Could it be that Stephan Muller, because of his unresolved problems with his own absent father, had projected his sense of responsibility onto his son, David? Maybe because Stephan had not been able to keep his own father, sons unconsciously became "bad" for him. Perhaps he had set up his own son to fail by sending him on impossible missions, unconsciously giving him assignments that were undoable, challenges that were insurmountable. There is, of course, another side to this Oedipal drama: David may have been rebelling, unwilling to submit to his father's wishes and thus (consciously or unconsciously) taking on the role of the incompetent.

Given this tangled web of motivation and action, how would Muller have been likely to perceive Houtman or any other consultant? As they do with therapists, people often transfer their feelings about significant figures in their past onto consultants. But even that provides only a partial answer. Would Muller think of Houtman as the "good uncle" of Muller's childhood, or would Houtman come to represent the deserting father or even the irresponsible and unreliable mother? Perhaps Houtman would take on all of these characters at once, or in turn. Whatever the upshot, the transference process would almost certainly affect the outcome of Houtman's intervention.

This case illustrates how, by putting an organization "on the couch," we can uncover a rationale for what would otherwise seem to be highly irrational behavior. In this case, it was the intrapsychic fantasies of the key powerholder that turned out to undergird a series of highly unusual management practices. Because of Muller's psychological characteristics, Houtman found the diagnosis of Vocatron's problems rather complex. Determining an intervention strategy, given the magnitude of irrationality in Muller's leadership style, was even more difficult. Because some of the organization's problems were extremely deeply rooted, a quick fix was out of the question. Indeed, even a more gradual organizational solution would have been difficult for Houtman to find. As for Muller himself, it is not clear from the case whether he was experiencing enough pain to want to change the situation. If so, maybe something more than a simple consultation would have been needed: professional psychological help might have been required to enable Muller to resolve his deep-seated hostility toward women and to create a more equitable management structure in his company.

Note

1 For a more complete analysis of this case, see M.F.R. Kets de Vries, *Organizations on the Couch: Clinical Perspectives on Organizational Behavior and Change*. San Francisco: Jossey-Bass, 1991.

Working with an entrepreneur
Life at the Chantel Corporation

One definition of a consultant is a person who takes your watch, tells you what time it is, and keeps the watch. If you believe some of the stories about them, consultants are a rather greedy bunch, providing little value and submitting steep bills. To add insult to injury, they are (some say) also lazy and incompetent, telling you what you already know.

If all this is true, Arthur Lawrence, a consultant hired by the Chantel Corporation, would seem to have fallen right into the honeypot. The client has stated that he needs some strategic marketing help, but the covert (but nevertheless clear) message is quite different: he does not want any interference in his company. The only thing he really wants is for Arthur Lawrence to give a positive recommendation to the government – one affirming that Chantel is viable and therefore qualified for government grants. The client is quite happy to pay the consultant his fees; after all, the government is going to pick up a substantial part of the tab.

This is the easy part. The difficult part is that the company is *not* fully viable; in fact, there are a host of problems. This poses an ethical dilemma for Lawrence. How should he proceed? Should he just take the money and run, or should he confront the client with the real issues?

Put yourself in the place of the people who work at Chantel. Imagine how it would feel to work in a company headed by someone who asks for one thing but wants another. What would it be like to work for an entrepreneur like John Husek, founder and president of Chantel? How would you cope with his leadership style? What kind of people would feel comfortable working for this type of leader? How would you describe the company's corporate culture? And most important, if you were the consultant, what would you do? How would you deal with this ethical dilemma while keeping your billing intact? Is your responsibility to the man who is paying for your advice or to the government, which may provide a grant on the basis of your recommendation?

THE CHANTEL CORPORATION

Arthur Lawrence, president of the Strategic Consulting Group, was thinking about the events of the past few weeks. He tried to organize his thoughts around the way his relationship with the Chantel Corporation had developed.

It had begun the previous month ago with a phone call from Ken Becker, vice president for operations at Chantel. During the conversation, Becker had asked Lawrence if he would be willing to do some consulting for the firm's lingerie division. Lawrence had first met Becker when Becker was a fast-track trainee (with a new MBA from a well-known business school) at one of Canada's larger apparel manufacturers. Lawrence had immediately taken a liking to him, enjoying his wit and quick mind. They kept in touch at intervals, and it did not surprise Lawrence that Becker's career had progressed rather rapidly; he recalled hearing that Becker had left a vice-presidential position to work for the Chantel Corporation, attracted by the challenge of expanding his manufacturing responsibilities to include financial matters and by the promise of eventually holding some equity in Chantel.

During the telephone conversation with Becker, it had become obvious that Chantel had an ulterior motive in turning to Lawrence as a consultant. Both the Québec and the federal governments in Canada had become very concerned about the future of the apparel industry. Canada's federal government, in an effort to modernize the industry, had set up an Industrial Renewal Board (CIRB). If a company was deemed eligible by this board, the federal government would pay 75 percent of the cost of a general consulting study to determine whether the company qualified for a government grant that would cover 25 percent of the cost of new machinery. A company could also become eligible for a grant from the Québec government to cover 25 percent of the cost of capital improvements that would increase employment.

Lawrence had quickly realized that Chantel wanted to use him as a means to obtain government financing, hoping to buy more machines and thereby increase capacity. Nevertheless, he had accepted the assignment; and in retrospect, he had to admit that his visits to the company had been far from boring. He recalled his first glimpse of Chantel: walking around a corner in a rundown section of the city, skirting some litter on the street, he had suddenly encountered the gleaming glass façade of an eight-story building that stood out among the surrounding walk-up apartments and tiny shops with faded fabric over their dirty windows. Inside the building, a modern tapestry hung in the reception lounge opposite four stainless steel elevator doors. When he reached the fourth floor (to which he had been directed), the noise of machines as he made his way through the cloth scraps strewn about reminded him that this was really an old-fashioned garment factory. Nearby, buyers at a fashion show were being served chocolate-dipped strawberries by a gracious, slender older man who turned out to be the owner-entrepreneur, John Husek.

Now, after interviewing most of top and middle management at Chantel, visiting the production facilities, and becoming familiar with the various product lines, the time had come to make some preliminary recommendations. Arthur reviewed his interview notes and read a recent marketing research report indicating that consumers were not satisfied with the styling of the company's products, the quality of the fabrics, or the workmanship and that retailers were dissatisfied with Chantel's service. When he had finished reading, Lawrence considered, with some apprehension, how to proceed.

Company history

The Chantel Corporation was established thirty-five years ago by the current president, John Husek, who was at that time a recent immigrant to Canada from Czechoslovakia. Starting as a small manufacturer of knitted underwear, the company had remained a relatively simple, vertically integrated knitting company, though it had machines that had been converted five years previously to serve the demand for material in the velour market. Sales and profits had boomed just after that conversion, as some of the executives nostalgically recalled; they were able to sell their products at any price and under any conditions. The primary executive team in the organization during that strong period consisted of John Husek and his nephew, Sid March, an industrial engineer.

Shortly thereafter, John Husek decided, against the advice of all his executives (as well as his family and outside advisers), to embark on a major expansion and modernization program. The result was a doubling of the size of the building and the installation of in-house dye and finishing facilities. The expansion proved to be more costly and disruptive than expected, however; there were major production and delivery problems. For the first time, Chantel had a small financial loss. The company, which had had cash reserves in the past, became dependent on the banks.

A year before the expansion, Sid March had become vice president of the lingerie division – a promotion that signaled a major shift in corporate responsibilities. John Husek had been using his son, Robert, as his assistant for special projects for two years (after cutting short Robert's liberal arts studies) and now promoted him to the position of vice president for operations, essentially Sid's old area.

Disagreements arose between Husek and March during the expansion period – over the new building, over March's salary and responsibilities compared to Robert Husek's, and over whether John Husek would indeed retire at fifty-five as he had once promised. After a year of increasing conflict, Sid March finally left the company. After fourteen years with Chantel, he decided to set up his own business. It was a painful separation for March, who had always looked up to his uncle. (His own father had died when March was very young.) After March's departure, an outsider named Moira Kelly assumed his position, but she too left the company after several years. At that point, Robert Husek took over as vice president of the lingerie division.

Now the Chantel Corporation was no longer the simple, vertically integrated knitting operation of the past. The new Chantel included the lingerie division, which was composed of two lines: the Chantel brand (for the mass market) and the recently added Faubourg line (for the "contemporary" consumer). Both an inexpensive children's wear division and, most recently, a swimwear department (which was to become a separate division in the near future) had been added. (For an organization chart, see Figure C3.1.) Although sales had grown from $15 million to $30 million in the four years prior to the expansion, Chantel nevertheless had had three successive years of losses that put a serious strain on the company's financial resources.

The lingerie/swimwear division accounted for approximately 40 percent of sales; knitted fabrics – the original Chantel business – contributed 30 percent, and children's clothes made up the rest. Both the fabric and children's wear divisions had recently made small profits, but with the departure of the executive responsible for children's wear (who left to join a direct competitor), the future of at least one of those divisions was in jeopardy.

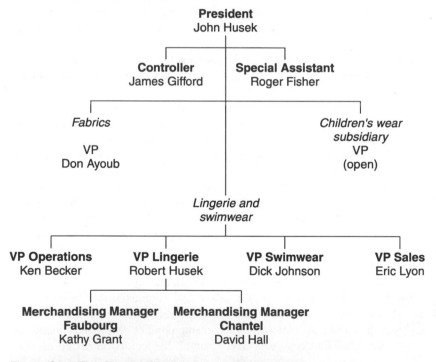

Figure C3.1 The Chantel Corporation organization chart

Executive relationships

The following are Arthur Lawrence's impressions of key Chantel executives based on his interviews with them:

John Husek, president

Lawrence's first interview was with John Husek, the president and majority shareholder. Husek described himself as a very impatient person, a fast decision maker. The present problems of the company, according to Husek, were caused by the general recession in the industry, high interest rates, market erosion by imports, the Québec government's wage structure,[1] and Bill 101 (the Québec law making French the official language of work).[2] But Husek felt things were taking a turn for the better; the new lines were doing well in the shops. He had hired Ken Becker to be responsible for both manufacturing and finance. He felt, unfortunately, that he had been too optimistic in his assessment of Becker's abilities. The new budgeting system that Becker had adopted had taken too long to implement, making for a total lack of information flow inside the company in the interim period and resulting in an absence of correct cost figures. The previous vice president of the lingerie division, Moira Kelly (the woman who had replaced Sid March), had taken advantage of that situation to make excessive purchases of useless fabrics; there was still $1 million worth of merchandise lying in storage. In spite of Kelly's claim at her departure that everything was fine, things had been quite the opposite. In the panic that ensued when it became clear what had happened, Becker had not been able to deal with the problems. Husek had had to cut down Becker's responsibilities and rehire as controller James Gifford, a man Becker had fired six months previously. At least this man, in Husek's opinion, knew how costing functioned at Chantel; Gifford could keep him informed of the operations in the company.

Robert Husek, vice president of the lingerie division

Robert Husek was a lanky, apparently relaxed individual. He started the conversation with Lawrence by saying that Chantel had hired too many people too quickly, leading to predictable adjustment problems. In addition, he said, the start-up costs of the many new operations had been high, and his predecessor had priced many styles below cost. Like his father, however, he thought that the company was posed for a turnaround. In hindsight, it almost seemed as if the major objective of the executives at Chantel over the previous few years had been to fill up the building. But that preoccupation was gone now; the building was at capacity. Moreover, he felt that the spring lines of both Chantel and Faubourg – quite in contrast with the previous year – looked great, and the buyers had not been shocked by the higher prices. This year, Chantel was going to make a serious effort to become more profit-conscious. In the past, the corporation had been practically giving the merchandise away. Robert Husek also said, as an aside, that he thought one of his main tasks in the company was to monitor his father's temperament.

Robert Husek initially did not want Lawrence to meet his subordinates. He claimed that they were too busy working with the introduction of the new lines and dealing with sales representatives. Only after Lawrence insisted that he needed information from these people to do a decent job in preparing the marketing part of his report did Husek give in. Lawrence thought that the push that made him change his mind was Lawrence's remark that if the sales representatives were really too busy, he would have to wait until more time was available (although that would delay the submission of the report, which would postpone government funding).

Kathy Grant, Faubourg merchandising manager

Kathy Grant was an attractive, soft-spoken, fashionably dressed young woman. She characterized Chantel as a large organization with a small-company attitude, where management by the seat of the pants was the norm. She described what she called a "funny" incident by way of evidence: when she was hired, she discovered that someone else had been simultaneously assigned the same job by the president.

In her conversation with Lawrence, it became clear that her contact with Robert Husek, her boss, was rather limited. She saw much more of his father, who often used her as a sounding board. She complained to Lawrence about John Husek's way of motivating people. In his efforts to get better results out of his executives, the president frequently told them how much better others were doing, a practice that was infuriating. If that did not work with a person (and the person was someone he wanted to keep in the company), he used money as a motivator. Grant mentioned that you went to John only with good news (unless a problem was extremely serious and you could think of no alternative).

According to Grant, the previous vice president of the lingerie division had made grave errors but was able to cover them up. This woman "would wrap John around her finger by telling him how terrific everything was." Grant said that she really admired John in spite of his weaknesses, because of his willingness to take risks. Robert, in her opinion, was quite different: a slow decision maker, he would check and recheck everything before making a move. She thought that he had a lot of common sense, but she was bothered by his complete lack of belief in planning. That lack often caused conflicts between the two of them, since she saw herself as a very organized person. Grant also mentioned that Robert's other two subordinates, Eric Lyon (the vice president for sales) and David Hall (the merchandising manager for the Chantel line), did not really get along, which certainly did not make life easier.

David Hall, Chantel merchandising manager

David Hall said he viewed the president as a planner and a thinker and enjoyed working for him. In his opinion, John Husek was a real chess player. Robert also got good press: Hall described him as having changed from an irresponsible young man just out of college to a real manager. He said that Robert had molded the people working under him into a real team.

Eric Lyon, vice president for sales

While attending a preproduction planning meeting of the Faubourg line, Lawrence was informed that Eric Lyon, who at that time was a sales director, had resigned to join a competitor. He had managed to have a few words with Lyon before his departure. Lyon particularly complained about David Hall's incompetence as a manager. He viewed Hall as one of the old-timers and felt that he did not really understand sales management, merchandising, or manufacturing (let alone their interrelationship). He described Hall as a person who withheld information and liked to surround himself with weak people. Lyon thought that Hall should have remained a designer; he was, Lyon claimed, a good example of the Peter Principle.

Lyon also complained about the lack of structure in the organization. What Robert Husek did all day puzzled him: "He just wanders around!" Unfortunately, the interview with Lawrence was cut short by Robert Husek, who barged in to say that Lawrence should not be talking to Lyon at this time. Lawrence was surprised to learn later in the day that Lyon had rejoined Chantel and had been promoted to the position of vice president for sales.

Dick Johnson, vice president of the swimwear division

Johnson had been with the company for only four months. He had originally approached John Husek with a large private-label order for swimwear. The president had seen an opportunity to set up a new swimwear division and had hired Johnson to run it. Johnson, previously a salesman, mentioned that he was attracted by the freedom that his new position offered. He felt that the Chantel Corporation had a lot going for it and saw great opportunities for synergy between his department and others. Lawrence wondered about that, since he had the impression that fabrics and customers in the swimwear division were quite different from those in the other divisions. He was particularly struck by Johnson's confidence in his prediction that he could bring his unit from start-up to $5 million profitable sales in one year, but perhaps this was possible: Johnson was supposed to be familiar with the industry.

James Gifford, controller

In his interview with Lawrence, the controller described Chantel as a potential gold mine. "The company now has terrific diversification, and with proper discipline and direction, it will go places." He described the president as a highly volatile, results-oriented man, adding that Husek was sometimes unrealistic in the amount of time he gave his managers to produce results. But Gifford felt that whatever else might be said about Husek, he was a great person to work for. He seemed to be rather philosophical about his strange career in the company – having been being fired by Ken Becker and rehired by Husek: "Becker was new, and I was in the wrong place at the wrong time. I just fell between the cracks, I guess."

Roger Fisher, special assistant to the president

Roger Fisher, an MBA, viewed himself as one of the old-timers, having been with the company for nearly ten years. He mentioned that he was among the many who had advised John Husek against the expansion program. "But John went ahead anyway. There was no way to stop him. After all, the man is a visionary: he had a vision of being number one in the country, and he challenged everybody to meet his goals. He had no idea at the time that the economy would turn sour or that velour would no longer be so popular." According to Fisher, Husek had wanted for years to erect the new building, the construction of which had depleted $9 million in capital. It was also his opinion that Chantel could really not scale down. Only when the building was filled up could the firm make money, but to do that effectively, more professionals were needed to run the place.

Fisher's main function at present seemed to be serving as Chantel's liaison to both the federal and provincial governments, with the objective of obtaining government grants. Since the company had created new employment for several hundred people by expansion and by taking over other businesses – firms that otherwise would have left the province or gone bankrupt – it qualified for government money. Chantel expected a major provincial grant, since the Québec government paid a subsidy for every newly created job. Husek had kept the bank, which was pressuring him about repayment of loans, at bay by pointing out that a significant amount of government money would soon be forthcoming. In fact, however, although the grant might alleviate to some extent the current financial strain on Chantel, Lawrence saw that there was a catch: if the grant was dependent on the number of people employed, it would be imperative for the company to grow, adding a further requirement for working capital.

When the discussion shifted to John Husek's management style, Fisher mentioned to Lawrence how difficult it was for his boss to delegate responsibility. Fisher remembered Husek once saying, "I gave a number of people a lot of rope, and look what they did to me: they almost killed me." Fisher wondered if Husek really trusted anybody, adding, "The man is just impossible to predict; he bypasses all the time. In case of bad news, he panics, goes fifty directions at once and gives urgent orders right down to the shop-floor level." Lawrence was quite concerned when Fisher confided to him: "You know, I don't sleep very well any longer. And it's all because of him. He's driving me crazy. It's so difficult to work for him. He listens to what I say as long as he wants to hear it; but if he's set against it, he gets me out of his office fast. Sometimes he comes into my office and yells at me, supposedly because I've done something wrong, but I know it wasn't me. I'm just a good whipping boy. I hate to say it, but there are times when I have the fantasy of lifting him up and dropping him out of the window."

Don Ayoub, vice president of the fabric division

The interview with Don Ayoub was a short one, characterized by Ayoub's suspiciousness. Ayoub was initially reluctant to talk to Lawrence, leading Lawrence to hypothesize that secrecy was a pattern found throughout the company.

Ayoub described himself as the right arm of John Husek. He viewed himself as the person who brought some realism to the organization. It was his opinion that there were quite a few rotten apples in the company. Some had left, however, and it had been good riddance; the Chantel Corporation would do much better without them. Ayoub felt that may of the difficulties the company found itself in could be traced back to these people, whom Ayoub had been instrumental in getting rid of. It sometimes upset him that Husek did not rely more on his services. Ayoub mentioned that it had been through his efforts that the ex-general manager of the children's wear subsidiary had not taken his people with him. Ayoub had managed to prevent an exodus by convincing Husek to offer those people shares in the subsidiary.

Ayoub felt that he would like to spend more time with Husek. After all, Ayoub had proved his worth by running the most profitable division. Unfortunately, it was only when the chips were down that Husek would come to him. Ayoub told Lawrence, "See how unsuccessful the latest whiz kid has been? Now I have to sort out the mess and help James Gifford with the costing system." He hinted that Husek had made him the informal vice president for planning in the firm. Ayoub also remarked that Husek should not really be concerned about his aspirations. His plan was to work a few more years for Chantel and then join a public service organization.

Ken Becker, vice president for operations

Ken Becker talked with Lawrence about his frustration in setting up the new budgeting system. He thought he had done an excellent job, but it seemed that John Husek had expected miracles from him: "Everything was supposed to be done yesterday." He admitted that his report might have been too sophisticated for Husek. Furthermore, he felt that Robert Husek's comment that he did not believe in such detailed statements, that all the information was not really necessary, had undermined Becker's report. Robert Husek's belief that meetings were a complete waste of time had also discouraged Becker's drive to hold more meetings focused on better coordination between the various functional areas and the divisions.

Becker mentioned that when he finally installed the new budgeting system and discovered that the Chantel Corporation was losing money, he suddenly found himself being blamed for everything. It was *his* fault that things were out of control. He was held responsible for the activities of the previous vice president for sales and merchandising, who had burdened the company with useless merchandise. Nobody seemed to realize how much time it took to analyze a new organization. Granted, he might have made some errors in the selection of priorities, but he felt that he had worked primarily on projects requested by the president.

He admitted that it was difficult for him to cope with the sudden change in Husek's attitude. Husek's current disdain was quite a contrast to the way he had courted him away from his previous employer. Husek now wanted Becker to concentrate his efforts on production, relieving him of his responsibilities for finance and planning. Becker's new mandate was to cut costs on the production floor by 20 percent in the coming year – a task he expected to be quite easy, given the mess his predecessor had made of the job. But he was somewhat anxious about possible interference by the president.

He sometimes regretted leaving his previous job. Of course, he had been offered more money and a possible share in Chantel. But he wondered aloud if Chantel was really his kind of place. He was getting calls from headhunters and was considering his next move.

COMMENTARY

To the reader, this case offers a great opportunity to get a sense of what it means to work for an entrepreneur. John Husek seems to be a textbook example of dysfunctionality. There was an early period when things went quite well, enabling Husek to build a successful enterprise. Now, however, things seem to be running out of control. While structural changes in the market certainly have had an effect on Chantel's bottom line, a major contributing factor to the company's problems is Husek's erratic leadership style and its effect on the organization. Husek has become quite self-destructive in his actions, apparently a victim of the psychological pressures that can derail leaders. Given his erratic ways, the future of the company is in serious jeopardy. But Husek does not see this. He hopes that the consultant's report will induce the Canadian government to bail him out.

The symptoms of dysfunctionality are prevalent in Chantel's three-ring-circus style of management. First, there is a lack of strategic direction. Presently, Chantel's products do not correspond to consumer's needs, and the company is not providing an adequate level of service to retailers. There are also liquidity problems. These can be traced to Husek's "edifice complex," which led him to build a monument for himself at a time when the wisdom of expansion in Québec could be seriously questioned. Another sign of bad news is that good people are leaving. Husek's nephew and most valued employee, Sid March, not only left but might even become a competitor (because of Husek's refusal to anoint him as his chosen successor and to honor his promise to retire at the age of fifty-five). The promotion of Robert Husek, who appears to be rather incompetent, undoubtedly also alienated March and other employees.

Husek's way of running the business leaves much to be desired. His talent for reality testing seems to be minimal. He is optimistic about the company's future at a time when all information indicates the opposite. Indeed, denial of unpleasant reality seems to be a pattern throughout the company. In spite of his contradictory report by the marketing research agency, Husek hangs on to his opinion that the new lines are welcomed by consumers. It is clear why his employees hope to bring him only good news: he has a tendency to kill the bearer of bad tidings. Moreover, Husek takes no personal responsibility for the mess the company finds itself in. Corporate difficulties are all caused by outside factors: the depression in the industry, high interest rates, imports, the high wages in Québec, and the province's language law.

John Husek is anything but an ideal boss. He has a very autocratic, dramatic leadership style. He is impulsive, has outbursts of anger, and frequently bypasses his own chain of command. Chantel enjoys no delegation or empowerment; Husek likes to control everything. He withholds information and oscillates in his opinions. He splits the world into people who are with him and those who are against him. One never knows what his position will be toward others: today you are a hero; tomorrow you are in the doghouse.

Naturally, such inconsistent, impulsive behavior does not make for a culture of trust. Instead, paranoid thinking prevails. There is a lot of infighting among Chantel employees, with a consequent lack of teamwork. Confusion exists about hierarchy (as revealed in the incident where two people were assigned the same job). The company suffers from high turnover as well: hiring and firing are the order of the day. The most competent people rarely stay. They disagree with Husek at their own peril. Apart from his unprepared son, only sycophants and rather dependent personalities seem to hang on.

We really do not know why Husek behaves as he does; we know nothing about his background, because he refused to discuss personal issues with Lawrence. The only information we have is based on the behavior we observe.

Of course, knowing what we do about entrepreneurs, we can make some inferences. Husek's grandiosity and mood swings are indicative of narcissistic problems; most likely he has a poorly established sense of self-esteem. His rivalry with his talented nephew also warrants attention. Apparently, Husek feels more in control of his less competent son than of March. These relationships raise questions about envy and Oedipal rivalry. How successful has Husek been in addressing these issues? Probably not very, if his behavior in his company is any indication. And what of his distrust of the people around him? There must be something in his background that would explain it. Answers to these types of questions can provide useful insights, as we saw in the case of Vocatron. In John Husek's case, however, we can only speculate.

If you were the consultant at Chantel, how would you proceed? Would you walk away from a sick patient? Would you be a "hungry" consultant and give Husek what he wants? If you chose to deal with the issues, how would you "package" your interventions?

The actual consultant in this case, Arthur Lawrence, did not walk away. He realized the trouble the company was in and saw that further government grants would just provide a stay of execution. Fundamental changes had to occur in the company to turn the situation around. Lawrence realized that to introduce more viable product lines was a high priority, but first the turmoil inside the company had to be reduced. The challenge he was up against was how to modify Husek's rather dramatic leadership style.

Lawrence suggested to Husek that he bring his nephew back into the business. Not only did March seem to have a calming influence on his uncle, but he also had considerable expertise in running the business. After a long, passionate discussion, Husek remained unpersuaded; he wanted to hear no more about it. He told Lawrence that he had plans for his son, and his nephew would only complicate matters.

To reduce the effort required to "feed the monster" – keeping the production facilities occupied – Lawrence suggested subletting part of the building, a recommendation that was also shelved. Lawrence made a few other suggestions as well – and all were snubbed. It became increasingly clear that no recommendation from Lawrence would be acceptable. It appeared that Husek's only interest was in receiving a positive appraisal for his company so that he would qualify for the government grants.

Deeply frustrated, Lawrence talked once more with Husek, going over a list of factors that he felt needed to be changed if Chantel were to become viable. He then summarized his recommendations in a letter. Soon after, he received Husek's response: a request that he postpone all further work for Chantel. A month later, Lawrence got a letter from a competing consulting group telling him that someone there had taken up his assignment. (See Figures C3.2, C3.3, and C3.4 for the correspondence between the three parties.)

Lawrence learned later that the company was doing better. When Chantel had come close to bankruptcy some months after Lawrence's involvement, Robert Husek put pressure on his father to bring Sid March back into the business. March was prepared to come back, but only on the condition that he would become president of the company and Husek would resign. Husek realized that he had no choice; either he agreed, or there would be no company at all. March, helped by Robert Husek, managed to turn the situation around. Chantel also had a stroke of luck: a major competitor went out of business, thus improving Chantel's market position.

As a final note, we can ask ourselves how effective Lawrence was in communicating the problematic issues. His analysis of the situation may have been correct, but could the same be said about the way he transferred the information? In consulting, as in psychotherapy, timing is everything. If the timing is wrong, the client will not listen. Moreover, there is a limit to the amount of information, particularly if it is unpleasant, that a client can handle at one time. Furthermore, before a client can even begin to assimilate advice, a certain degree of trust has to be built up. A working alliance with the consultant has to be established. That was certainly not the case in the relationship between Lawrence and Husek.

But perhaps Lawrence never had a chance. He was dealing with deep-seated problems at a time when the crisis in the company was not yet serious enough for Husek to feel the need to take action. There was not yet enough pain in the system. But Lawrence could have been more of a Machiavellian in his actions. Out of principle, he did not want to take the money for going through a ritualistic exercise; the money would then have been a sort of bribe. He did, however, give Husek sound advice about his nephew Sid March, which Husek eventually took to heart. Quite possibly, Lawrence chose to act in a confrontational manner in order to disentangle himself from a seemingly impossible situation.

Notes

1 At the time, minimum wage in Québec was 20 percent higher than in other parts of Canada.
2 The Partie Québecoise with its separatist program and restrictive language legislation was in power at this time.

Personal and Confidential
Mr John Husek
President
Chantel Corporation

Dear John:

After interviewing your executives over the past few weeks and reviewing the most recent collections, I have reached certain conclusions. Some of these thoughts have been discussed with you, but I feel they should be put in writing to enable you to review them carefully.

The spring Faubourg lingerie line seems well designed and simplified, and it should have some success if all goes well. The line has used some of the directions suggested in the market research report. This also seems to indicate that Kathy Grant and the Faubourg designer are adapting to the demands of the marketplace and developing the necessary expertise.

The Chantel lingerie line is much more embryonic, and there appears to be some difficulty in communication between the executives and the sales organization. Even though there has been some increased last-minute demand, the unavailability of timely and sufficient fabric for desired styles will make it impossible to satisfy these orders in time.

The most serious problems I have found are organizational rather than marketing or merchandising problems. I believe it would be difficult for Chantel to develop a marketing plan until these organizational issues are resolved. They involve your own management style and Robert's lack of certain managerial skills and expertise. In short, the Chantel Corporation needs organized and professional leadership. Sudden and unexpected changes in responsibilities, high executive turnover, rapid shifts in decisions, and the bypassing of executives are making it impossible to plan for and meet the needs of the marketplace. Internal conflicts are being patched over rather than resolved.

In consequence, the morale of your executives is being affected. They are becoming frustrated and discouraged. In addition, our survey indicates that your sales force and customers are rapidly losing confidence in the Chantel Corporation.

I have made the following suggestions to you:

1 Try to hire a successful lingerie executive to run the Chantel division. If such a person is available (whatever the cost), the leadership provided should ensure the long-term survival of the division.
2 Try to obtain the Canadian license for a well-merchandised brand from Europe or the United States on a royalty basis to serve as a bridge to learn sources, patterns, styling methods, and planning and production techniques and to obtain a name to help open doors.
3 Robert should either be given more limited responsibilities or obtain an MBA to equip him with necessary managerial skills needed for the significant responsibilities you would like him to undertake. The latter option is preferable.
4 You must refrain from bypassing your executives and from rapidly shifting direction. It is vital to let your executives manage their areas with less direct intervention from above.

The only alternative to the above actions would be to drastically reduce the size of the lingerie division (or close it) and concentrate resources and management time on the remaining (profitable) divisions. Problems in lingerie are affecting other divisions adversely by draining resources, etc. This alternative may not represent a choice but may be forced upon you as events unfold, unless a dramatic change in Chantel's internal environment occurs.

I believe that the potential strengths of your organization will result in eventual success, provided you make the necessary changes in atmosphere. I feel that you should deal with these matters with a sense of urgency.

I will be available to discuss these issues further at your convenience.

Yours sincerely,

Arthur Lawrence
President, Strategic Consulting Group

Figure C3.2

Mr. John Husek
President
The Chantel Corporation

Dear John:

Confirming our telephone conversation of last week, you have asked that I postpone all further work on the CIRB project for two reasons:

1 Your people are busy with the development of the lines and selling and should concentrate on these things for the moment.
2 Some events will clarify themselves in the marketplace to give us a better idea of direction.

I am very pleased to hear that the initial reaction to the Chantel line has been so good.

You also mentioned that your need for government assistance will be for the purchase of equipment for the fabric division. I have pointed out that we have not really had the opportunity to study the market of the fabric division properly and therefore cannot make a recommendation of such nature.

Please let us know when you want us to continue the study.

Sincerely,

Arthur Lawrence
President, Strategic Consulting Group

Figure C3.3

Mr. Arthur Lawrence
President
Strategic Consulting Group

Dear Mr. Lawrence:

At the request of the management of the Chantel Corporation, I will be conducting and directing the CIRB project from a general standpoint. My discussions with the management of Chantel have convinced me that the relationship between you and that organization has deteriorated, apparently as a result of your criticism of the management and organization of the company, as well as the great variance between your marketing projections and the company's recent experience with the new collections.

In order to avoid arguments at a personal level and to complete the restructuring plan for Chantel within the time constraints of CIRB, Chantel will not require further input from you on the project other than a proper accounting of the number of days worked and a written debriefing report of the work done to date.

Yours sincerely,

L. Johnson
President
L. Johnson and Associates, Consulting Engineers

Figure C3.4

B. SYMBOLIC PARRICIDE

Rashomon in organizational life
The Fashion Shoe Company

The consultant hired by Frank Faulkner, chairman of the Fashion Shoe Company, is going to have to be a real organizational detective and diplomat. Many recent incidents at Fashion Shoe seem to defy rational analysis. The company is a hotbed of politics and intrigue, with upset following upon upset. While the president, Bill Farnsworth, has been on a three-week vacation, Faulkner, who is also the controlling shareholder, has been running amok, making one unexpected decision after another. A sales manager was fired, a newly opened plant was closed, and the vice president for manufacturing (an executive who has been with the company since its inception) was almost axed. Now Frank Faulkner has asked the consultant to tell him whether or not he should fire Farnsworth, who is just back from his travels and due to return to the office. What is going on in this company? Why is Frank Faulkner acting in such a strange way?

In Akira Kurosawa's movie *Rashomon*, four different protagonists – a bandit, a murdered nobleman (through a medium), his wife, and a woodcutter – look at a recent event, each from a different perspective. Although the film is initially very confusing, by carefully analyzing the four contradictory stories, the viewer can eventually solve the puzzle of what really happened.

Perhaps the confusing incidents at the Fashion Shoe Company can be deciphered in a similar way. This case study gives Frank Faulkner's perspective, but you, as an armchair consultant, should think about the points of view of some of the other executives in the company. You might, for example, compare how Frank Faulkner, Bill Farnsworth, and one or more of the vice presidents see things. How would each of these people describe the developments in the company? What would be their interpretation of recent events?

Another question worth exploring is the extent to which the behavior of the executive group is a direct result of Frank Faulkner's actions. Why did Faulkner not make the choice for the new president himself instead of letting the candidates for the job decide? Why has Faulkner physically moved away from the company's offices? Given the degree of political infighting, what can be done to keep the young "tigers" in line? Furthermore, is Bill Farnsworth's position as president salvageable, given Faulkner's ambivalence about him? Finally, as the consultant, what recommendation would you give to Faulkner, and how would you present that information? (Keep in mind John Husek's hostility toward Arthur Lawrence in the Chantel case.)

THE FASHION SHOE COMPANY

In June 1995, Frank Faulkner took on the newly created office of chairman of the board of the Fashion Shoe Company. He was the controlling stockholder in a business that his father had started about thirty-five years earlier. Upon his father's death in 1987, Faulkner, then twenty-four years old, became chief executive officer. In addition to the stock bequeathed to him, he purchased outstanding stock held by other family members; he also acted on behalf of his mother, who owned the remaining 50 percent of the shares.

Faulkner's plan was to free himself from operating responsibilities in the company by becoming chairman so that he could turn his attention to a program of product diversification and corporate acquisitions. In addition to accelerating the company's growth, Faulkner hoped to go public as a means of increasing his wealth, providing for estate planning, and offering stock options to attract and hold able executives who were, in his words, "professionals."

The company had an enviable growth record in the 1980s. From a small business that manufactured women's shoes for private-label distribution, the company grew exponentially, increasing its sales and profits by more than 600 percent. It introduced a "Fashion" brand-name program, established marketing and design functions backed by national advertising in magazines and on television, increased its full-time sales force from about ten to sixty people, and introduced sophisticated management control systems. While achieving this expansion, Faulkner managed to attract executives from leading competitors who were interested in building a business under Faulkner's leadership.

William Farnsworth, currently the company president, was the first "outsider" to join Fashion Shoe after Frank Faulkner became chief executive in 1987. He was an aggressive salesman with intuitive approaches to product design and marketing. Farnsworth succeeded in selling to several major retail chains, and he was also instrumental in developing several design innovations that provided product identification for the Fashion lines.

Farnsworth's appointment to the presidency occurred shortly after Faulkner decided to pursue acquisitions and ultimately to offer stock to the public. Faulkner described the circumstances surrounding the naming of a new president as follows: "There were three candidates for the job of president: Farnsworth, Garland (the vice president for manufacturing), and the man who was the controller and treasurer. I called a meeting of these three men and told them of my plan to become chairman of the board. I said, 'One of you will be president, and I want you to select the man. Go into a room and decide among yourselves who should be president.'" Faulkner felt certain that the group would name Farnsworth.

The three candidates, though about the same age, were vastly different in background and personality. Ralph Garland had been with the company since its inception and had worked closely with Frank Faulkner's father. Since the business primarily manufactured shoes in accordance with customer orders for customer brands using customer designs, the success of the business had thus far depended upon meeting cost estimates, quality standards, and delivery promises. Garland was conscientious about managing the plant and assumed responsibilities beyond what might be expected of an employee. He had been devoted to Faulkner Sr and had often visited his house, both to talk business and to play with Frank almost as uncle to nephew (if not father to son). When Faulkner Sr retired from the business at age forty-eight, Garland ran the business, checking by telephone with Faulkner Sr, who had moved across the continent from the plant and its offices.

Frank Faulkner was uncertain why his father had retired so early and moved so far from his business. The ostensible reason was a heart condition, but Frank felt that it was just as possible that his father was a hypochondriac.

During the period following the retirement of Faulkner Sr and up until his death in an automobile accident, the company's sales and profits were on a plateau. Garland saw himself as a plant manager producing goods for a selected number of retail accounts and servicing their needs for women's shoes to be sold under each store's brand. While attending to costs and delivery schedules, Garland thought of his plant and the people it employed as members of a family. He knew all the employees by name and kept himself informed of all their personal joys and tragedies. He customarily opened his plant at 6:00 a.m. and – except under unusual circumstances – was the last to leave the building twelve hours later.

The company controller – a man who came into the business about the same time as Farnsworth – was the second candidate for the job of president. While Faulkner believed that Garland had only moderate interest in becoming president, he believed that the controller was ambitious and wanted the job. The controller was a tense, irritable person who, while conscientious in his work, was not the type of "professional" Faulkner would have preferred in the position of controller (let alone president).

The three men held their meeting and, by the process of elimination, named Farnsworth as president, largely because of his experience in marketing and his personal aggressiveness. Shortly after becoming president, Farnsworth, with Faulkner's concurrence, asked the controller to resign because of shortcomings in his performance. Faulkner arranged, through Fashion Shoe's public accounting firm, to place the controller with another company. Not long after his resignation, the controller became seriously depressed and killed himself.

Faulkner not only accepted the decision to name Farnsworth president but also gave him freedom to run the business. About six months after Farnsworth became president, Faulkner established a new office for himself in a sophisticated building a taxi ride away from the Fashion Shoe offices. Faulkner believed his move "uptown" would clear the way for Farnsworth to become president in fact as well as in title. This move would also, Faulkner believed, help him concentrate on his own long-range planning and on acquisitions.

Faulkner took only his secretary with him, leaving the president and the five vice presidents, as shown in the organization chart (Figure C4.1) to carry out the program he had initiated for the Fashion Shoe Company.

That program consisted of the following steps, initiated about a year before Faulkner became chairman of the board:

1 Designing new styles and new footwear lines and establishing the Fashion brand name through a magazine and television advertising program.
2 Upgrading the line so that it could be sold in department stores and retail chains catering to higher-income groups.
3 Building a new sales force of bright young people who would be selected for their potential rather than their best-yet performance in selling to shoe buyers in prestige retail outlets.
4 Opening a new plant at some distance from the existing plant in an economically depressed area that could supply a workforce at wage rates below the current level in the industry (a plant initially intended to manufacture the new lines, reserving the old plant for the more established lines of shoes).

The five vice presidents shown in the organization chart in Figure C4.1 were, with the exception of Garland, of the "new breed" that Faulkner hoped to attract to the company. He viewed them as "professionals" who were intensely competitive – people who were capable of exposing weaknesses elsewhere in the organization as well as carrying out their own functions.

James Markham, the controller, was the most recent addition to the group of vice presidents. He had had considerable background in management control and Markham valued his experience in working as a subordinate to "sharp and aggressive" general managers. In joining Fashion Shoe, he hoped to improve its reporting and controls, but he also looked forward to spending increasing amounts of time working with Faulkner in his acquisitions program.

The next most junior vice president (in terms of experience with Fashion Shoe) was James Doyle. He had been with the company for less than two years, having been hired by Alfred Corwin. Corwin, currently vice president for private-label sales, had been vice president for sales and marketing before assuming his current position. Corwin hoped to utilize Doyle's aggressiveness to build the sales force needed to promote the Fashion brand line to prestige accounts. According to Faulkner, Doyle had managed to "outmaneuver" Corwin, forcing a decision from Faulkner to rearrange job responsibilities and titles. This reorganization, which occurred in the spring of 1995, resulted in naming Doyle as vice president for sales, George Jensen as vice president for marketing, and Corwin as vice president for private-label sales. These three vice presidents were, in effect, equal in status, reporting directly to the president. (Formerly, both Jensen and Doyle had held the title of "manager," reporting to Corwin.)

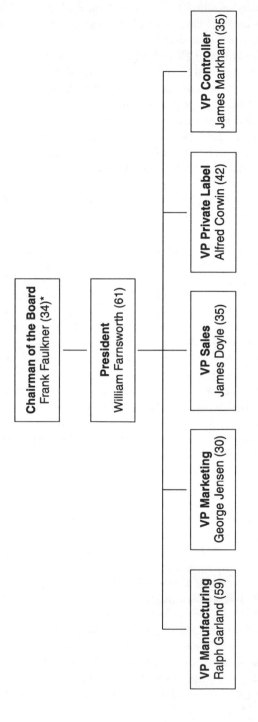

Figure C4.1 Fashion Shoe Company organization chart, June 1969. *( ) designates age

In explaining this reorganization to the consultant, Faulkner said he believed that he would have lost Doyle if the title of vice president – with its direct line of responsibility to the president – had been withheld.

Faulkner had become aware of Doyle's expectations when he received a call from him at 5:30 one morning – not a conventional hour for conducting business. Both men were out of town at the time, staying in the hotel where the company was about to hold an important national sales meeting to introduce the new marketing plans and to stimulate sales representatives to meet the sales targets established for them. Faulkner acceded to Doyle's request, but he felt that the promotion could not stand alone: he believed it was necessary for him to appoint Jensen as vice president for marketing simultaneously, since Jensen and Doyle seemed competitive with each other. In Faulkner's words, "Jensen and Doyle don't like each other. They're both hungry, aggressive, and out to make a name for themselves. Where they both agree is in wanting to push aside and get rid of the tired old men."

Jensen was responsible for developing the product lines and marketing plans for each selling season. He worked with the company's advertising agency and was largely instrumental in moving into television advertising. When formulating the initial plans for television, Jensen convinced Faulkner that the company should fire its advertising agency: it was, in Jensen's opinion, unsuitable for work in television. Faulkner accepted this recommendation, though aware of the fact that the head of the old advertising agency and Farnsworth were close friends and work associates of long standing.

Shortly after Faulkner moved his new office in 1995, he began to feel uneasy about the implementation of the plan that he had formulated in conjunction with Farnsworth and the vice presidents. While dollar sales stayed even with comparable periods in 1994, they fell below the budgeted level. Of even more serious concern to Faulkner was the realization that profits would go below the amount realized in 1994. Faulkner recognized, however, that both sales and profits had been impacted by the company's new strategies of dropping "low-end" accounts, increasing advertising and marketing expenses, and adding to the sales force (since there was an unavoidable delay before any new salesperson's sales rose to the level where the individual would pay for him- or herself). He was also concerned about Farnsworth's ability to lead the "young tigers" who reported to him as vice presidents. Faulkner studied the figures into the spring of 1995 without taking specific action. He began to act, however, when Farnsworth left in April on a three-week trip abroad with his family.

Faulkner spent two consecutive days in the Fashion Shoe offices and conducted interviews with executives and employees at various levels to get a closer view of what had contributed to the disappointing results of early 1995. He also conducted an "exit interview" with a product manager who had resigned – a man who was critical of Farnsworth's leadership and downright damning of one of the sales managers who had been close to Farnsworth. Faulkner, upon learning that Jensen and Corwin were also critical of this sales manager's performance, decided to take "dramatic action" to indicate his concern about the sales and profit performance in early 1995. He discharged the sales manager.

Another decision that Faulkner made during Farnsworth's vacation was to close down the new plant. It had failed to meet its production schedule, although Farnsworth, at last report, was still expressing optimism about meeting its quotas. Faulkner first appointed an investigative committee of three, including Jensen (who reported an impending "disaster"); he then went to the new plant with this committee and announced that he was closing it down immediately.

During Farnsworth's vacation period, Faulkner also conducted a whirlwind visit to various key accounts to reestablish his feel for the marketplace. Upon his return from this tour, one of the company's product managers came to him to report a conversation he had had with Garland, the vice president for manufacturing. According to this product manager, Garland had suggested that he visit Faulkner to criticize Jensen's performance as head of the marketing department. The product manager said, in addition, that Garland had indicated that he would persuade Faulkner to name this product manager as Jensen's successor.

Faulkner felt angry upon hearing this report from the product manager. He was disturbed over the political infighting that seemed to have erupted and concerned about the possibility that the new plant had fallen victim to company politics. Faulkner asked the controller, Markham, to go to the factory with him to see Garland. He especially wanted Markham along because Faulkner felt "emotional" (something Markham had never been accused of) and doubted whether Garland should remain with the company.

According to Faulkner, he began by confronting Garland with the report from the product manager. At first, Garland countered this report with his own version, which was quite different. He then conceded that the reported version was accurate but added, "I was really testing [the product manager's] loyalty." Upon hearing this, Faulkner exploded: "I just plain pinned Garland to the wall," he said. "Then Garland began to confess his sins and said to me, 'I'm with Fashion Shoe all the way. I'll keep my nose clean; I'm with you, Frank.'" Faulkner detected sincerity in Garland's words, and even though he still had doubts about Garland, he decided to keep him with the company. "After all," he reflected, "I used to play with him as a kid. We have a strong emotional tie."

At the conclusion of Faulkner's investigation, he prepared a detailed memorandum outlining his criticisms of the way the company was being run and the various decisions he had reached during Farnsworth's absence. He sent this memorandum to Farnsworth's house on the day he returned from his vacation.

Shortly after sending this memorandum, Faulkner met with a friend and business associate to whom he described his recent experiences as chairman of the board of the Fashion Shoe Company. This friend suggested that Faulkner call in a consultant he knew who specialized in problems involving personality conflicts among executives.

Faulkner accepted this suggestion readily. In meeting for the first time with this consultant, he reviewed the events described above, asking the consultant to undertake a study and then to recommend whether he should discharge Farnsworth (and if so, which contender he should then select as the new president).

COMMENTARY

The case of the Fashion Shoe Company offers a good illustration of how rational and irrational processes in management overlap. It also indicates the extent to which a top executive's inner theater can influence the decision-making processes in an organization. In addition, it demonstrates how an individual's dysfunctional leadership style can lead to organizational pathology and eventually endanger the survival of an enterprise.

This case presents us with a real psychodrama. The interpersonal dynamics that are usually repressed (or at least suppressed) in organizations are in this instance fully acted out. Here unconscious motivations provoke action and collusive behavior. A central theme in this case is symbolic parricide. The theme is an Oedipal drama: the wish of a younger man to "kill" and replace a father figure.

Given the power that top executives wield, unconscious conflicts can become displaced and externalized and may then be acted out in a larger setting – private dramas appearing on a public stage. In this instance, Frank Faulkner, the instigator of the psychodrama, is able to engage others in a collusion to act out his theme of killing the father.

We learn that the corporate controller is "killed" (committing suicide after being forced to resign), Corwin is "killed," Garland is almost "killed," and Farnsworth is now set up for the "kill." This repetition compulsion – the need to repeat an emotionally charged event – can be seen as a belated form of mastery, as Faulkner tries to work through his ambivalent feelings toward his father. But Faulkner's actions have serious consequences: reality is distorted, and the company is in danger of being led into disaster.

This situation reveals a complex layering of rationality and irrationality. What appear at first sight as rational acts are actually covers for irrational behavior. For example, why does Faulkner detach himself from day-to-day operations to become chairman and then move to another office (albeit located close to the company)? The rational explanation is that he wants to show his executives that he is serious about delegating authority and responsibility. Moving uptown is (he says) a symbolic act demonstrating that he does not want to interfere in their activities. In his new role as chairman – so the rational explanation goes – Faulkner plans to devote all his energy to product diversification, corporate acquisitions, and preparations for a public stock offer.

Faulkner's actions appear to be well thought out. Upon closer scrutiny, however, we can see a great difference between the rational reasons given by Faulkner for his actions and his true motivations (at least some of which may be outside Faulkner's conscious awareness).

Interestingly enough, the moment the new president turns his back and goes on vacation, Faulkner can be found back in his old office, busily undermining his successor. Suddenly, Faulkner sees disaster everywhere. He encourages the speculation that under its new leadership the company is going down the drain.

And given Faulkner's power base, his attitude toward corporate developments seems to be contagious: other executives concur, joining the fray. Obviously, according to Faulkner's logic, he has no choice but to intervene. He realizes now that it was unwise to leave things to others. Farnsworth was not the right man for the job after all.

We can ask ourselves, however, whether the situation under Farnsworth necessitates this kind of panic. Is the situation really so dramatic and unexpected? After all, the variations in sales and profit figures are in part a result of the new program Faulkner put into effect himself. Is it too much to expect that it might take this new program some time to fall into place? Low-end accounts have been dropped; a new sales force, which will not be fully functional for some time, has been put into place; advertising and marketing expenses have increased; and a new plant (with predictable start-up problems) has been built. Given the way Faulkner acts, we can infer that his moves are irrational – unconscious and born out of conflicts within himself – but put into the language and form of logical business planning.

This does not negate, however, the strong possibility that Faulkner is essentially correct in believing that he needs to diversify and strengthen the base of his business and to give his products brand identity and a strong selling base in order to enhance the profits and the market position of the Fashion Shoe Company. The point is that Faulkner's corporate planning and strategy are influenced by personal motives that are outside his conscious control.

"Killing older men" is only one of the themes arising out of Faulkner's inner theater. Other themes can be deciphered in studying the case. Faulkner has a tendency toward grandiosity, for example, reflected in his plan to increase the size of his company. Again, many rational reasons can be found for expansion, but they do not rule out the possibility that underlying Faulkner's arguments for growth is his need to deny and externalize fears of weakness and inadequacy.

Another theme that Faulkner translates from unconscious conflict to action is this: "The world is dangerous, hostile, and competitive, and one must be on guard to kill before being killed, to devour before being devoured." Faulkner's use of aggressive language and his emphasis on competition are symptoms of this attitude. How does Faulkner manage to persuade others to help act out his delusions? How do his unconscious needs set the process of *folie à deux* into motion? One explanation is that Faulkner may select, consciously or unconsciously, executives who share many of his fears and defensive requirements; in other words, he may recruit at two levels. Another is that Faulkner may be very talented at communicating his fears and needs to others, in turn stimulating them to participate. His imagery of "young tigers" and "tired old men" seems to be contagious: the young tigers are eager to oblige their leader, as the political infighting in the company demonstrates.

Abdication is another interesting theme in this case. Faulkner feels that his father abdicated his responsibilities by retiring at such a young age and moving so far away. This perceived abandonment may color Faulkner's attitude toward older men. Resentfully, Faulkner accuses his father of being a hypochondriac. Ironically, though, Faulkner himself abdicates responsibility in appointing a new president. In addition, he takes Markham with him to act as his front man in the confrontation with Garland, and he hires a consultant to fire Farnsworth.

The most flagrant sign of abdication is Faulkner's decision to relocate his office. Just when the effectiveness of his new product program is going to be tested, he physically removes himself and shifts the responsibility for the program's outcome to someone else. When evidence of problems arises, Faulkner blames others (even for results for which he was largely responsible). Realizing his mistakes, he acts in a whirlwind fashion to deflect attention from the risks involved in the business planning decisions he has made.

Will Faulkner listen when the consultant presents his report? Is it possible (or desirable) to suggest to him what his unconscious conflicts might be and discuss why they are acted out? Can someone explain reality to a person who is behaving irrationally? The problem here is how to say things to Frank Faulkner so that he can use and hear the information, how to address the issue of the spillover of unconscious conflict into the corporate domain. In attempting to convey his impressions, the consultant must tread lightly. Given the nature of Faulkner's inner conflicts, the consultant, if he is not careful, may find himself being "killed" as well.

The consultant would do well to move gradually from surface issues to in-depth interpretations. He could start with secondary problems such as the following: the energy spent on politics, symptomatic of the company's lack of boundaries; and the degree of infighting which indicates that nobody is really in charge of the company (Faulkner having installed a president whose authority he undermined from the beginning with the bizarre selection process). Because the setting of boundaries is the responsibility of the chief executive, the rules of the game have to be redefined by the chairman himself. Faulkner should be made aware of the fact that his own behavior is encouraging the younger executives to run wild. To stop this pattern, the company needs a solid dose of reality and some explicit rules and limits.

The political infighting is a crucial issue. The energy of the vice presidents should be directed outward to fight the competition, not inward to fight each other. We have only to recall the incident of the early-morning telephone conversation to find an example of an out-of-control power play. The fact that it happened at all implies that Faulkner may have overtly or covertly encouraged such activities. Another ominous sign is his comment that the vice president for marketing and the vice president for sales do not like each other. Because these functions are very much interdependent, Faulkner should work to resolve this conflict. If no solution is forthcoming, one of the vice presidents should be moved into another position.

The consultant would do well to find out who is really responsible for the spectacular growth record of the company. Is it Faulkner or Farnsworth, or is it the synergy between these two senior people? This is important to know in making recommendations. If Farnsworth is largely responsible for the company's success, as seems to be the case, a strong effort should be made to keep him in the company. If not, in light of the present situation, it may not be worth the effort to try to salvage his position.

Whatever he does, Faulkner should make up his mind whether he wants to be actively involved in running the company or not. As we have seen, there is a great difference between what he says he wants and the actions he takes – a result of the scripting in his inner theater.

The consultant could begin to address Faulkner's personal shortcomings by asking him to decide upon his own degree of involvement. If he prefers a hands-off approach, he should be made aware of its implications. Is he prepared to truly hand over authority and responsibility to the president? If the role of chairman is really satisfactory to him but he still wants to be involved in certain decisions, these interactions should be handled through the president.

Given Faulkner's personality, the most realistic suggestion is to encourage him to become actively involved in the business again. In his role as chairman, the temptation to interfere may be too great. Better to have the organizational power structure match the reality of the situation.

Many of these recommendations must be made to Faulkner's rational side. He may not be willing to follow these suggestions, however; the forces in his inner theater may be too strong. After all, the consultant was hired for the specific purpose of firing the president. Faulkner's need to "kill off" older men may again come to the fore. To help Faulkner control his unconscious tendencies, the consultant may need to make him aware of some these themes, though psychological interpretations are often difficult to swallow. Making Faulkner understand his central role in creating the upheaval in the company will require a lot of repackaging of ideas, insights, and preconceptions.

Faulkner's behavior at the Fashion Shoe Company presents in a very dramatic way the dysfunctional use of power and politics in an organizational setting. It gives insight into the origin of collusive practices, illustrating how certain intrapsychic themes become externalized and enacted on the stage of the corporation. What started as a problematic father–son relationship turned into a major soap opera that threatened the very existence of the family firm.

Exorcising a ghost
The Dunor Corporation

It all began with a rather standard request by Bernard Lambert, the president of the Dunor Corporation, for recommendations to make the company's executive committee function more effectively. Clearly, this group had not been working productively together. But there was more to come. Didier Anzieu, the consultant/psychoanalyst hired to sort things out, also had to deal with the president's strange demand that he give a psychological examination to one of the top Dunor executives to determine whether that executive was mentally capable of handling his job. What lay behind this bizarre request, of course, was Lambert's unspoken desire to find an excuse to get rid of the executive.

While reading this case, imagine yourself in Didier Anzieu's shoes. As you, the beleaguered consultant, walk around the company and talk to the different protagonists, you may notice that there are a number of "wounded princes" hanging around, executives who feel wronged for not having been chosen as president after the founder-entrepreneur was forced to retire. And to increase the general confusion of the situation, the person who is president does not seem to be convinced that he is the right man for the job. He keeps abdicating his role, adding considerably to the political unrest in the company. To top it all off, the ghost of the "retired" entrepreneur seems to be haunting Dunor's corridors. As a matter of fact, though, this man is anything but a ghost: he lives only a stone's throw away from the company's premises. But time for your assessment is short: the company is floundering while its executives spend their energy fighting each other instead of going on with the business at hand.

Finally, you realize what the key question is: What is the real problem here? Does it have to do with the functioning of the executive committee, as the president believes? Or is there something quite different going on? And how should you go about solving this problem (once you figure out what it really is)?

THE DUNOR CORPORATION

Didier Anzieu,[1] a psychoanalyst and management consultant, was wrestling with a knotty question: What recommendations should he give to Bernard Lambert, president of the Dunor Corporation, who had recently asked him to visit the company and advise him about two problems: how to make the executive committee function more effectively, and how to let go of an executive who had been promised a permanent position in the company.

The Dunor Corporation is a medium-sized firm in the light metal industry with its head office and factory in Douai, France. The company was started forty-five years ago by Albert Peltier, who is described as a workaholic – a self-made man who was very hard on himself and others. He is portrayed by those who knew him as a rather inflexible person, someone who could be very tough and who had a strong autocratic streak. His temper was notorious. When Albert was in charge of the company, he visited the factory each day and talked to every worker personally in his own dialect. Many of these employees still vividly remember how he would shout at them for the smallest mistake, accusing them of slacking off. By all accounts, he ran the company with an iron hand and was both loved and hated by his employees.

Unfortunately, Albert was not able to move with the times. He overlooked many financial and manufacturing opportunities, preferring to stick to comfortable routines. Consequently, his leadership of the firm eventually led to financial difficulties and aroused the board's concern. According to several people, the board's loss of confidence in Albert had a deep emotional impact on him and may have contributed to his subsequent physical illness. This illness and its effect on Albert only made the company's financial situation deteriorate further. When, after seeming to recover, Albert became ill again, he decided that it was time for his younger son, Jean, to succeed him. Albert had, in fact, been planning this for some time, having persuaded Jean to join the company several years before. His son, he said, would be better equipped than he to introduce modern management practices.

Albert lived in a large mansion owned by the company. He had been allowed to continue using the house, located next to the factory, after his retirement. A small gate at the end of the garden led directly into the factory grounds, making it possible to enter the factory without using the main entrance. This was the entrance Jean used when he moved into the house with his father after Albert decided that he should be his successor. Albert seemed to have pinned all his hopes on Jean.

Albert's older son, Michel, had disappointed him by refusing, some years earlier, to go into the family firm. Albert had then managed to convince his younger son to join him, in spite of Jean's reluctance to break off the career he had just begun in a credit institution. Since technical problems were not Jean's forte, his father promised him the presidency and hired Xavier Trudeau to take care of manufacturing.

Anzieu had noticed during his recent consultation at Dunor that the telephone on Albert's desk was directly connected to the factory. In spite of claims of non-interference, it seemed that Albert was still kept closely informed of what was going on in the factory. During Anzieu's visit, Albert had remarked that when he had first become ill and been forced to stay in bed for several months, it had been his son who, with his help, had successfully run the factory. Others in the corporation, however, had spoken differently about Jean's abilities to Anzieu. They were of the opinion that Albert had crushed his son.

After Albert's retirement, things did not, in fact, turn out quite as he had planned. The board of directors asserted itself, appointing the sales director, Bernard Lambert, president instead of Jean. The company was then officially run by an executive committee consisting of four people: Bernard Lambert, Jean Peltier, Robert Coffin (the chief foreman), and Xavier Trudeau (head of manufacturing).

Lambert, aged forty-five, had a degree from a commercial college. In his previous position as sales director, he had been located in Paris to be near most of the company's biggest clients. The board of directors, by the time it chose Lambert as president, included a number of members of his own family, which held a majority equity position in the company. After he became president, Lambert remained in charge of sales but moved to Douai.

Jean Peltier, aged thirty-two (and son of Albert, the founder), had a law degree and was now director of personnel. The board, in choosing Lambert over Jean as president, cited his father's mistakes in managing the firm and Jean's own mediocrity as the reasons for their choice. Furthermore, the majority of the board expected Lambert to make drastic financial changes to improve the company's profitability. Lambert and the board promised the disappointed Albert that his son would always have a management position in the company. Jean, meanwhile, continued to live with his father next door to the factory even after he married and had children.

Robert Coffin, aged sixty years, who as head foreman did not have a managerial position, had become a de facto member of the executive committee because of his knowledge of and experience in the company. He was one of the most senior people in the factory, with forty years of expertise. Albert had recognized his abilities, promoted him, and eventually made him his right-hand man.

Xavier Trudeau, aged forty-eight, had received his training at a technical institute and was now director of manufacturing. He had been recruited by Albert ten years before, when Albert had first decided to make his son his successor; and he had developed the manufacturing side of the business during the company's expansion, overseeing a reorganization of the factory. Now Trudeau worked mainly in research, leaving the day-to-day management of manufacturing to Robert Coffin. Trudeau was very concerned about self-improvement. He had taken a course on how to direct meetings, which had led Lambert to suggest that he chair the executive committee meetings.

From Lambert's conversations with Anzieu, it became clear that the former thought the executive meetings were too long and not very effective. A considerable amount of time seemed to be taken up by arguments between Jean, Robert Coffin, and Xavier Trudeau. Because they were so unproductive, the meetings were held further and further apart, and eventually Lambert had been forced to stop them altogether. He now made decisions by himself, informing the others afterwards about what he had decided. The executive committee meetings had been replaced by individual meetings that Lambert held with each of his three managers separately. Lambert felt that he had a good relationship with each of them; it was only the relationships between them that seemed not to work.

Lambert said that he had been very satisfied with his life in Paris. He had not had many responsibilities, and he had been very successful in sales. He had not in any way lobbied for the position of president. Rather, it had been given to him by the board to stabilize the situation in the company. He had accepted the position because he had a sizable financial stake in the company himself, but now he felt guilty towards Jean, whose position he had taken. Because of these feelings, he had given Jean as much independence as possible. It seemed, however, that Jean could function effectively only under strict control (such as his father had imposed).

Lambert told Anzieu that he felt vaguely uncomfortable with the people in the company. He saw himself as a newcomer, a Parisian who did not really understand the northerners and who was a stranger to the factory. He never ventured onto the shop floor, using the excuse that he was too busy with other matters. He also told Anzieu that he felt incapable of asserting himself as Albert had done. He wondered if the other employees would ever be able to forget that he was a usurper. At times he even wondered if the others would unite against him.

The executive team – except for Jean, who was always excluded – held lengthy conversations about how to reorganize the company and improve the profit picture. But the three men were unable to communicate well among themselves. Coffin and Trudeau had very much the same temperament: both were very assertive and flew off the handle easily. Arguments would go on all day, although in the end everyone usually managed to make up. In spite of their disagreements, these managers seemed to respect each other's way of working.

This respect did not seem to extend to Jean. His reputation was one of laziness and incompetence. Others blamed him for mislaying files and failing to resolve the problems in his domain – problems related to recruitment, performance appraisal, salary administration, office allocation, and so on. His procrastination and incompetence had led to serious problems in other departments and had caused great annoyance. Coffin and Trudeau frequently had violent confrontations with Jean, which only seemed to make him worse. Now Coffin and Trudeau had developed the habit of joining forces to get at Jean, if possible bypassing him altogether. Jean was aware of this and tried his utmost to get back at them. The warring parties continually put obstacles in each other's way, each going to great lengths to show the other up. The atmosphere had become so hostile that Trudeau and Jean now communicated only by memo, even though their offices were next door to each other. Given the increasing tension, Coffin and Trudeau had managed to convince Lambert that Jean was incompetent and should be dismissed for the good of the company.

Lambert told Anzieu that he had tried to help Jean organize his work. He had also tried to act as peacemaker in the conflicts between Jean and his colleagues. Unfortunately, he witnessed in Jean the same management problems of negligence, forgetfulness, and procrastination that the others complained about, the only difference being that his relationship with Jean had always remained polite.

Lambert now faced a difficult moral dilemma that bothered him greatly, and he could not see a way out of it. He felt torn between his promise to protect the old president's son and his duty to make the company succeed and the management team work well together. He was concerned about Jean's intellectual capacity: he wondered if a certain childhood illness might have had an effect on his brain. He asked Anzieu if he could give Jean some kind of psychological examination that would prove him incompetent. In Lambert's opinion, doing this would solve the problem once and for all. He admitted, however, that it was unlikely that Jean would willingly submit to such examination, and he felt that he would have no right to force him to do so.

In reflecting on their conversation, Anzieu wondered whether this strange request for a consultation by a third party was really a way to blame one individual's "psychopathology" for what was really a group problem. He wondered whether Jean had been put in the role of scapegoat so as to relieve the tensions of the group.

COMMENTARY

The major issue that seems to preoccupy the members of the Dunor executive group is succession – or, to be more precise, failed succession. To all of them, the succession question is still an unresolved problem. Unconsciously, and maybe even consciously, Albert still seems to be the boss.

Each of the key players continues to think of Albert as the true leader, the only one who has really proved himself in the company. In spite of his retirement, Albert still seems to be watching over everything from next door while his former subordinates fantasize that he – and only he – knows everything and holds the reins. From his close observation post, linked to the factory by its network of telephones, Albert seems to hear everything. Somehow, he is still controlling the minds of his executives as he did before retirement. At any moment, they expect to hear his booming voice.

Not only is the "ghost" of Albert still haunting the corridors, but each of the four members of the executive committee considers himself Albert's heir and rightful successor. These men are now fighting over the spoils of the company. No wonder the executive committee does not work!

The purported reasons for the existence of this executive committee are laudable: information sharing and power sharing. If the committee meets regularly, the executives can inform each other about what they are doing and make decisions jointly (so that everyone is committed to shared goals). Committee meetings theoretically also create a sense of team spirit and a feeling of belonging. Unfortunately, the members of the executive committee are unable to deal with real management problems because they are preoccupied with the "hidden agenda" – that is, the question of who is going to be the true successor of Albert.

As the situation stands now, Lambert does not dare to exercise his power. Trudeau, Coffin, and Jean each attempt to show, in their own way, that Lambert has no authority over them. Even worse, they unconsciously try to destroy, through subtle (and sometimes not so subtle) sabotage, the usurper's capacity to rule.

In spite of his resignation, Albert remains the de facto leader, a man admired but also hated. During his official tenure, his autocratic way of running the firm created a certain amount of resentment, as did his abrasiveness. When he was running the company, there was no doubt that only one person could be in charge. When Lambert was selected as the new leader, the others – wanting to avoid a repetition of the previous regime – banded together to restrain his power. Under the pretext of obtaining a more democratic form of leadership, they instigated anarchy. Yet all the anarchists could feel both Albert's condemning presence and his absolute desire that Jean should succeed him. The others must have sensed Jean's desire to take what belonged to him.

If it had been as simple as that, Jean might soon have become president. When we come into the story, however, the idea of having Jean at the helm is creating a considerable amount of ambivalence among the other executives, who fear the emergence of a second Albert. After having got rid of one tyrant (or at least having relegated him to ghostly status), they find the possibility of another one hard to take. The only apparent solution to this dilemma is to force Jean to leave by making his life impossible.

Moreover, by tyrannizing Jean, the other managers can take their revenge both for Albert's tyranny and for the tyranny that they would expect from Jean. For years, Albert has ruled over Lambert, Trudeau, and Coffin with an iron hand. Now he even wants to impose his son – a small, unobtrusive, intelligent young man – on them. Unconsciously, they are taking their revenge; they will make the son pay for all the suffering the father has caused them. It is now their turn to make Albert suffer. And what better way is there than to wound his fatherly pride? They humiliate him by demonstrating to him that he has an incapable son. They even question the son's mental state, going so far as to hire a psychoanalyst to assess his stability. This is their way of telling Albert that he has failed. We may hypothesize that there is an enormous amount of lingering resentment toward the dethroned Albert among the members of the executive committee.

Other factors also need to be taken into consideration. After having been with the company for such a long time, Coffin is upset at being suddenly subordinated to a newcomer, a Parisian, a "commercial." Trudeau too is resentful. He was hired to support Jean, the heir apparent. In his eyes, then, the implication is that he is more capable than Lambert. *He* should have been chosen as president (or at least been the de facto president under Jean). This resentment of the interloper, which Trudeau and Coffin do not dare to show through open hostility toward Lambert, is communicated through subtler forms of expression.

Thus we can see that the company is suffering from both a leadership and a psychological breakdown. It seems that all the players prefer to let the boat sink with the whole crew aboard than to let a rescuer take over; they choose mass suicide over Albert's symbolic resurrection.

The confusing thing is that on the surface all the executives show good intentions, an example being their willingness to stay and work late each evening. Their shared fantasy of displaced parricide, however, steers them away from rational action. Instead, they collude among themselves, playing destructive games. They see themselves as acting very rationally and accuse the others of irrationality, failing to recognize their own responsibility in the matter.

As a matter of fact, the retired boss is perceived as a more powerful figure than he really is. (An absent or deceased boss is often idealized and, through that process, can become even more powerful than he or she was when actually in control. The image of authority becomes stronger as the authority him- or herself becomes less concrete through absence.) We can also see – now that Albert has retired, and given his history of abrasiveness – that the others are finally free to hate him. However, the boss's old subordinates (the Old Man's "sons") are unable to give up this double image of admiration and resentment.

The question now is what to do about this mess. As a consultant, how can Anzieu bring the hidden agendas out in the open? What is the wisest way to go about it?

In this particular case, Anzieu decided that he had no choice but to begin by working with the members of the executive committee to help them distinguish fact from fantasy, to identify and place the different fragments of the puzzle, and to allow the executive team to work out a more realistic way of functioning. He began by scheduling two meetings each with Trudeau, Coffin, and Jean. In addition, he had one meeting with Albert and three with Lambert.

In their meetings, Anzieu helped Lambert realize that he should begin to really take charge during the executive committee meetings, that he needed to assert his authority in a clear way. His subordinates were running wild because he had failed to define the rules of the game.

Anzieu also explained to him that the team's difficulties with Jean did not stem from a lack of intellectual ability on Jean's part – after all, he had been able to earn a law degree – but had a more psychological origin. Lambert had to realize that he had been treating Jean like the boss's son. He had not acted as a president should toward a subordinate. These discussions helped Lambert recognize that *he* was the new boss.

Anzieu decided that both Coffin and Trudeau needed a short lesson in the psychodynamics of organizations. They had to understand more about Jean's background: how he had been brought up, which of his ambitions had been encouraged, and the disappointments he had suffered. They had to be shown not only how Jean's background had led to negative reactions but also how their own attitudes made the situation worse. They had to see that they had engaged in self-fulfilling prophecies, setting traps for Jean.

Trudeau had difficulty with these explanations and did not let up in his hostility toward Jean. In an effort to defuse the hostility, Anzieu asked him to put together a list of all the mistakes Jean had made. When this was done, the consultant showed the list to Jean and asked him to react to it. Anzieu then returned and gave Jean's replies to Trudeau, leaving him to draw his own conclusions. He had to discover that the "surface" issues of these conflicts with Jean were trivial compared to the deeper emotional issues, which had blown everything out of proportion. Trudeau had to realize that the conflicts could easily have been resolved through reason and give-and-take. Moreover, he had to accept the fact that if the differences in opinion persisted, the president was going to take on the role of arbitrator.

Coffin, on the other hand, accepted Anzieu's interpretations immediately. He had known Jean since birth and had seen him grow up. He had no difficulty understanding him and seeing what role unconscious fantasies played in his actions. Without immediately telling Anzieu, he took the first two steps that would help solve the crisis.

One evening, before dinner, Coffin went to see Jean and acted in a fatherly manner toward him. This, rather than his previous aggression, was a more natural way of behaving for an old factory worker who had introduced the boss's youngest son to factory life. Coffin's change in behavior eventually helped sort out the differences that were making relations between personnel and manufacturing impossible. Then, after dinner, Coffin went to see Albert. He had not dared to speak to him for six months, fearing that he would have to tell him that his son was a good-for-nothing. He had also been afraid that the old man would reprimand him in his usual forceful manner, reproaching him for entering into a conspiracy against his son. Thus Coffin now went to Albert under the pretext of needing a solution to a problem with the municipal brass band (which they took turns directing). Delighted to be together again, the two had a relaxed and general conversation about the problems at the factory. Albert reaffirmed his wish not to interfere (in order to avoid embarrassing his successor). Coffin made him understand that if his son persisted in his passive-aggressive behavior, this would inevitably lead to his dismissal.

Released from his bondage of authority by Albert himself, Coffin was finally convinced that the only real boss would henceforth be Lambert. And Albert, prepared beforehand because of his meeting with Anzieu, understood that. He also realized that rather than listening complacently to Jean's recriminations and his long-winded accounts of the injustices he was suffering at the factory, he had better help his son face up to reality (just as he himself had done more than a year previously when he was forced to resign in Lambert's favor).

Anzieu's most decisive talk was with Jean. The meeting with him was more spontaneous than the consultant had imagined. Anzieu found that Jean had believed his father's promise until his resignation; he had never had any doubt that he would eventually succeed his father. He had therefore felt that the compromise worked out between his father and the board was a personal betrayal. Because he believed that what was promised to him was owed to him, he did not think of himself as a personnel director; instead, deep down, he felt that he was the true president. Lambert was therefore nothing more than a usurper, as were all his colleagues. They were all trying to obtain the position of president; they all wanted to deprive him of his legitimate legacy.

Jean, meanwhile, was biding his time, waiting for the day when his true rights would be recognized and the usurpers, incapable of directing the firm, would finally call on him. Jean continued to believe that only a direct descendant of Albert had the ability to manage the firm. When Jean was not granted the position of president, he decided angrily not to act properly as personnel director, neglecting his job through sullenness and procrastination while wallowing in self-pity and offended dignity. Through a kind of unconscious sabotage, Jean was showing that without him at its head, the factory would go downhill. What he did not realize was that by behaving in this resentful way, he was contributing to his own downfall.

Having made Jean clarify for himself the reasons for his behavior – his hanging onto a shattered hope, his bitterness and resentment toward the colleagues who he felt should have been his subordinates, his unconscious desire to destroy the factory that had been taken from him – Anzieu then described how the others saw his behavior: to them it proved not only his inability to be president but also his inability to be personnel director. While he was destroying the factory, he was at the same time destroying himself professionally. When Anzieu explained this, Jean defended himself each step of the way: he did not like being confronted with a truth that had never before been brought out into the open. Up to this point, Jean had had only the merest inkling of the true situation, having been blinded by his illusions. He recognized, however, that Anzieu was making valid points. From the following day onward, he began to work in the true sense of the word. He made a list of tasks to be done in order of their priority and submitted it to Lambert for discussion.

Given this progress, the executive committee meetings could begin again. Lambert's real assumption of the presidency, coupled with the change in Coffin's and Jean's attitudes, isolated Trudeau. Eventually, he had no choice but to acknowledge that he had been wrong and to stop trying to play the boss. He became once again more willing to help.

Lambert, who was still worried about his own ability to lead, asked Anzieu to attend several executive committee meetings. He wanted him not only to be an observer but also to play a more active, guiding role. Anzieu refused, though reassuring Lambert at the same time. He told him that since the unconscious puzzle had been solved, it was now up to him to take on the role of president and to solve the problems by taking rational action. This was possible now, since his colleagues were finally playing a role that corresponded to their functions.

We can see, then, how Anzieu's intervention consisted of bringing about an exposition of an "irrational" interpersonal theater – that is, making the unconscious conscious. The situation that existed at Dunor echoes the mythical adventure that Sigmund Freud described in his book *Totem and Taboo* (Freud, 1912–13). In that story, rival sons unite to kill the father, each one renouncing through their joint act the absolute power that their father has held. After doing so, however, neither son can renounce the other; their shared action leads them to become interdependent, to have common norms and goals and shared roles. This is similar to the situation at Dunor after the father, Albert, was "murdered" in his forced resignation as president.

The executive committee was able to function effectively for eighteen months. During that time, the necessary management decisions were taken to bring the company back on course. And then? If you have been viewing things from Anzieu's perspective, you may not be surprised at what happened next.

Lambert, the newcomer, was not able, given his personality, to impose his authority and define the new rules of the game. Because the authority of the Old Man continued in the minds of his former subordinates – both because they craved his strong leadership and because Albert wanted (unconsciously) to continue as boss – these transference reactions toward Albert reinforced Lambert's uncertainty and timidity. He managed to muddle through for some time, but only because of Anzieu's intervention. Once the group problem was solved, Lambert was increasingly troubled by personal doubts and dilemmas. After eighteen months of struggling, he had learned his lesson and handed in his resignation.

This case indicates that in complex management situations, unconscious collusions have to be "decoded" to make groups function more effectively. Group dynamics functioned at Dunor as they sometimes do within families: the members of the executive committee created the myth of the scapegoat, and Jean was singled out for ritual sacrifice.

Group fantasies are inevitable, in both successful and unsuccessful groups. To make group dynamics more effective, however, everyone must come to recognize these emerging shared fantasies, analyze their structure, grasp their function, and establish processes by which they can be identified and dealt with on an ongoing basis.

Note

1 The only name in this case not disguised.

C. ENVY, SPITE, AND SIBLING RIVALRY

Case 6

Who is the leader?
The Nadia Corporation

The Nadia Corporation was dealing with a number of real problems – loss of profitability, lack of leadership, and a demoralizing atmosphere – when Joe French, a management consultant, was called in to help the company. But Joe found, as have many consultants in family business, that the stated problems of the company were really symptoms of other problems simmering beneath the surface. Joe knew, from years of experience, that unless these underlying problems were taken care of, solving the surface issues would not turn the company around.

Readers of this case may be somewhat surprised by the reluctance of two of the children to take over the helm of the company from their father. Perhaps subliminally these children know something others are not yet aware of – that it might not be possible to be a true leader in this company that has too many leaders already.

This case offers an opportunity to observe the consequences of various "unholy triangles" and to see that chaotic family dynamics do not come without repercussions. From the consultant's point of view, the question is what French can do to help unravel the various "games" the family members play. Are there inferences he can draw about the linkages between the personal and business spheres? To understand this interplay, he must first be able to figure out what the various key players really want. What are their fantasies, what conscious and unconscious wishes do they have? What is going on in their inner world? And even if the consultant manages to decipher some of the various hidden (and not so hidden) agendas, what kind of advice will these people listen to? Is it possible to stop the relentless perpetuation of these dysfunctional family myths?

THE NADIA CORPORATION

Joe French, senior partner of Advitex, a strategic consulting firm, was sitting behind his desk letting his mind wander over the events of the previous week. What was he going to tell two of the principals of the Nadia Corporation, who were about to visit him? What was really going on in their company? Once more he ran through the interview notes in his mind. He had recently seen everyone except the president, who had chosen to take a holiday during the time that Joe visited the firm.

The executives Joe met with explained that the Nadia Corporation was losing profitability. In addition, the management structure of this family firm seemed to be confused. Financial and other data on how the company was doing were not readily available to the managers of the firm. The president, Peter Johnson, was secretive and had frequent fights with the other managers of the company – especially his sister, Nadia. Morale in the organization was low. Three presidents in the past five years, family conflicts, confusion about who was making decisions, lack of confidence that the new president could lead the company into a new market, rumors that the company would be split up into three parts – all these factors contributed to a tense and demoralizing atmosphere. How had this come about?

Company history

The Nadia Corporation had been started thirty years before by Steve Johnson, Peter's father, who believed that there was a market niche for elegant, high-quality, lightweight luggage. His idea proved to be a good one, and his first product line was an immediate success. The company had had almost a constant rate of growth since then, reaching a sales volume of $60 million and employing over four hundred people in its two factories.

As the Nadia Corporation expanded, Steve brought in two of his younger brothers, Bob and George, to help run the company. They were followed by the two children of another brother, now deceased, and – about a decade ago – by two of Steve's own three children, Nadia, the oldest, and Tony, who was four years younger.

Although many people admired the founder's business acumen, old-time managers in the company spoke of his mercurial temperament. They recalled in particular how the first of his younger brothers, Bob, who stayed with the company only a few years, bore the brunt of his wrath when things did not go well. Steve would embarrass his brother in front of others and afterwards tell all and sundry, "Since I pay him, I can yell at him." He was, however, much more considerate toward the youngest of the brothers, George.

In the more recent history of the company, two events stand out. Five years ago, Steve suffered a serious heart attack that made him decide to change his lifestyle. He withdrew from the day-to-day management of the company and bought a second home in southern France. There he could be found, particularly in the winter months, devoting much of his energy to golf. He still maintained an office at the company, however, and was in daily contact with his children.

Following this change, Steve's brother George had taken on the presidency. According to most of the other executives, George's style differed sharply from that of his older brother. George had a much more consultative approach; he was not as authoritarian as Steve. Many executives Joe interviewed noted, however, that Steve had mellowed after his semi-retirement.

After George became president, the company was run on a product management basis by Nadia and Tony (Steve's two children) and Steve's two nephews. One of the nephews, Henry, was considered a star in the industry. In addition, Peter, Steve's third child (two years younger than Nadia but older than Tony) joined the company after a four-year stint in the Unification Church as a devotee of the Moonies. The ownership of the company remained in Steve's hands.

A few years later – in other words, just a couple of years ago – another crisis occurred when Steve's two nephews asked for part ownership. Steve, supported by his brother George and their accountant, refused, feeling that there was not sufficient room in the company for five owners. The two nephews left angrily. After their departure, Steve transferred his shares in equal parts to his children. He continued to hold control over the voting shares, however.

The two nephews, having received some financial help from George, set up their own company, Duvon, in order to compete directly with the Nadia Corporation. Feeling torn between the warring parties, George resigned as president. Like his brother Steve, he retained an office at the company.

After considerable hesitation, Steve and George (still involved, though not at the helm) made Peter, the last family member to join the company, the new president. Although Nadia was offered the presidency first, she refused. Given the workload the position entailed, she felt that she would have to give up her personal life if she took on the presidency. Moreover, she felt that her talents were needed more in sales and merchandising. She also admitted later that she was concerned with how she would compare, if in charge, with her highly visible cousin Henry. She doubted whether she could live up to her father's expectations. Her other brother, Tony, who was also offered the position before Peter, felt at the time that he was indispensable in manufacturing. In addition, it was his opinion that from a seniority point of view, his older brother should be the first to receive the offer.

Peter accepted the presidency, an appointment Steve favored. Steve believed Tony too gullible to be president, basing his opinion on Tony's investment in a computer system that had proven very costly. Steve described Peter's management philosophy as typified by such statements as "If it ain't broke, don't fix it," which was much more to his liking. However, Steve had once been heard to say (several years earlier) that his dream was to see Nadia take on the presidency, a statement that had been brought to her attention.

Peter's role as president was sometimes confusing to outsiders. Nadia and Tony were running their own show, and Peter's father and uncle were still very present. In addition, a partner of the company's accounting firm seemed unusually involved in the affairs of the company. Joe French had been quite intrigued on hearing this accountant's constant use of the pronoun "we" when describing his role at Nadia.

Current developments

Although some Nadia Corporation executives confessed to Joe French that they had looked at the choice of Peter as president with a certain amount of trepidation (because of his checkered background), most were of the opinion that a remarkable transformation had taken place in him soon after he took over. Although they acknowledged that it had taken him some time to learn the ropes, they felt that he had grown into his new job very quickly – especially given his prior ignorance of the business. After their initial uncertainty, then, many of the executives were impressed by his accomplishments. Some attributed great wisdom to even the most banal inquiries made by Peter. Almost every decision he made was affirmed with comments such as "He surely sensed how to enter that market" or "Without his intervention, we'd still be arguing about the viability of that investment."

After the realignment of the organization, the company initially prospered. Certain problems did arise, however. Some executives noted that Duvon – the cousins' competition – was merchandising almost identical lines aimed at the same customers, sometimes actually copying the designs of the Nadia Corporation. Despite this direct competition, the three Nadia principals ignored Duvon's existence. In the meantime, Duvon was steadily gaining market share and eroding the Nadia Corporation's competitive position; Nadia's profitability was slipping.

Some executives were concerned about the negative aspects of their president's leadership style once the bottom line started to suffer. They acknowledged that he was a rather secretive, shy individual, reluctant to share information with the other executives. For non-family members, financial information such as profitability by product line was particularly hard to come by. Peter seemed to be afraid that if others found out how profitable the company was, he would be asked for raises.

Others questioned the soundness of some of Peter's measures in cutting costs. Many of the executives, including the principals, also complained about the lack of positive feedback (indeed, in the case of some personnel, the lack of any feedback at all) from the president. They felt that this lack might have been the reason some of the key people had left the company.

Some executives wondered about the president's almost daily contact with his father (by phone, generally). They found regular visits by Peter's Uncle George only marginally less disconcerting. Others questioned the role of the accountant, whose possessive attitude added to the general confusion about who was running the company.

Although many executives felt that there must be some deeper meaning to Peter's frequently enigmatic remarks about business developments and desperately tried to make sense out of them, others became bewildered and demoralized. The general feeling in the upper echelon was that policy should be more formally established and that decisions should be made more quickly.

Peter's withdrawn, uncommunicative style became of even greater concern when the company decided to augment its presence in the European Economic Community (EEC). There were a number of problems in the planning of that venture caused by Peter's failure to transfer information to key players in the company – a failure that could eventually have serious legal consequences. Some managers (including Nadia and Tony) began to wonder whether Peter, as the main executive responsible, had the right personality makeup to engineer such a major venture.

Moreover, some executives were annoyed at Peter's occasional derogatory remarks about the abilities of women. These comments, combined with a tendency to ignore the normal chain of command, had led to a number of serious blowups with his sister. Clashes between Peter and Nadia had become the order of the day. A typical scenario: Nadia, who was known for having quite a temper, indulged in an emotional outburst, complaining of having received information from thirdhand sources about certain actions Peter had taken that would directly affect her work. Peter reacted to these accusations in a withdrawn, apparently unemotional manner. Tony's anxious attempts to mediate in these instances met with very little success.

The conflict came to a head when Peter scheduled a series of meetings concerning the EEC launch, committing his sister without first consulting her. Nadia's reaction had been a flash of anger: she shouted, "I don't like being told what to do!" She also accused Peter of letting details related to the EEC plan slip.

These conflicts reverberated throughout the company, leading to an increasingly tense atmosphere that affected both morale and productivity. Lunches in the executive dining room, originally a place for banter and the frank exchange of ideas, became painful affairs. Peter would disappear from the office for long periods, returning looking run-down and dejected. Eventually, the situation deteriorated to such an extent that the family began to consider whether the company could be split into three parts so that each sibling could go his or her own way. Whether this was a viable option (with product lines and functions so interrelated), however, was questionable. And such a split would make the three siblings extremely vulnerable to the competitive onslaught of Duvon. Furthermore, their father (who was, after all, the company founder) would not countenance such drastic action. He felt that everyone was exaggerating the situation and that there was no crisis to speak of.

It was at this point that Tony asked Joe French, who had previously done some work for the company, to give his thoughts on what to do. Although French was able to schedule a series of interviews with the principals immediately, Peter explained that he would be gone when French arrived: on the advice of Uncle George, who felt he needed a rest (since he seemed seriously stressed), he was leaving with his uncle for a fishing trip in Argentina. French was not too concerned, however, since he remembered talks he had had with Peter at other times.

Family background

Apart from clarifying the company situation, during his meetings at Nadia Joe French developed a better idea of the Johnson family history. From all information, it appeared that Steve had been something of an overpowering father, a person who "made the house tremble when he came home." His wife – the mother of Nadia, Tony, and Peter – had made a great effort to keep the children out of harm's way.

That marriage was not a happy one. Conflicts between the parents were the order of the day. Steve had a very traditional view of the role of women: they were supposed to stay at home, cook, clean, and take care of the children. His wife obliged, taking the back seat and having very little say in Steve's activities. As the conflicts increased, intensified by Steve's affairs with other women, his wife finally divorced him. At the time of the divorce, Nadia was fifteen years old.

It appeared that all the children had had a hard time dealing with their father during those years. Nadia always felt that her father had really wanted a boy in her place. Peter, who had been a sickly child, tended to stay at home under his mother's care, though when he grew older his father took him out to go hunting, to get him away from her influence. At Peter's adolescence, things had soured between the two. Peter grew long hair, his marks went down at school, and he started to drink and take drugs. To add insult to injury, he flunked out of college (although he was always considered the brightest of the children). Eventually, he joined the Moonies, who – for four years – forbade him to talk to his father. In the meantime, his father shifted his interest to his younger son, Tony.

A repeated complaint of both Nadia and Tony was that their father would play favorites, turning them against each other and using them as a wedge against their mother. They also resented the fact that their father embarrassed them in front of others, using criticism as his only form of feedback.

Nadia grew up thinking that she was nobody's favorite, with Peter close to their mother and Tony close to their father. She felt that she had to manage all on her own and prove herself to the world. Moreover, because of all the turmoil, she often had to take care of the other children. Fortunately, according to her own reports, she was the pragmatic one in the family. If, for example, she had to take care of things when her father had one of his fits of depression and disappeared for days, she was resourceful enough to handle the task. Nadia mentioned that her relationship with Peter had never been very good. In the business, for example, she felt that Peter automatically rejected anyone she hired. Privately, she confided that she wondered if Peter actually hated her.

Nadia and Tony felt that Peter was most like their father, similar in not sharing information and in disappearing at times. They felt that Tony was the only one who saw eye-to-eye with their father.

Of the three children, only Tony was married. Peter had had a number of transitory relationships with much younger women – "girls" who tended to admire him and cater to his whims. Only once – at a time when most who knew him felt he was more confident – did he have a relatively stable relationship. According to Tony, Peter had only one close friend from childhood. As for Nadia, she had had a series of unsuccessful love affairs and still hoped to have a husband and children. She was thirty-six at the time of the interviews.

Steve seemed to be particularly concerned that his son Peter, if under too much stress, would return to the Moonies. Other executives also wondered how Peter would fare outside the company if indeed it was split up. Would he be able to handle himself emotionally and financially? They questioned, however, whether Peter's departure from the company was a real option. On many occasions, when pushed about his future role – after he had made a caustic remark about wanting to run a fishing camp, for example – he had expressed a strong wish to stay on and contribute to the success of the business.

With all the different issues once more clear in his mind, Joe French wondered how he should tackle the Nadia Corporation's problems.

COMMENTARY

The overt problems that the Nadia Corporation faces are such issues as a drop in profitability, a confused management structure, and low morale. These problems, however, are only the tip of the iceberg. Underneath, many other issues seem to be simmering. Steve's reluctance to make a true break with the company, for example – as evidenced in his tendency to use many subterfuges so as not to transfer power – is contributing greatly to the present malaise in leadership.

Two events were instrumental in contributing to the company's present loss of its sense of direction: Steve's heart attack (which forced him to give up day-to-day management of the firm) and the departure of Steve's two nephews (one of whom was a real star in the business).

Although these two events brought things to a head, the psychological balance among the key players in the company had always been rather fragile. Previously their conflicts had remained rather contained. Now, with the off-and-on presence of Steve, everything is gradually falling apart. Fighting among the family members is creating morale problems throughout the company. What is the role of the different protagonists in the perpetuation of Nadia? That is now the important question.

Closer analysis makes it quite clear that the present group dynamics and the interpersonal relationships among the principal actors are, in fact, rooted in the family background. Early life experiences led to unresolved family conflicts, and these now color adversely the relationships between the members of top management. That being the case, it may be helpful to have a look at the major protagonists.

Steve Johnson

Steve Johnson, the founder-entrepreneur, is also the father of the current president, Peter. Steve's other two children also hold strategic positions in the company. Because Nadia is responsible for sales and merchandising, and Tony, the youngest, is head of manufacturing, good communication among the three children is essential for effective company functioning. Steve's brother George, in spite of his resignation from the presidency due to a conflict of interest, also seems to play an important role in Nadia's management.

For the first twenty-five years, the company was run by Steve, who is described as having been a rather overpowering, autocratic leader. However, Steve also had good business sense, which led to the early success of the company. Indeed, his autocratic style was probably suited to the needs of a small entrepreneurial firm. The disadvantages of Steve's leadership style manifested themselves only as the company reached a more mature phase in its development. The corporate culture that had developed as a by-product of his style turned out to be too entrenched to adapt to his brother George's more consultative approach. We can conjecture that Steve had stacked the company with yea-sayers, not people who had a mind of their own.

Steve-the-father is very much like Steve-the-boss. According to all accounts, he was an overpowering father in the early years. He played favorites with his children, turning them against each other and using them as a wedge against their mother. We can only speculate about the kinds of unholy triangles Steve created when the children were growing up. And the games continue in adult life: Steve has surrounded himself with his family members at work, thus extending his role as superior/boss into the family and likewise his role as father into the company.

Steve-the-husband was no better. His traditional view of women's role in society led to intense conflict between him and his wife and resulted in a divorce when the children had not yet reached adulthood. Perhaps his wife was not able to handle the different games Steve played in the family, and she appears not to have been strong enough to play an effective role as buffer. All of these factors – particularly Steve's attitude toward women – reappear in the company dynamics.

Steve's sudden heart attack and its aftermath – his retirement from the day-to-day management – made it very clear that succession had not been one of his priorities. Even now, after his semi-retirement, Steve is unwilling to let anyone else manage his "baby." For example, he refused to give shares to his capable nephews when they asked; and although he transferred his shares to his children, he has kept control over the voting shares. Moreover, he manipulates both Peter and Tony in order to have a hand in running the company.

From a "fantasy" point of view, we see how Steve wants to keep control of the company at all costs. In spite of statements to the contrary, he is not letting go. And notwithstanding all the turmoil his actions create in the company, he stubbornly holds on to the myth of harmony among the family members. If you would believe him, everything is all right between his children; there is nothing to worry about. Of course, trying to keep control from a distance can be very costly: the golf course is not the place to take the pulse of the business.

Peter Johnson

From the information in the case, it appears that a major theme in Peter's life is the search for a father, be it his Uncle George, the Moonies, or now, belatedly, his own father. Peter also seems to suffer from a certain amount of persecutory anxiety.

Peter's role in this family drama highlights the importance of the family members' early life experiences in explaining the Nadia Corporation's current difficulties. Initially, Steve tried to "make a man" out of him; then, having failed, he turned his attention to his younger son, Tony. Peter, who was weak and sickly, felt much more compatible with his mother, but he deemed himself a failure for not having fulfilled his father's expectations. Rejected in adolescence by his father, he dropped out of the competition and sought solace in drink and drugs, eventually joining a sect that seems to have been a symbolic father replacement.

Peter became stereotyped in the family as the incompetent brother, and from young adulthood on he played that role to the hilt. However, he has now returned as the prodigal son, trying to win back his father's attention. Given the way he is portrayed by other family members, we could hypothesize that there exists some kind of unconscious conspiracy among them to find something for him to do, to keep him out of trouble. What better job to give him than make him the president of the company!

There is another unconscious conspiracy at work: Peter's appointment suits everybody's needs. As president, Peter remains vulnerable, insecure, and dependent on Steve. Because Peter does not have what it takes to be president of a company, Steve stays in control. Nadia and Tony benefit too: they have a graceful way out of accepting an impossible job – one in which they would have their father and uncle hanging over their shoulders, intruding into their decisions.

The fact that the presidency was offered to Peter only after being rejected by both Nadia and Tony increased Peter's need to prove himself as the right successor. One might wonder, however, whether Peter even really wants to be president of the company. Is being president in order to resolve the difficulties in his relationship with his father a sufficiently strong motive? Of course, Peter may not be savvy enough to realize the lame-duck nature of his appointment. But even so, one reason for his willingness to accept the job was that it gave him an opportunity to work more closely with his father. Having failed earlier in life to live up to his father's expectations, he may be looking for a second chance.

Peter's daily consultation with Steve on business matters illustrates his dependency. At times – as a way of feeling more powerful – he tries to mirror his father's behavior. And Steve, seemingly pleased at having again become closer to his rebel son, is using him as a proxy in order to continue to run the company himself.

However, the atmosphere of envy, spite, vindictiveness, and competitiveness in the early life of the siblings, exacerbated by the father's talent at playing favorites, has been transferred into the working environment. Steve's absence and Peter's arrival have shaken the previous carefully maintained equilibrium. Open warfare is breaking out between the children. Their actions seriously affect the atmosphere within the company, as indicated by the climate of suspicion and the regressive behavior of a number of employees who mindlessly idealize some of Peter's actions.

The impact of their parents' divorce and of Steve's misogyny is reflected in Peter's present attitude toward Nadia. Peter's hostility toward his sister may be deepened by his feeling that his mother was never strong enough to stand up for him or protect him from his father.

Nadia Johnson

Nadia, as the oldest child in the Johnson family and as a female, had to struggle all through her childhood for attention and recognition. The idea that her father had really wanted a son and her corollary sense of rejection reinforced her resolve to prove herself and to win a place of honor among the family members.

As a result of her parents' conflict and subsequent divorce, many of the responsibilities in the household were transferred to Nadia. This curtailed her childhood, forcing her to grow up quickly. Too early in life, an unfair share of responsibility was given to her. This feeling of a lack of balance in her relationships may have lingered on in adult life. Too much giving and too little receiving may have left her with a continuing sense of the unfairness of life.

Nadia's only male role models were her domineering father, one weak brother, and another brother who was probably too young to relate to as a man. The narcissistic injury of being nobody's favorite and the lack of adequate role models (a manipulative father contrasted with a weak mother) are symptomized at present in her difficulty in establishing a significant relationship with a member of the opposite sex. She seems to have a knack for selecting the wrong men. Obviously, her "internalized" father image – anything but a soothing influence – is not a helpful model in partner choice. Being put in an adult role prematurely may also have left Nadia with a sense of inadequacy. The situation certainly filled her with resentment toward her father. Getting even with fathers (real or symbolic) seems to be a major theme in her life – an activity that now seems to be displaced toward Peter and that has had unfortunate outcomes with the men in her romantic life.

Knowing her father's attitude toward women's role in society, Nadia may feel that she is a failure for not being a wife and a mother. She lives in a world of internal contradictions. On the one hand, she wants to prove herself to her father and brothers; on the other hand, she is afraid of risking failure by meeting this objective. She handles the contradiction by convincing herself that what she really wants is to have a family. But is that her true desire? And does it have to be a zero-sum game? The knowledge that her father's dream was to see her take on the presidency of the company adds another element of confusion and insecurity to her life. What if she should do so and fail, as she feels she has in her personal life? Is her insistence on having a family her way of rationalizing her refusal?

Nadia at work is not much different from Nadia at home: she transfers her emotions vis-à-vis her father and brothers into the working environment. It may be that her resentment of Peter is a displacement of her feelings toward her father. Knowing that she cannot afford to resent her father directly, she transfers her frustrations onto her brother Peter, who might seem to her to be her father's clone.

Obviously, Nadia's relationship with her father remains unresolved. At the age of thirty-six, she still continues to play the role of "nobody's favorite." One part of her personality resents playing this role – a resentment that is manifested in her constant clashes with her brother. The other part of her personality prevents her from taking more constructive action by making her believe that she would not be able to meet her father's expectations. Nadia's lack of self-confidence and fear of failure ultimately rob her of a sense of satisfaction from her real business accomplishments.

Tony Johnson

As the youngest child in the Johnson family, Tony seems to be the most balanced of the three. Last in line, he was supported throughout his childhood – initially by his mother and then by Nadia. He was also his father's favorite at a critical stage in his development. This support resulted in his being more secure about himself than his siblings can be said to be.

In the family, as in the business, Tony has taken on the role of mediator. Not belonging to any side, he can analyze the situation in a more rational way. Indeed, he was the first one to recognize the need for an external consultant. Basically, he would like to get on with the business. He, of all his family members, seems to be least affected by images of the past.

One might wonder if Tony's image as a mediator could help him fulfill a possible dormant wish: to be his father's successor. Tony rejected the presidency when asked; and this may have been the right response at the time, given his place in the family. But this does not preclude his acceptance of the job at some later juncture.

George Johnson

George's role in the Johnson family drama is superficially that of the "nice guy." Being in the shadow of his dominant brother, he tries to protect himself and the others. His consultative approach as president of the company, however, did not match the corporate culture established by the previous president and founder, Steve. At times the soundness of his decisions seems to have been open to question. Not supporting his nephews in their request for shares in the company is one example. Could not some kind of arrangement have been made? The offer of financial help to those same nephews in setting up a company of their own (prompted, perhaps, by guilt feelings) may have intensified the family drama. And consider his timing in taking Peter on a fishing trip while the consultant was visiting the company. Such action clearly illustrates the confusion between family matters and business matters – confusion that has turned out to be a major problem at Nadia Corporation.

The present situation, characterized by turmoil, lack of clear guidance, weak leadership, internal conflict, and overall confusion, is a fertile environment for an outsider (in this case, the accountant) to gain power and influence. The metaphor of the two parties fighting while the third wins accurately describes the role of the accountant. Under such circumstances, it is not surprising that the company has lost its sense of direction and that business issues such as the EEC launch are not given due importance.

This analysis of the interpersonal relationships among the principals at the Nadia Corporation – relationships rooted in early childhood – gives us some idea of how manifest management problems in a family-owned business relate to latent psychological factors. The question then becomes what can be done about them.

Obviously, the linchpin in this particular drama is Steve himself. Steve has to be persuaded that he needs to let go. He should be made aware of the fact that the present situation does not augur well for the future of the business. If things continue as they are, the company will be soon out of business.

In addition, Peter should be convinced that managing a company is not really for him. He should probably be doing something more in line with his abilities. Somehow he must be made to realize that he is in over his head at Nadia, a realization that may endanger his already fragile sense of self-esteem.

Nadia or Tony should be convinced (if their father is really prepared to let go) to take over the helm of the company. The consultant first has to assess, however, how deep the conflicted feelings are between these two siblings. For example, if the theme of unfairness is too much of an issue to Nadia (her inability to sort out her personal life being a giveaway), perhaps she should not remain in the company but instead should go her own way. To stay on in the family business, with its background of triangulation and other dysfunctional family dynamics, is not the way to become a person in one's own right. Too many memories will come back to make true separation possible. For Tony, on the other hand, the ghosts of childhood in the family business will probably not be overly problematic.

Epilogue

The three siblings continued to work together for some time. The presence of the consultant, who was subsequently asked back to consult on other matters, seemed to have calmed the situation down; there was less open conflict in the company. After a number of consultations, however, Peter realized the impossibility of his present position; he decided he was not presidential material. Since money was not a problem, he made up his mind to withdraw completely from the business and put his energy into running a fishing camp in British Columbia. Some time later, Nadia too made the decision to get out. She adopted a child and took a less pressured job. She sold her shares to her brother Tony, who found himself in total control of the company.

Case 7

Alice in Wonderland
Roland and Stone Inc.

John Bursk's description of what is happening at Roland and Stone has a kind of Alice in Wonderland quality. Bursk, the protagonist in this case, reveals considerable naïveté about organizational life in the surprise he experiences as he encounters the course of events in this new corporate world. He is only now beginning to realize that what you see is not always what you get. Perhaps a focus on surface issues has led him to ignore important underlying factors in this evolving corporate drama.

This case touches on a number of interesting issues, many of which we have all faced when considering a new job. Choosing a new position is not easy, especially since it demands that we take account of a host of factors related to person-organization fit – that elusive compatibility between our personality and the culture of the organization. Complicating such decisions is the fact that there are as many *emotional* dimensions to "fit" as there are rational and logical aspects.

Now Bursk has chosen his job, and we can ask how astute he was in assessing the company's dynamics. Why did he not realize sooner that Roland and Stone was in the middle of an internecine war? Could he not have seen problems coming?

In reading this case, try to put yourself in John Bursk's shoes and reflect on what he should have paid attention to before joining Roland and Stone. How did he get himself into the pickle he finds himself in? Ask yourself, too, what is really happening in this company. How did the trouble begin? And finally, think about what John Bursk should do now.

ROLAND AND STONE INC.

In September 1995, John Bursk, vice president and general manager for wholesale sales at Roland and Stone Inc., was feeling frustrated by the firm's lack of direction and by the uncoordinated sense of responsibility among its officers and senior executives. The sales representatives of the company, a wholesaler and retailer of high-priced men's shoes, seemed to think of themselves as independent contractors. The senior vice president for marketing operations, to whom Bursk reported, was surprisingly indifferent to market trends in the shoe industry. Little if any reporting relationship was evident between outlet discount stores and the controller's office or between management and warehouse employees. And yet at the last meeting of the executive committee, none of these issues had been seriously dealt with.

Bursk had been hired for his present job in the spring of 1994 by George Roland, the president of Roland and Stone. The company had just closed down the manufacturing plant on which it had built its reputation as a high-quality, customer-oriented business dating from the late nineteenth century. Spiraling costs in the domestic shoe industry and shifts in consumer preferences from high-*quality* to high-*fashion* shoes had forced this change. Since the death of its two founders, the company had been owned and continuously managed by members of the Roland family. George Roland was the grandson of one of the founders, whose widow had managed the company with a firm hand until her son Neville had learned enough as her assistant to take over on his own. Neville (the father of George Roland) had continued to serve as company president for thirty-five years after his mother's death, until he himself died in 1988 and was succeeded by his three sons (as co-owners with their mother).

Neville Roland was still fondly remembered by long-time employees as the boss who knew all of them by their first names, who kept a watchful eye on operations, and who personified the firm's industry reputation for quality and individual service. One old-timer recalled that Neville Roland used to be able to "come into the shop, spot the one pair of lousy shoes on the floor, and know who was responsible."

John Bursk, before becoming vice president and general manager for wholesale sales, had been a successful salesman of high-priced jewelry in the New York area. He had been attracted to Roland and Stone by an advertisement in the *Wall Street Journal*. Although Roland and Stone was in an entirely different kind of business, the position of directing wholesale sales seemed to John Bursk like a welcome opportunity to expand his managerial abilities while drawing on his sales experience. After one telephone conversation with George Roland, Bursk had come up to the home office for an interview with Roland and Jeremy Maxwell, a consultant to the company. Though he initially thought it strange that he did not meet any of the other officers at that interview, Bursk decided, after Roland explained the current setup of the company and its evolution from a manufacturer of quality shoes to a merchandiser of retail and wholesale lines, that meeting the others was not especially important.

George Roland's hope was that the major decision to close the shoe factory would restore profits for Roland and Stone. Between 1988 (when he and his brothers, Jim and Dean, became owners) and 1992, net income after taxes had stayed at approximately $800,000. In 1992, net income dropped; and in the following years, the company suffered sustained losses. Sales remained constant at around $36 million through 1994, however. The company borrowed at a 10 percent interest rate against the cash surrender value of life insurance on the Roland brothers; this source provided considerable unused debt capacity.

When George Roland called back to offer Bursk the position, he proposed a salary that approximated Bursk's present income; $120,000 plus 1 percent of increases in wholesale sales. The job seemed to present the kind of challenge that Bursk wanted. His first responsibility would be to coordinate the efforts of the wholesale sales force of fifteen people and to assist Joseph Hale, senior vice president for marketing operations, in strengthening the product lines, developing new sales tools, and managing product promotion.

George Roland had told Bursk that "the independent operator who purchases 200 to 400 pairs of shoes a year represents the backbone of our wholesale business." Sales representatives were assigned to regions throughout the United States. They were remunerated on a straight commission basis of 7 percent; their earnings ranged from $40,000 to $160,000 a year. Three of the salespeople were also allowed a guaranteed salary draw that consistently exceeded their commission.

In his first few weeks at Roland and Stone, it became obvious to Bursk that there was very little communication between Jim Roland (the oldest brother), Dean Roland (the youngest brother), and George, who was president. Each brother owned a 25 percent share in the company (with the balance held by their mother) and theoretically contributed a comparable share to the company's management. George, with a master's degree in chemistry, was more educated than his two brothers and had learned the business from working as his father's assistant. Jim had come into the factory only reluctantly when his father insisted; he had started in the lower ranks of production and worked his way up to the skilled but non-managerial job of leather buyer. In conversation, he was likely to talk more spiritedly of the time when he had been a young Air Force flight instructor than of the family business. Dean started to work for the company during summer vacations which led to a permanent arrangement.

Bursk learned that only after Neville Roland's death had the three brothers worked out an agreement about their managerial roles. Dean Roland, who said he had never had much chance to "work with Dad in learning the business," became executive vice president for retail store operations. Jim, initially in charge of the factory, became executive vice president for marketing when the factory was closed down. It was understood that each would have a high degree of autonomy. (Figure C7.1 shows the organization chart in 1995.)

Gradually, the executives who had worked under Neville Roland left the firm as frictions developed in both the retail store operations and the factory between the old-timers and Jim and Dean Roland. When the wholesale marketing director ran into problems with Jim Roland, he was fired but not replaced. Dean Roland fired two regional managers of retail sales on the grounds that they could not get along well with other people, although they had been with the company for over ten years.

However, Dean Roland had strong support from Phil Tomey, another long-

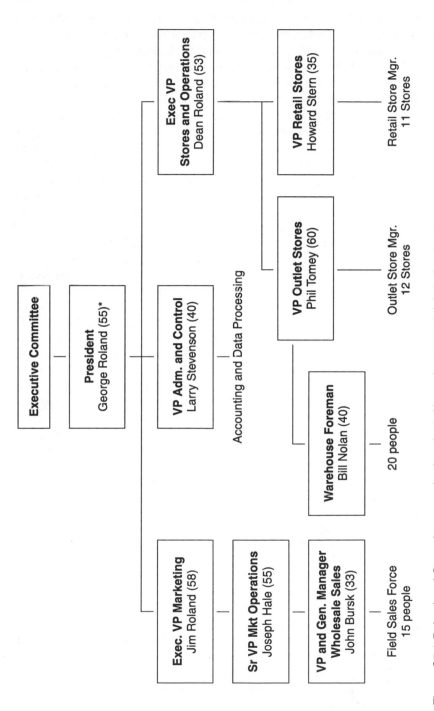

Figure C7.1 Roland and Stone Inc. organization chart, November 1983. * ( ) designates age

time employee, who was now vice president for outlet stores. In 1991, Dean and Tomey had decided to add to the company's retail outlets by opening a discount outlet store for the factory's unacceptable shoes. It became profitable, and under the stimulus of its success, they decided to devote more time to opening up stores of this type in other locations. As of September 1995, Roland and Stone had twelve outlet stores and eleven traditional retail stores.

When Bursk took charge of the wholesale sales force, the sales representatives covered regions that served approximately 8,000 men's shoe stores through a total of 3,000 accounts. All the sales representatives called Bursk two or three times a week to keep him up to date on sales in their territories. They reported on which styles were selling well, what mixes of the 200 to 250 shoe samples were being shown to dealers, and what the overall fashion trends seemed to be. At the semi-annual sales meetings, the sales representatives proposed new styles. Bursk's plan was to spend about one week each year in the field with each of the fifteen salespeople. He sent out two or three bulletins a week that gave them trade information on product-line changes, fast-moving styles, pricing adjustments, sales goals, individual sales performance, special promotions, competitors' styles, and opportunities for new accounts (for example, when a competitor's sales forces was shaken up).

One of the first things John Bursk noticed when he looked over the accounts was the large proportion of independent dealers who ordered only one to ten pairs of shoes a year – a far cry from the 200- to 400-pair orders that George Roland had said were the backbone of the business. During Bursk's field trips, he found that many of the sales representatives tended to make decisions for their retailers, and many of them focused on certain accounts where they felt confident that the clients would take their advice on merchandising techniques. Bursk began to question whether the sales territories were still appropriate and whether the system of giving salespeople straight commissions on dollar sales had any effect on attracting new customers.

Bursk was also skeptical about the effects of contract manufacturing on Roland and Stone's product quality image. Since the factory shutdown, the main suppliers of shoes were a number of contract manufacturers and a buying cartel in Brazil. Product quality was uneven and unpredictable, and delivery from suppliers had been unsatisfactory. The combination of poor deliveries and rapid style changes led to inventory shortages, which inevitably hurt the company's reputation for customer service.

Reporting procedures at Roland and Stone were so informal that Bursk felt up against a barrier when it came to getting his ideas heard. Hale, the senior vice president for marketing operations (to whom he was supposed to report), had had no purchasing experience up to the time the factory closed down. He now coordinated shoe purchasing. Although he spent a lot of time at trade shows, he preferred to rely on his own intuition about styles rather than on industry statistics, having been an award-winning stylist himself. Hale seemed uninterested in what Bursk had to tell him about new styles or the success of new product lines or the products of competitors. When there was an important decision to be made, Bursk noted that Hale took the issue directly to the president, bypassing Jim Roland (who was his executive vice president).

On the few occasions that they had worked on projects together, Jim Roland had seemed quite detached, perhaps even absentminded, to Bursk. A memo that Bursk once sent him about a possible change in a supplier had never been answered. Jim was not in his office much, in fact, and was generally inaccessible. His associations with other officers of the company appeared to be limited to lunchtime meetings with his youngest brother and Phil Tomey. Rumors floated about that Jim Roland had a drinking problem.

In the warehouse operation, Bursk found a lack of any reporting arrangement between management and employees. Eventually, he was told that Tomey and Dean Roland maintained informal relations with Bill Nolan, the warehouse foreman, who was also a member of the Teamsters union. Nolan had had a hand in bringing the union back when the previous warehouse supervisor was discharged. Offices and warehouse were in the same building complex, but communication between them was all by telephone.

After a few visits to the warehouse to check the inventory of specific lines, Bursk thought he understood warehouse operations. When an order was received from the order department, the warehouse receptionist combined the new order with past orders and compiled a packing list to pull shoe boxes from a multitude of storage racks. The order would be shipped the same day if all the shoes were in stock. When some were not, the available shoes were sent and a back-order list was made. One of the warehouse clerks would send the order department a copy of orders shipped and items ordered.

Administration and control were handled through Larry Stevenson, vice president and controller, who had joined the company a few years earlier. He supervised retail accounting, data processing, general accounting, credit and collection, and the miscellaneous office staff and had recently begun to reorganize the data-processing system. At the executive meetings, he presented a monthly profit and loss statement on each of Roland and Stone's retail and outlet stores.

In discussions with John Bursk and Howard Stern (vice president for retail stores), George Roland repeatedly expressed his concern about the Roland and Stone brand image and the difficulty of maintaining a consistent product policy nationwide. In contrast to their retail stores, their discount outlets were yielding significant profits, but Bursk wondered about the effects of discount operations on Roland and Stone's brand name. He was also skeptical of the retail stores' policy of holding on to a brand image of a conservatively styled older man's shoe in the present-day fashion-oriented market. Each store manager seemed to have complete control over his store, but Bursk discovered in discussions with retail store managers that they were not informed of their own monthly profit and loss statements.

The company's product-line policy for the retail stores extended only to the design of new styles. Product/price mix decisions between their retail stores and the factory outlets were made daily by Phil Tomey, who also had responsibility for store inventories and the location of sites for new stores.

When Bursk raised some of his concerns about retail store operations during a lunch meeting with Howard Stern, he was astonished at Stern's angry reaction. Stern hotly denied responsibility for the situation, referring repeatedly to "those secrecy mongers."

Each month, the executive committee of Roland and Stone Inc. held a meeting attended by the three Roland brothers, Joseph Hale, Phil Tomey, Howard Stern, Larry Stevenson, and John Bursk. Jeremy Maxwell, the consultant recommended by the two banks that handled the company's accounts, also attended. (The two banks had given Maxwell authority over the company's loans.) During each meeting, Maxwell drew up "action assignments" for the executives after each specific issue had been discussed. At the next meeting, these same issues would be discussed again under the heading of old business. If an issue came to a vote during one of the meetings, Dean and Jim Roland and Phil Tomey would nearly always vote against any proposal backed by George Roland. Although the meetings were chaired by George, Bursk remembered a comment Maxwell had once made to him: "Hell, I'm just trying to get the company going, to push the boys into action and set George straight!"

Concerned about the competitiveness of the product line, Bursk had made a strong plea during the last meeting about the need for three to four new lines every forty-five days. To his astonishment, Dean Roland exclaimed, "I need three to four *stores* in that same period!"

In view of the troubling lack of focus in the company, Bursk was trying to decide what possible steps he could take to improve the situation and develop an upward trend in sales and profits.

COMMENTARY

It is obvious that John Bursk entered a hornet's nest when he accepted the position at Roland and Stone Inc. If he was looking for a real challenge, certainly he could not have asked for more. But he was naïve in joining the company; he should have done more homework before signing on in order to understand its dysfunctional interaction patterns. The secretive, rushed way in which he was hired should have given him an indication of the political gamesmanship that prevailed.

In this case, we are introduced to a family firm besieged with problems. Sibling rivalry, unconscious collusion, alcoholism, and depression are all on the agenda. The case dramatically highlights how family firms can turn a potential transitional space into a psychic prison, their inmates confined by interdependence, the reinforcement of past and present conflicts, and past hurts that are repeatedly acted out in the present. The fact that all three brothers work in the family firm accentuates their interdependency and aggravates a situation from which there is no escape: there is no neutral setting in which they can experiment with independent behavior.

The executives in this company seem to be on a very self-destructive course. At the center of the drama stand the conflicting relations among the three Roland brothers, whose dealings are colored by envy and sibling rivalry. These men seem never to have grown up; they still act like children, perhaps because of their ambivalent attitude to their now-deceased father. Neville Roland created his sons' conflict-laden interrelationship by not allowing them to become adults and by symbolically imprisoning them in his company. The brothers' attitude toward Neville seems to be a mixture of anger at their father, who forced them to act in certain ways (such as joining the company) and placed them in positions of dependency, and guilt over their negative emotions. We can say very little about the role the boys' mother played in all these interactions; it may have been substantial, but it is not revealed in the case.

Although old relational issues are at the heart of Roland and Stone's current pitiful state of affairs, two external events contributed significantly as well: the death of Neville Roland and the subsequent closing of the manufacturing facility. Let us look at each in turn.

We can infer from this fragmented case that Neville Roland had a strong, decisive personality. He not only built the company into a successful enterprise, but he also exerted a strong influence on his sons, particularly the eldest, who was more or less forced to join the company. In view of his autocratic leadership style, it is unlikely that Neville Roland gave much responsibility to his sons. The death of a CEO is always dramatic, but in the case of offspring involved in the business who are excessively dependent upon the father, death becomes a truly traumatic event. At Roland and Stone, complete responsibility for the management of the firm was suddenly placed on the shoulders of three sons who were not properly prepared for such a task.

As with many entrepreneurs before him, Neville Roland had not paid much attention to succession. Because letting go of power must have been an unattractive alternative to him, no specific succession plan was put into place. He was unwilling to make a clear choice while he was alive – an omission that is now costing the company dearly.

Under their autocratic father, the three brothers had toed the line. When he died, however, the equilibrium between them was suddenly broken and many long-suppressed emotions were brought out into the open. We can only speculate about the succession fight that led to George Roland's being formally named president (thereby bypassing his older brother). And the fight continues: being formally made the president does not mean that the others accept George in that role.

The second major incident that enormously affected the behavior of the executives in the company was the shutdown of the manufacturing facility. Why this decision was made is not really clear from the case. Executives may have been reacting to structural changes in the industry or addressing manufacturing problems that resulted from poor management. Whatever the cause, this decision had a great impact on the organization, because it meant a readjustment in behavior of some of the principal characters in the company. Clearly, the company experienced great difficulty shifting from a manufacturing orientation to a merchandising orientation, and many of the firm's officers were unable to make this transition. Expertise once useful suddenly became immaterial, and men who were previously respected for their knowledge were forced to question themselves in unaccustomed ways.

While the closing of the manufacturing facility may have been a rational decision (because of changing environmental conditions, for example), it can also be looked at from a psychodynamic point of view. Because the factory was the pride of their father, one might argue that the children's closing it down was a statement of independence, a provocation, a retaliatory act (though not necessarily a conscious one).

Regardless of the reasons for the closure, such an action has another side to it: it comes with a price. It may have led the brothers to think that they had let their father down, and this may have left them with a considerable feeling of guilt.

Of course, if unconscious retaliation was the underlying reason for the factory's closure, the men ended up cutting off their nose to spite their face. For Jim Roland, at least, closing the plant took away the main source of his self-esteem. His problems in coping with this change – the frightening discovery of finding himself obsolete and the ensuing guilt about failure – may have contributed to his depressive symptoms of work paralysis, general apathy, and alcoholism.

Whereas the change led to depressive symptoms for Jim, the two others found different ways of expressing themselves after the death of their father. But given their inbred dependence on their father, they would have found going it alone difficult because of their lack of confidence. Because Neville Roland did not instill self-confidence in his sons, they were never able to attain a true state of autonomy. In order to do what they want in the present, they need the help of father surrogates: Jeremy Maxwell for George Roland and Phil Tomey for Dean Roland. Dean seems to be completely dependent on Phil Tomey (the two seem inseparable), while George is highly dependent on his consultant.

Unfortunately, insecure executives usually do not surround themselves with capable subordinates. As a matter of fact, a number of the more capable managers at Roland and Stone at the time of Neville's death were soon fired. After all, they had been hired by the Roland brothers' father; no further offense was needed. Three of the more senior remaining executives seem to be quite ineffective, and probably the company would be better off without them. Joseph Hale, like Jim Roland, has been unable to make the transition from a manufacturing to a merchandising orientation; Phil Tomey does not have the presence of mind to distance himself from the fraternal fights; and Howard Stern does not make an effort to disseminate information to his retail stores. In their defense, one could say that these people are also victims of the dysfunctional culture created at Roland and Stone by the three brothers – an ambience that does not allow people to grow.

George Roland appears to be somewhat aware of the problems in the company. Although reality testing is not the strong point of any of the three brothers, George at least seems ready to have a go at it; he is willing to listen to his consultant, for example, who seems relatively capable. And George took action when he hired John Bursk, realizing that Jim Roland's department was in need of reinforcement. Unfortunately, in spite of his good intentions, George has a hard time dealing with his brothers and does not know how to stop the fraternal fights. The secrecy and haste in the hiring of Bursk is only one indication of his problems. Still, perhaps George had no choice but to act the way he did; with his two brothers on an (unconscious) collision course, they might have sabotaged any open attempt George made to reinforce the merchandising function.

This collision course is epitomized by Dean Roland's destructive management of the retail stores. These stores get short shrift; all Dean's attention is focused on the outlet stores, which were his idea not his father's. This may be a way of expressing, and belatedly displacing, Dean's anger toward his father.

While Dean Roland's destructive behavior seems to be active, Jim Roland deals with the loss of self-esteem in a more passive way, through depressive reactions. Occasionally, he responds actively – for example, when he colluded with Dean to sabotage George's proposals and thereby impeded the progress of the company. The collusion of Dean and Jim against George is the cause of a variety of problems:

- deterioration of the company's financial position
- lack of adherence to a formal organization chart and lack of established reporting procedures ("bypassing")

- weak sales organization
- lack of a clear strategy vis-à-vis retail and discount stores
- cannibalization by discount store sales of wholesale and retail store sales
- inadequacy of the purchasing function
- deterioration of the company's quality image
- lack of understanding of the fashion market
- lack of price/product policy for retail stores
- lack of accountability of outlet stores (because of prevailing secrecy)
- a commission system that does not encourage the search for new customers
- sales territories that may be outdated
- overabundance of small wholesale accounts
- outdated inventory and ordering system
- strained relationship between warehouse and main office (with brothers afraid to confront the warehouse supervisor, whom they see as an authority figure)
- obsolete inventory.

As the previous checklist illustrates, there are a number of problems to be confronted at Roland and Stone. These problems, however, are merely the tip of the iceberg. Only if the dysfunctional family dynamics are resolved will it be possible to tackle the business problems. A key issue is how to break the existing stalemate between the two camps represented by the three brothers within the company.

The question now, though, is what action John Bursk should take. The most capable people in the company appear to be George Roland, Larry Stevenson, and Jeremy Maxwell (the consultant), so it seems advisable to work with them. Although Maxwell fosters George Roland's dependency needs, he seems to have some influence on the other two brothers. As a matter of fact, he seems to be the de facto chairman of the board. (Of course, the influence of the banks – who may or may not use Maxwell as proxy – should not be forgotten.) A coalition of Bursk with the consultant, whereby they would work jointly on the various problem areas, may be one way of revitalizing the company. Bursk can also play on the dependency needs of the other two Roland brothers and take on a constructive support role.

Change takes place gradually when not precipitated by catastrophe. In this case, however, the pull of the status quo may be unusually strong: there is the real possibility of a "secondary gain" – in the form of unconscious pleasure derived from continuing a seemingly painful situation – as far as the three brothers are concerned. This implies that Bursk should proceed carefully so that he can create a measure of reality by bringing the unconscious to consciousness. If he moves too fast, too many resistances will come to the fore as the different groups "dig in," to the detriment of the company. In situations of this kind, one cannot assume, notwithstanding the bad financial position the company finds itself in, that rationality will prevail. Of course, if Bursk moves *too* slowly, the company may soon be out of business.

It might be a good idea for Bursk to start with problem areas that are not too heavily loaded emotionally. Focusing on real problems could be a learning process for the hostile parties and might give them a more realistic outlook. But Bursk also needs to remember that it is important to seek a balance in making changes, because too much partisanship may harden established positions.

With Jim Roland, someone may even need to suggest professional help as a way of dealing with his depressive reactions and loss of self-esteem. In his case, it seems obvious that early retirement would be advisable; but given his position as a major shareholder, he may resist that alternative. Professional help, financial incentives, and a meaningful alternative activity may be factors of persuasion, however.

As far as Dean Roland is concerned, his "fixation" with discount stores should be dealt with in a non-threatening fashion. (Remember Dean's explosive response during an executive meeting with Bursk.) Again, taking advantage of his need for dependency may be the starting point.

There are a number of other realistic alternatives. One is for one brother to buy out the other partners (including the shares of their mother); a second alternative is to split up the company; a third is to sell the company. Because these old family feuds are deeply rooted, the most effective solution may involve getting the different parties out of each other's hair. Their forced togetherness only rubs salt into old wounds. The time may have come for each brother to go his own way.

There is, of course, one final alternative: if the principal officers of the company remain unwilling to confront reality and continue to act out past conflicts, bankruptcy is the most likely scenario.

The sins of the parents
Steinberg Inc.

This case about the grocery giant Steinberg Inc. is a sequential case consisting of three parts. The purpose of this division is to create an optimal learning experience for you, the reader, making you reflect on things as they happen and encouraging you to try to envision suitable solutions for the emerging problems. Reading the three sequences in one stretch would not only defeat this educational purpose but would rob you of the excitement of an evolving real-life "soap opera." Using your imagination, you can ask and investigate many intriguing questions after each sequence.

After having read the first part, for example, ask yourself who you think Sam will choose as his successor. Will he nominate anyone at all? If he does, will this person be a family member or someone outside the family? Whoever it is, do you think this person will have a chance to make his mark with Sam around? Will Sam still be pulling the strings from behind? And who would you nominate if you were Sam? Who, in your opinion, is the right person to lead Steinberg after Sam?

After the second part, you can ask yourself these questions (and more): What do you think of Sam's choice? How well did his selection of a successor prepare the company for Sam's eventual death? Do you think that the events that followed could have been prevented had Sam made a different choice? What is your impression of the role of Mitzi and her relationship with Jack Levine? How do you think the way Ludmer treated Mitzi influenced events?

In retrospect, after the third part (Steinberg Inc. (C)), how do you explain the roller coaster that Steinberg embarked upon after Sam's death? What role did Ludmer play in the whole affair? What was Mitzi's part? Which of Sam's mistakes contributed to the ruinous consequences? What should he have done differently to prevent them? In general, as a family business owner, what can you learn from Steinberg Inc.? What kind of potential problems does it suggest in your firm? What solutions do you envision to prevent the outcome seen in this case?

STEINBERG INC. (A)

Snow piled up in drifts outside the old clapboard hotel as the top executives of Steinberg Inc. got down to the real business of the weekend. "Mr Sam" – Sam

Steinberg, the company's founder and driving force – was nearing sixty-five years of age and would soon be stepping aside as president into the newly created post of chairman. The purpose of this weekend meeting at Palomino Lodge, the Steinberg retreat in the Laurentian Hills north of Montreal, was to decide who would replace Sam at the head of the corporate empire he had created.

The executives were to debate the subject of Sam's successor, but there was no question where the final decision lay. Sam had built his retailing and real estate empire from a single family grocery store, and he controlled the public company absolutely. In the end, his would be the only vote that mattered.

Inside the meeting room, the atmosphere was charged. Everyone around the table knew that they were debating not only the company's future but also each individual's. Several of the senior executives – all present – were qualified to take over the reins from Sam, and it was almost certain that one of them would be the next president of Steinberg Inc. As they argued over the company agenda for the coming years, they were also jockeying for position in the succession sweepstakes.

Behind the maneuvering was one central question: Would Sam Steinberg allow control of his company to pass to someone outside the Steinberg family, or would blood ties decide who would be next to hold the top job?

The beginnings

Sam Steinberg was six years old when he came to Canada with his family in 1911, a penniless immigrant fleeing poverty and anti-Semitism in his native Hungary. It was from the dirt-poor streets of Montreal's old Jewish quarter that he began his incredible climb to riches. Yet the true origins of Sam's empire were not in Montreal but back in the old country before Sam was even born, in the difficult life of his mother.

Ida Steinberg was born Ida Roth, the oldest girl in a poor family of one son and seven daughters. Ida's mother ran the family while her father concentrated on religious studies. What childhood Ida had was cut short when both her parents died before she was fourteen years old. As the eldest daughter, she struggled valiantly to look after her siblings and keep her family together. Ultimately, it was too much for her, however, and the Roth children were separated and sent to live with various relatives.

Ida went to live with her uncle near the town of Debrecen, where he ran a general store. Working in the store gave the industrious Ida her introduction to the retailing business.

At age eighteen, Ida was married to Vilmos Sternberg – an arranged marriage, as was customary in the Jewish community in Hungary. Like Ida's father before, Vilmos was an impractical man, preferring religious studies to his sometime job as a baker. A tiny but hugely energetic woman, Ida managed the growing household. She gave birth to four children in rapid succession. Sam, the second, was born on Christmas Day in 1905.

By 1911, Ida had decided that a better future for her family lay in the New World. Two of her sisters had already made the voyage to Montreal, and stories of vast opportunities circulated through Hungary's hard-pressed Jewish community. So Ida packed up husband and children and sailed for Canada, selling all the family's possessions to pay for the passage. Ida's brother and two more sisters joined them on the journey. They landed in Québec City, where an immigration officer somehow changed their family name from Sternberg to Steinberg.

If the new Steinbergs had expected a life of milk and honey in Canada, they were disappointed. The family lived crammed together in one room of a cold-water house, renting out the other rooms to raise precious pennies. They were always poor, a situation not helped by Vilmos's decided disinterest in work and Ida's considerable fertility (two more Steinberg boys were born during the family's first three years in Canada).

It was at least in part Vilmos's troublesome reproductive tendency that led Ida to decide to separate from her husband shortly after the birth of her last child in 1914. Vilmos left to live alone in a rooming house in Montreal's east end, where he worked as a caretaker in a small synagogue and pursued his religious studies. For the children, their father practically ceased to exist; Ida became the head of the family.

To make ends meet, Ida opened a small grocery store in 1917 on The Main, the strip of St Lawrence Boulevard that was the center of Montreal's immigrant community. All the family worked in the tiny store – Ida, her six children, two of her sisters, and one nephew – and they all slept above it. The children took orders, bought produce, delivered groceries and stocked shelves in the store that operated sixteen hours a day, six days a week. Ida did more than anyone, working from dawn to dusk to provide for her family and above all to keep them together.

Her forceful personality dominated all aspects of business and family life. She lived by an ethic of hard work and honesty. She believed in treating customers well, allowing them to buy on credit when they needed to and always giving them something extra for their money. It was Ida's unwavering belief in the value of treating customers well that was largely responsible for the immensely strong customer loyalty enjoyed by Steinberg Inc. in later years. Ida's rules for life and business also profoundly shaped the outlook of young Sam, who would forever quote his mother's maxims to senior Steinberg executives. Years after her death, Ida's portrait still hung on the wall at the head of the Steinberg boardroom.

The empire is born

Sam Steinberg's brief flirtation with formal education came to an abrupt end at the age of fourteen, when he was kicked out of school because of his annoying habit of answering questions before the teacher had finished asking them. The expulsion did not bother Ida, who was pleased to have Sam helping out more around the store. Neither did it bother young Sam, who was delighted to have the chance to turn his full attention to the family business.

It did not take long for Sam to make his first mark. That same year, on his own initiative, he undertook the first expansion of the family business. Seizing a sudden opportunity, he rented the store adjacent to his mother's grocery, knocked out the wall between the two, and in a stroke doubled the size of both the store and the family's living quarters.

Soon after, Sam again moved to enlarge the business, buying another store in the more fashionable, fast-growing Outremont area of Montreal. He chose his younger brother Nathan to manage the new store, starting a pattern of using expansions of the business to provide jobs for family members. Sam called the new premises "Store Number One."

Ida, who gave Sam the money for his new ventures, reminded him that the business was there to keep the family together. "Sam, you must look after the boys," she told him.

Throughout the 1920s, the Steinberg stores flourished, building on their reputation for high quality, innovative retailing and square dealing. Sam's personal life also blossomed. In 1928, he married his first cousin, Helen Roth, daughter of Ida's brother Lewis, who had come to Canada a few years earlier. From his in-laws, Sam acquired not only a wife but also more family members he felt obliged to provide for. So he expanded the business again. He went into partnership with Helen's father, whose fruit store in Outremont was transformed into a Steinberg grocery store: "Store Number Two." As family demands kept growing, so did the business, with Sam adding two more stores by 1930.

As Sam's star rose, Ida gradually faded from the company scene. Years of grinding work had taken their toll on her body if not her spirit, and she suffered from angina and other complaints. In 1931, on the insistence of her family, she retired from daily operations and her first small grocery store was closed. Ida was never really happy on the sidelines, however; she missed the bustle of daily business. During Passover in 1942, she contracted pneumonia and died suddenly. She was fifty-seven years old.

When the Great Depression hit North America, Steinberg's base of loyal customers allowed the company to continue to grow while the big grocery chains were retrenching. In 1931, Sam opened three new stores, filling market gaps left behind as the majors retreated.

During these years, Sam also confirmed his reputation as an innovator in the Québec food business by bringing the first self-service grocery stores to the province. This store format had already been introduced in Ontario and in the United States, and to Sam's mind it seemed suited to the Depression era. By allowing customers to pick out groceries for themselves and cutting out the traditional order-taking and delivery functions, Steinberg's could reduce its prices sharply and undercut its competition drastically. The business grew by leaps and bounds, setting new sales records and adding outlets.

The expansion of the business was matched by the growth of Sam's own family. Helen bore Sam four daughters: Mitzi in 1929, Rita in 1932, Marilyn in 1933, and Evelyn in 1938. During these years, Sam worked tirelessly, traveling constantly and supervising every detail of his business; yet he somehow made time for family dinners and special events.

The onset of the Second World War meant an end to Steinberg's steady growth, as food rationing and labor shortages brought hard times to the grocery business. The family hunkered down and waited out the war, steadfastly refusing to participate in the price gouging and black marketeering of those years. The company's wartime conduct helped to cement still further both its reputation for integrity and the loyalty of its customers. It emerged in the postwar era ready to embark on its greatest period of growth.

The boom years

During the late 1940s, Steinberg's regained the momentum it had lost during the war, opening new stores and winning still more customers. During the war, the company had bought a lot of real estate at bargain-basement prices, looking ahead to later expansion. When the boom years of the 1950s arrived, Steinberg's was ready.

By 1952, the company was booking over $70 million (Canadian) in sales and had profits of over $1 million. That year Sam launched by far the most ambitious expansion scheme in the company's history – a $15 million plan that would see thirty new giant supermarkets opened in just five years, one store every two months.

Key to the company's rapid growth in this period was another of Sam's innovations, the suburban shopping center. Steinberg's began developing integrated shopping complexes anchored around a company supermarket, the idea being that the presence of other retailers would increase the number of customers. Montreal's financial community was skeptical, but the resounding success of the first Steinberg shopping center in the new suburb of Dorval, west of the city, silenced the critics.

Until the 1950s, Steinberg's had financed its growth with internal funds. Now the company needed access to much larger financial resources to pay for its massive building program. This posed a problem for Sam, who refused outright to give up absolute control over his company. At first he dodged the question, issuing $5 million in debentures (instead of shares) in 1952. In 1955, the company issued another $5 million of securities, this time in the form of preferred shares.

Finally, about to embark on another ambitious round of expansion in 1958, the company issued $8.5 million of participating equity. But still Sam would give up none of the control of his company: against the advice of his lawyers and bankers, he issued non-voting shares. These forays into the public capital markets, coupled with the sheer size of the business – by 1960 the company had ninety-two stores along with its burgeoning real estate and warehousing operations – meant that Steinberg Inc. was looking more and more like a large public company (with all the formality and bureaucracy that that entails).

Sam's leadership style

If Steinberg's began to look like a public company on the outside, on the inside it was quite another story. Sam still ran the company very much like a small family firm. The archetypal entrepreneur, Sam was the center of everything, driving the company forward with his energy and vision. Those who worked closely with Sam said that his business sense bordered on genius and that he had an amazing capacity for absorbing and retaining information. They also said that he was a workaholic with an intolerant, egotistical streak that made him very difficult to work for. Though Sam's vision and uncanny sense for market opportunities earned him the respect of his employees, he was occasionally known to blunder: forays into the Ontario food business and the launch of a chain of discount department stores were among the more prominent and costly of his mistakes.

Sam drove his employees as hard as he drove himself, and there were few executives who had not suffered under one of Sam's characteristic tongue-lashings. His was a world of creative chaos, where formal management systems counted for little and his whim was the order of the day. As the company grew exponentially, Sam continued to keep track of every aspect, often taking decisions that circumvented those executives nominally responsible for a given part of the business. Sometimes it seemed that the whole company still reported directly to him.

Yet Sam inspired enormous affection and loyalty among many of his employees. A man of great integrity, his personal code of behavior shaped the corporate culture of Steinberg Inc. Sam cared deeply for the welfare of his workers, helping them when they faced financial difficulties, calling on them in the hospital when they were sick, attending their weddings and funerals. He was a benevolent dictator, a man both loved and feared by those who worked for him.

Nowhere could Sam's contradictory nature be seen as clearly as in his treatment of his family. He was the unquestioned patriarch of his extended family, and he looked out for the interests of all its members to the point of interference. To his brothers and other family members who worked for the firm, Sam could present the image of the bullying father, shouting at them at the top of his lungs and disparaging their work in front of others. To a greater or lesser degree, all family members were cowed by Sam. One brother, who was a senior executive at Steinberg's, was so intimidated by Sam that he used another, non-family executive as an intermediary to ask his brother for a raise in pay.

But if Sam was bossy and demanding with his family, he was also unquestioningly and aggressively loyal to them. Sam might berate his brothers, but he would defend them fiercely against attacks from others. Urgent family matters always took priority over business, and secretaries quickly learned that telephone calls from family members always went straight through to the boss, whatever else might be happening. He was always ready to help a family member in need. At home he was devoted to his wife, Helen, and he was an indulgent – maybe too indulgent – father to his four girls.

Sam's paternalistic concern for his family's well-being carried over into hiring and promotion practices in his company. Sam was determined that there would always be a job for any family member who wanted or needed one, which turned out to be a lot of them. There were no scandals involving disastrous management by family members, but there was a widespread belief that many Steinberg employees owed their positions more to who they were than to how competent they were. This did not bother Sam. In his mind, the company had been created to serve the family's needs, and that was just what it was doing.

But there was a high price to be paid for using the company as a family job pool: the pervasive nepotism at Steinberg Inc. contributed in large part to a disturbingly high turnover among talented executives. Dozens of bright young managers cut their teeth at Steinberg's and then left for firms where they saw greater long-term potential for their careers. In Montreal, the company was known among its former employees as the University of Steinberg.

The succession question

Sam Steinberg may have been the absolute ruler of his family and his business, but not even he could withstand the march of time. He was getting older, and he knew as well as anyone that one day he would have to hand over control of his company. Finding someone to fill his central role in the company, Sam knew, would be an all but impossible order.

With no obvious solution in sight, confident in his own abilities and stamina, Sam repeatedly swept the question of his successor under the carpet. It fell to his senior executives to raise the issue again and again at annual executive reviews, pushing Sam to prepare for a clear and orderly succession.

Perhaps non-family executives believed that succession planning was a chance to change fundamentally the way the business was run, sensing that the company had grown to a point where it needed a professional manager instead of an entrepreneurial genius at the helm. Perhaps they also saw the succession issue as an opportunity to break, or at least weaken, the family's stranglehold on power in the firm. They knew that real influence at Steinberg's still lay not with the executives in their offices but with those members of the family inner circle who gathered at Sam's spacious Westmount home Friday nights for Sabbath dinners.

For his part, Sam would have dearly loved to have had a son to carry on in his footsteps and keep the Steinberg name at the head of the company. But to Sam's regret, his marriage to Helen had produced only daughters, and – despite the shining example of his own mother – Sam never seemed to consider his daughters as possible successors. Indeed, he never encouraged them to be anything other than housewives. When his oldest daughter, Mitzi, left the kitchen to gain a law degree and finally entered the family business, she did so entirely on her own initiative.

Looking around the wider family, Sam could see other possible successors. Arnold Steinberg, the bright son of Sam's brother Nathan, had distinguished himself in the family by being the first to get a higher education, earning an MBA from the Harvard Business School. Arnold was still relatively young, however, and had blotted his copybook by spearheading a misguided and expensive diversification scheme in France. Nevertheless, he was among the most able of the pretenders to the throne.

If nephews did not provide the right grist, Sam could look to his sons-in-law. All four of them had worked for the company at some point. Only two were serious contenders, though, and one of those had recently quit the scene. Leo Goldfarb, the savvy, aggressive husband of Rita, had shone brightly as a vice president in the company's real estate division since joining in the mid 1950s. He saw himself as presidential material and felt that Sam agreed. In 1968, however, with his marriage shaky, and with the sense that his way to the top of the company was blocked by others, Goldfarb quit the firm.

This left Mel Dobrin, the clever if somewhat plodding husband of Sam's oldest (and most forceful and aggressive) daughter, Mitzi. An accountant by training, Mel had joined the company on the grocery side and had climbed steadily upward through the corporate ranks. He knew the business inside and out and was a solid administrator.

A few non-family executives also stood out as possible successors. Irving Ludmer, another brilliant performer in the real estate division, had risen, like Sam, from his origins as a child of impoverished immigrants. Despite having a university degree in nuclear physics, he enjoyed a special intimacy with his street-smart boss. The major strike against him was his age: in 1969, Ludmer was just thirty-three years old.

Other candidates included James Doyle, the straight-talking former Ford Motor Company executive who was a vice president and Steinberg Inc.'s general counsel, as well as a trusted adviser of Sam. Also high on the list was Jack Levine, a company veteran and Sam's right-hand man.

In 1969, Sam was sixty-four years old, and the unpleasant task of naming his successor could be put off no longer. He would have to decide whether to keep the job of running his company in the family, turn to one of his non-family executives, or go outside the firm for a new chief executive. All the contenders were present at Palomino Lodge that cold weekend in March at the meeting Sam had called to help him choose his successor.

STEINBERG INC. (B)

"This is not the most qualified person we're selecting," Sam Steinberg explained to one of his non-family executives shortly after naming his son-in-law Mel Dobrin to succeed him as president of Steinberg Inc. "It may be in the best interests of this corporation to have a professional manager. But I've had so much fun building and running this business that I wouldn't deprive my family of doing it."

With this blunt admission, Sam confirmed what many already suspected. As long as Sam was around – indeed, for the foreseeable future – family would always come first at Steinberg's, even though it was now a large public company responsible to thousands of shareholders. For Sam, appointing Dobrin was the least unattractive solution to an intractable problem. He simply was unprepared psychologically to either surrender control of his company or see it pass out of family hands. Inside the firm, many said that Sam was also incapable of standing up to his oldest daughter, Mitzi, Dobrin's wife. By appointing the solid, dependable, but uninspired Dobrin to the presidency, he could keep family peace while maintaining personal control of the company through his compliant son-in-law. The appointment of Dobrin coincided with the beginning of a long, drifting decline at Steinberg's. It would be unfair to blame all the problems on Dobrin or his appointment, however; many of the management sins of Sam's era were coming home to roost, and strong new competitors were making their presence felt on the scene. But Dobrin's appointment did speed the onset of the decline, and he was wholly incapable of providing the leadership needed to reverse it.

The most obvious effect of Sam's choice of a successor was a marked acceleration of the company's already serious problem of brain drain. For many talented executives, the appointment of Dobrin was the last straw. In the ensuing months, Steinberg's lost the services of a number of its best managers, including top real estate lawyer Morgan McCammon, executive vice president William Sherman, and Sam's special favorite, Irving Ludmer.

One veteran executive who chose to remain was Jack Levine, the retailing wizard who for years had been Sam's right-hand man. Many thought Levine was the most qualified to step into Sam's shoes, and he was deeply disappointed to be passed over. But Steinberg's was his life's work, and he stayed on out of loyalty to Sam and the firm.

For his part, Dobrin never enjoyed any real power during his term as president and indeed was often undercut by Sam. At first, Sam routinely made executive decisions as if nothing had changed. Even when he finally started to withdraw somewhat from the daily operation of Steinberg's, he would still telephone his son-in-law several times a day just to keep tabs on everything. Shortly after Dobrin became president, Levine was made executive vice president of retailing with the same salary and job description as Dobrin, further blurring the lines of control in the firm.

Steinberg Inc. executives of the period remember Dobrin as a passive president who showed little knack for leadership or strategy. Managing through committees, he admirably sought to build consensus among executives but failed to provide the necessary impetus or direction. A short-term profit orientation took root in the firm, and risk taking and initiative disappeared. Little investment was made to counter the threat of rising competition, and combative unions ran roughshod over the company. A profound malaise set in as Steinberg's drifted aimlessly through the 1970s, living off past accomplishments.

That malaise turned to despair in May of 1978, when Sam died of a heart attack. He had suffered chest pains in 1976 and since then had scaled back his involvement in the business. But his almost palpable presence had remained, holding the company together and reassuring its workers that there would always be a solution to a problem. Suddenly "Mr Sam" was gone, and with his passing the company seemed to lose its very soul.

Steinberg Inc. employees were shocked. Many wept. When Sam was buried, his workers swelled the ranks of the 2,000 mourners who filled the synagogue and lined the streets of Montreal to pay their last respects. In an emotional sense as well as a literal one, the father of the company was gone.

The interregnum

In the weeks after Sam's death, Dobrin moved quickly to provide a sense of continuity and competence in the company. To his credit, he stepped aside as president, moving into Sam's role as chairman and chief executive. For Dobrin's replacement, the company turned to Jack Levine, the veteran who had been passed over for president nine years before. By 1978, however, Levine no longer wanted to be president. He accepted the job only out of loyalty to Sam, to help preserve what his friend had built. He would come to regret his decision.

Levine faced a number of serious problems. The competitive environment was getting ever tougher. The loss of Sam hung like a pall over Steinberg's, and his memory competed with Levine for authority and legitimacy in the company. It may also be that Levine, probably the most capable and innovative of Sam's senior executives, had seen his best days by 1978. However, Levine's greatest difficulty came from the family, in the person of Sam's oldest daughter, Mitzi Dobrin.

Following Sam's death, Mitzi had become the de facto head of the Steinberg family and the center of power within Steinberg Inc. The only Steinberg daughter with a university education, she was also the only one working in the family company: in 1973, Sam had parachuted her in to run Miracle Mart, the money-losing discount department store chain. At that time, Mitzi had no experience in retailing, and Levine firmly opposed the appointment, telling Sam it was a bad idea. Mitzi never forgave him for that, and soon the two were fighting openly in executive meetings.

After Levine became president, politics became the order of the day at Steinberg Inc.; factions formed quickly, and executives sought to curry favor with the respective camps. Meanwhile, the core business went from bad to worse: by the early 1980s, the once unassailable Steinberg's had slipped into third position in the Québec grocery business behind Metro-Richelieu Inc. and Provigo Inc.

In 1982, a tired and dispirited Levine announced his resignation. Again the family, led by Mitzi and Mel Dobrin, huddled to choose his successor. By now, the situation at Steinberg's had become so grave that family members were prepared to contemplate "the unthinkable." In October of that year, after extensive consultations with executive headhunters, the family agreed to appoint a complete outsider to run Sam's firm. Peter McGoldrick arrived on the scene like a much-needed breath of fresh air. An experienced executive who had previously run a chain of food stores in Virginia, McGoldrick was a large, gregarious man with a winning manner and an impressive bearing. To the beleaguered foot soldiers at Steinberg's, he promised change and momentum, as well as an end to the bickering that had been draining the life from the company.

It was a promise he could not keep. McGoldrick's brief tenure as president was an unmitigated disaster. The politicking continued as fiercely as ever, and Mitzi moved to consolidate her power within the firm, assuming the role of executive vice president for corporate and legal affairs. In that position, she seemed to many to be the de facto president, undercutting McGoldrick's authority and dividing the executive body.

If Mitzi made life difficult for him as president, McGoldrick himself was responsible for the catastrophe that ultimately made his position untenable. Back in the 1960s, in a brilliant strategic ploy conceived by Jack Levine, Steinberg's had stunned its competitors and seized an enormous market share with a "Miracle Pricing" program of deep-discount grocery prices. Now, in 1983, McGoldrick gave the go-ahead to another such scheme, which this time involved giving customers coupons worth 5 percent of their purchases good for the next time they shopped at Steinberg's. The idea was that the lost revenues would be more than offset by gains in market share, as had happened before.

But times had changed since the 1960s – margins were much tighter in the food business – and this time Steinberg's could not rely on catching disorganized competitors asleep at the wheel. When Steinberg's surprised everyone with its coupon program in March 1983, all it did was touch off a bitter price war with competitive chains, both of which had lower cost structures than Steinberg's. Metro-Richelieu immediately matched the coupon program; Provigo began giving instant rebates in cash. Steinberg Inc. gained no significant market share whatsoever. By the time the coupon plan was ignominiously put to rest three months later, the fiasco had cost Steinberg's $18 million in operating profit. Nine months later, McGoldrick was gone.

New hope

Now the company seemed to be in freefall. Without purpose or leadership, it was hemorrhaging money and talent. Analysts began to wonder if there was a future at all for the empire Sam had built. Into this desperate situation stepped the new president, Irving Ludmer.

After leaving Steinberg Inc. in 1971, Ludmer had gone on to become one of Québec's leading real estate developers and a rich man in his own right. In 1983, he had rejoined Steinberg's to take control of its drifting real estate subsidiary, Ivanhoe Inc., after many months of concentrated lobbying by his old friend, Sam's nephew Arnold Steinberg. Intelligent, decisive, and driven, Ludmer seemed the company's best hope in time of crisis. After much consideration, Ludmer had agreed to take the job as president, but only on condition that he be fully supported by Mitzi.

The situation at Steinberg Inc. was rapidly becoming critical: in the past five years, the company's share of the Québec grocery market had slipped from 28 percent to 17 percent. The very depth and urgency of the crisis facing the company probably worked in Ludmer's favor, since executives and directors alike knew that serious changes were needed. And Ludmer, the former company *Wunderkind* (and Sam's special favorite), was a man who could deliver change.

When he took over, many doubted that even Ludmer could halt the decline of Steinberg Inc. But he confounded all the skeptics: in his first full year as president, Ludmer quintupled profits, and Steinberg Inc. shares more than tripled in price. On his first day on the job, he flushed out the executive suites, pruning deadwood and cutting costs. He then began a huge program of renovating Steinberg's dilapidated stores, bringing them up to date with the style of the 1980s; he radically changed shop formats, introducing up-market full-service counters and specialty food sections; and he oversaw the transformation of Steinberg's perennial loser, the Miracle Mart discount department stores, into the affordable fashion outlets known as M Stores.

Most of all, though, Ludmer needed to rebuild the corporate culture at Steinberg's, which had become very conservative and risk-averse. He sought to bring back some of the entrepreneurship and responsibility that had characterized Sam's reign. It helped that in many ways Ludmer was cut from the same cloth as Sam. Like Sam, he was bright, single-minded, and relentlessly energetic, and he inspired enthusiasm in his subordinates. Also like Sam, he was seen as egotistical and opinionated, and he drove his workers hard. Ludmer was not easy to work for, but he certainly possessed the qualities of leadership that the company had been lacking for so long. To many at Steinberg's, he was a messiah, anointed by his ancient association with Sam, come to lead the company back to glory.

Ludmer was a determined man who would brook no interference in his running of the firm, be it from his executives or from the family. It was perhaps inevitable that he would eventually come into conflict with Mitzi. Her power base in the company was challenged by his ascendancy, and she began to reassert herself in company affairs. Push came to shove and finally spilled over into direct confrontation in September 1985. Ludmer, the architect of the dramatic turnaround in the company's fortunes, bluntly told Mitzi that if she did not resign, he would. The board of directors, which was chaired by Mitzi's husband, backed Ludmer. On September 6, Mitzi resigned as executive vice president, though she remained a director.

At last a Steinberg Inc. president had full power and a free hand to run Steinberg's his own way. Under Ludmer's leadership, the company began to pull together, free of the divisive presence of overt family power in the executive suite. The way looked clear for the company finally to become a truly professionally managed firm.

STEINBERG INC. (C)

As the Steinberg company began to recover some of its sense of purpose, the Steinberg family began breaking apart. The process turned into a bitter public squabble and ended up destroying the company that Sam had built.

At the root of all their troubles was money and the power that goes along with it. The seeds of the battle that would destroy Sam's family were sown many years earlier, when Sam had first organized his estate so that ownership of his company would be handed over to his children when he died. Ironically, part of the motivation behind Sam's estate planning was to keep his family together after he was gone.

Back in 1952, Sam had divided most of his assets into equal trusts for each of his four daughters and their children. The bulk of Sam's control block of voting shares was placed into a holding company called Rockview Investments Inc., which in turn was owned equally by the trusts of the four daughters. Altogether, this represented 40 percent of the firm's voting shares.

Sam retained full voting control of these shares during his lifetime, along with the 12 percent he still held personally. The logic behind this structure – the brainchild of brilliant tax lawyer Lazarus Phillips – was to put off indefinitely the capital gains taxes that would normally be charged on shares passed on to new owners. The terms of the trusts provided that the capital would be held for each daughter until her oldest child reached twenty-five years of age. Then half of the capital would be held for the children and the other half would go to Sam's daughters. The daughters all became trustees of each other's trusts.

This system worked well while Sam was alive and even for some time after his death. The voting shares were kept together and voted as a block by Helen, while family and friends served as trustees for the various trusts. There were minor irritations, however, because the daughters had different views on how they wanted to invest and manage their portions of the money accruing to the trusts and on how they wanted to spend the proceeds. For the most part, though, the process worked smoothly. While Mitzi went to work in the company, Sam's third daughter, Marilyn, took over effective control of the management of the trusts.

The problems began in earnest in 1985, after Ludmer ousted Mitzi from Steinberg Inc. Sidelined, she began to assert herself in Marilyn's preserve: the management of the family trusts. More critically, Mitzi started looking for ways to sell Steinberg Inc. It seemed that, having lost the power struggle with Ludmer, she had no more interest in the company and wanted to sell out. In 1985, she tried to offer the company to Vancouver businessman Jimmy Pattison and financier Sam Belzberg, without success. Alarmed, Sam's other two surviving daughters, Marilyn and Evelyn (Rita having died of cancer in 1970), joined together to stop Mitzi from selling the company.

It is impossible to tell how much of what happened over the several ensuing years was motivated by genuine business disagreements and how much stemmed from bitter rivalries between competitive sisters. What is clear, however, is that there followed a series of escalating confrontations, with each side seeing provocation in the acts of the other.

In 1986, Mitzi tried to convince her sisters to sell some of the non-voting shares held by the trusts, which at the time were trading at nearly $50. They refused, thus asserting their control over the trusts. Then Mitzi suggested separating the main asset of the trusts – the 40 percent of voting shares held in Rockview Investments – thus giving each sister effective control of her own inheritance. Again, Marilyn and Evelyn refused. Arguments intensified over which professional managers should advise the trusts, and the Dobrin children began to ask for more control over the funds held in trust for them. The dispute became more and more bitter, with the Dobrins convinced that the others were maliciously withholding rightful control of their assets. For their part, Marilyn and Evelyn believed that Mitzi simply could not abide their challenge to her hitherto dominant role in the family.

In 1986, Marilyn and Evelyn took two actions that led to a family confrontation. In the fall of that year, they asked Irving Ludmer for seats on the board of Steinberg Inc. Ludmer declined the request, but it remained a direct and open challenge to the Dobrins, who until then had always represented the family's interests on the board.

The two sisters also decided to take administration of the family trusts away from the firm of Phillips & Vineberg, which had been their father's lawyers and was currently the employer of Mitzi's son-in-law Sam Mintzberg. This was too much for their long-suffering mother, Helen, who intervened to try to stop the transfer. Marilyn, who of all the daughters had always been closest to Helen, wound up in a bitter argument with her mother; they did not speak to each other for almost two years.

Attempts by other family members to mediate the dispute failed, and both sides became increasingly hostile. Then, in 1987, Marilyn and Evelyn, who had cemented their voting control of the family trusts, managed to push through a motion breaking the voting agreement that gave Helen the voting rights for 40 percent of shares held by the trusts along with the 12 percent left to her directly by Sam. Helen was served legal notice of the intention to break the voting arrangement in July of that year, thirty-five years after Sam had created the trusts. This meant that the control block was broken, which represented a material change for the company and thus had to be reported publicly. So the family feud became public knowledge, and the stock market began to smell a takeover in the making.

The first offers were not long in coming. The Weston Group, which runs the giant Loblaw's food chain in Ontario, approached Ludmer with a $1 billion offer for the company in August 1987. Ludmer wanted to keep the company together, although he saw the sale of Steinberg's as perhaps the only means of resolving the bitter family dispute. The Dobrins were interested sellers, although Mitzi had reservations about control of Steinberg's leaving Québec. Marilyn and Evelyn did not want to sell, however, and the offer was never pursued. Not long after, a family business meeting degenerated into a screaming brawl, and all civil communication between the warring parties ceased.

The last vestiges of privacy were stripped from the battle on December 30, 1987, when Mitzi shocked everyone by filing a lawsuit to have her sisters and their husbands removed from the management of the family trusts. In the statement of claim, peppered with catty personal comments, Mitzi accused her sisters of "gross negligence and reprehensible neglect" in managing the trusts. In February 1988, Canada's national newspaper, the *Globe and Mail*, carried interviews with the battling sisters, which deepened the acrimony of the dispute. A well-known Montreal editorial cartoonist satirized the unseemly spectacle by portraying the Steinberg sisters as sodden mud wrestlers.

For Ludmer, the all-out war between the sisters made it difficult to ensure stability inside the company. Talk of takeovers always leads top executives to consider other employment options. This situation notwithstanding, as long as Marilyn and Evelyn were determined to block the sale of the company, Ludmer had a good chance of keeping it together. But he lost this advantage, touching off the final disintegration of Steinberg Inc., when he fired Marilyn's son Billy Pedvis during an executive shakeup in 1988. Billy was highly regarded in the family, and even the Dobrins objected when he was let go. Marilyn was furious at the treatment of her son, and gradually her attachment to the company began to weaken. Ironically, the family began to find some unity again in its resentment of Ludmer.

The final eighteen months of Steinberg Inc. as an independent company were marked by an on-again, off-again battle for control of the firm. It began in earnest with a bid from Oxdon Developments Inc., a consortium of Toronto developers and financiers keen to get their hands on Steinberg's prized real estate assets. In late January 1988, Oxdon made its first bid for Steinberg Inc.: $50 for the voting shares and $40 for the non-voting shares. In early February, the board invited other offers for the company. Ludmer and Arnold Steinberg were deluged with proposals from leveraged-buyout firms that wanted to finance a bid headed by the pair. Nothing came of this idea because of the family's refusal to enter such an agreement with Ludmer and Arnold Steinberg. Ludmer preferred to keep the company intact, and for a while it seemed he would get his way: the family rebuffed the Oxdon bid, saying it might consider an offer at the inflated figure of $100 per share. The board then announced that it would seek other ways of "maximizing shareholder value."

This bought time, but not much. In March 1989, Oxdon appeared again with an unsolicited second bid for the company. It was clear that Oxdon would break up the company if it succeeded in gaining control, so Ludmer turned to the powerful Québec public employees pension fund, the *Caisse de Depots et Placements*, in search of a long-term investor to buy out the Steinberg family and keep the company together. Jean Campeau, the head of the *Caisse*, wanted to keep control of Steinberg's in Québec, but even more he wanted its prime real estate assets for the *Caisse*. Campeau found his solution in the person of Michel Gaucher, the high-profile Québec entrepreneur who headed Socanav Inc. The

Caisse agreed to back a bid by Gaucher, in return for the opportunity to buy the Steinberg real estate portfolio.

Oxdon did not retreat gently from the fight. In late June 1989, it came back with a bid of $75 per voting share and $50 per non-voting share. The family preferred to sell to a Québec company, however, and Campeau played to these patriotic sentiments. On July 8, the Steinberg family entered into a lock-up agreement with Gaucher, accepting a bid of $75 per voting share and $51 per non-voting share (provided Gaucher could complete his financing by July 21). Gaucher had won. Last-minute court challenges from Oxdon delayed the transfer of control but did not change the outcome. On August 22, 1989, some seventy-two years after Ida Steinberg opened her first grocery store on St Lawrence Boulevard, Gaucher bought Steinberg Inc. for $1.3 billion.

COMMENTARY

In order to understand what happened to the Steinberg empire, we have to delve deeper into the personality of its major driving force. The clue to this fairy tale, with its bitter ending, can be found within Sam Steinberg himself. What kind of person was he? What were the motivations behind his actions? How did his personality makeup steer the creation and growth of his empire? How did it influence its downfall? How did the strengths and weaknesses of one single person influence the lives of so many others? Could the mistakes he made have been avoided, or was Steinberg Inc. doomed from its very beginning?

The first Steinberg store obviously grew out of the necessity for the family's survival. Sam's promise to his mother to always take care of his family was to guide his every move. Though it was the main reason for his initial success, it was also the first nail in the coffin of Steinberg Inc. We may wonder whether Sam could have failed to realize that his intention to always put the family first, even at the cost of the company, was in fact endangering the family's well-being in a most dramatic way. Did he really not understand that there would be no golden eggs to provide for his family if he let the hen who lay them die? What was it that made a man of Sam's intelligence so unreceptive to certain things?

There seems to be a direct connection between Sam's crucial childhood experiences and some of the mistakes he made later on. The absence of a strong father figure, for example, affected his outlook and his behavior. Ida, her life made difficult by two equally weak men, seems to have compensated for this to a certain extent by purposefully raising her sons to be different from her father and husband: strong and capable of providing for the family. As favorable as the strong personality of his mother proved to be for young Sam's success as an entreprencur, the lack of a father he could look up to as a role model during his childhood and early adult years seems to have affected Sam's attitude toward authority. Oedipal victories, as we have seen, come with a price. In some ways, Sam became his own father, extremely independent-minded, not needing anyone. At the same time, he must have yearned for a strong, dependable male figure.

That yearning may have created in Sam the tendency to idealize men he perceived as strong and powerful. But because Sam's need for idealization sprang from his own psychic makeup (and was thus beyond rationale), it was rarely supported by reality. When it came to his idealized figures, Sam's sound judgment could be clouded, often resulting in unnecessary damage to the business. One notable incident happened in 1959, during negotiations with the powerful chairman of Grand Union. Sam allowed himself to be influenced by the formidable reputation of the union chairman long before meeting him in person and was thus unwilling to put up a fight against the outrageous claims of the union. This resulted in substantial overcharges to Steinberg's on the part of the union – overcharges that Sam could have avoided had it not been for his admiration for, and awe of, the "great man." The generous wage settlements that

Sam agreed upon during those negotiations were one of the most crucial mistakes he ever made; they had long-term negative effects on Steinberg Inc.

Another major mistake of his own making was the way he dealt with the issue of his successor. There is more than one reason to be found for Sam Steinberg's reluctance in this matter. The first of these is his single-mindedness and perseverance. Although his firm belief in himself as the only person capable of making important decisions worked well for the company in the beginning when it was crucial to ensure growth and profitability, it turned into a double-edged sword later, when the company was forced to maneuver on stormy waters without a suitable captain. Given Sam's reluctance to let go of control (because the company was so much a part of his core identity), he gave his potential successor a Herculean task.

Given his need to be in charge, we can imagine how it must have felt for a man like Sam to evoke the (far-off) day when he would not be able to pull the strings of the company anymore. Endowed with an immense amount of energy and at the peak of his strength, he refused to face the fact that the day would finally arrive. His chosen solution was the conventional one: he preferred to stick his head in the sand and continue to believe in his own immortality. Even though we cannot be sure about this, he may unconsciously have wanted the Steinberg business to go to the grave with him (as long as his family was provided for), so strongly did he identify with "his" stores.

The lack of a male heir was another factor that provided Sam with a good excuse not to think of a possible successor. (However, we can speculate that a male heir would have had considerable difficulty growing up under such a strong father.) Most likely, it never occurred to Sam that one of his daughters could take over the business one day. The myth of stereotyping was very much in operation. Women, in his eyes, were the weaker sex and belonged in the home (if not the kitchen) and had nothing to do in a boardroom. The keen observer may discover a seeming contradiction in Sam's view of the role of women, however. Given the fact that his mother was an extremely hard-working woman who herself set the essential foundations for the business, it is interesting to note Sam's attitude toward the role of his wife and daughters in connection with the business. Perhaps seeing his mother work day and night triggered in Sam a strong determination not to let his own wife or daughters experience similar hardships. Even though he did discuss important business issues with his wife (sometimes even following her advice) and often took his daughters with him when visiting the stores in an effort to instill in them pride in "their" stores, he never seriously thought about letting any of them take more than a token place in his empire. His daughters, growing up with this openly expressed attitude, were probably conditioned to believe that any aspirations on their part to join the family business were in vain and that they would have to content themselves with a more traditional female role. Not surprisingly, when his oldest daughter, Mitzi, rebelled against this, deciding to study law, she encountered serious disapproval from Sam, who expressed his scorn about such "unwomanly" practices.

Interesting conclusions can be drawn in studying the dynamics of the core Steinberg family. It is remarkable to note how Sam and Helen Steinberg failed to instill in their daughters what they had grown up with themselves: the strong sense of keeping the family united that is so prevalent in most Jewish families. The Steinberg parents, after reaching a certain level of material comfort and security, fell into the same trap so many other successful entrepreneurs before and after them have encountered. Having come from the slums of The Main, they did not want their children to experience the fear of failure and poverty they grew up with. Instead, the girls were spoiled rotten. They were indiscriminately lavished with expensive gifts from very early childhood on. Never having learned to fight for anything, they took everything for granted. The non-material values so important for their character development were considered unnecessary, as was a solid education. An upbringing such as theirs obviously does not make for healthy, stable personalities.

The childhood environment of the Steinberg sisters seems to have been characterized by tensions between them from early on. Four female children, a strong, authoritarian father (who was absent most of the time but overindulgent when present), and a rather weak mother (who appears to have had little control over the girls) make for a problem-rich situation. Sibling rivalry was a destructive force strongly prevalent among the sisters as they competed for the favors of their father. With Mitzi being her father's and Marilyn her mother's openly declared favorites, the seeds were sown early for the bloody battles that were to take place between the two girls. Helen's personality does not seem to have helped to alleviate the situation. The docile Helen was the forceful Sam's perfect complement. As a wife, she was everything Sam could ever ask for. As a mother, however, she failed to provide the necessary holding environment to the girls while they grew up. Later on, she was cast from side to side in the war between her daughters and finally symbolically "stepped upon"; all her remaining power was taken away by her own brood. The viciousness of the daughters' fights, the all-consuming strength of their vindictiveness, the way they turned against their own mother – these factors raise disconcerting questions about the kind of emotional environment they must have experienced as children. It is characteristic that the only time they were able to unite was when faced with a common enemy, Ludmer.

Mitzi's personality probably deserves the most attention. Being the oldest daughter, and given Sam's well-known attitude toward women, Mitzi must have been frustrated at not having been born a male. An extremely ambitious person, she must have frequently fantasized about life as Sam's son and rightful successor. Possessing a certain degree of ruthlessness and a strong fighting spirit, Mitzi did not easily accept the hopelessness of her situation, however. She invested all her energy into competing with her sisters for their father's favors and emerged the clear winner. Having achieved the position as the favorite of the most special and outstanding man she knew and admired must have reinforced her narcissistic fantasies of being special, different, and better than others.

It is unfortunate for Sam, Mitzi, and Steinberg Inc. as a whole that Sam was blinded by his own prejudices and did not recognize the potential he had in his oldest daughter. Instead of channeling Mitzi's ambitions in a constructive direction, Sam overlooked them. Mitzi's bitterness over this turned into a destructive driving force. Her unspoken wish to follow in her father's footsteps drove Mitzi with a vengeance that neither Ludmer nor anyone else who tried to get into her way had reckoned with. She was out to win, even if winning meant the destruction of Steinberg. She assumed the role of the spoiler. A wrong had been done to her – the withholding of the coveted job of president – and nobody else was going to enjoy what she could not. If she could not get what she wanted, nobody was going to. Under the right circumstances, she could be very vindictive and spiteful. In this situation, we see an example of how entrepreneurs can turn the constructive into the destructive and potential into waste when it comes to their children.

And how did Sam deal with others when it became clear that he would have to make a decision about his successor? In spite of the elaborate discussions during the board meeting in the Laurentian Hills, where each executive tried to assert his secret succession agenda, it was clear to everyone that Sam himself would set the rules of selection. He did so by appointing Mel Dobrin as his successor, after rejecting everyone else as inappropriate. The major criterion for his choice was crystal clear: as a male family member, Mel was the perfect candidate for Sam, the only real contender (since Sam's nephew Arnold Steinberg had blown it in Sam's eyes). Mel Dobrin, as Mitzi's husband, was the most prominent male member of the family, competent or not.

As a weak personality in awe of Sam, Mel was the easiest of the Steinberg Inc. executives to steer. Led by his need to remain in control, Sam could not help but choose a weak successor. His own personal interests blinded him to the effect his choice would have on the company, though that effect was quite clear to the other board members. From the point of view of the other senior executives, Mel Dobrin was an incompetent individual who got the job for being a member of the Steinberg family. It might have appeased the others had Mel been able to show qualifications for the job; but since he was not, many of the most capable and promising executives abandoned the company, causing considerable bloodletting of good executive material.

After Sam's death, Jack Levine followed the departing Dobrin as president. Levine would have been a good choice had he been promoted earlier; he was the most suitable candidate to succeed Sam initially. However, both his disillusionment at being passed over for Dobrin at the time of Sam's choice and the flow of years under the bridge had eroded his fighting spirit by the time he became Steinberg Inc.'s president. It was not that, though, that brought him down: his downfall, like that of those following in his footsteps, was caused by Mitzi.

Irving Ludmer, the next president (after the short but disastrous intermezzo with Peter McGoldrick, in which Mitzi played her usual destructive role), made the same mistake as Levine: he raised the scorn of Mitzi Steinberg. Ludmer, however (unlike the tired Levine, who had the ghost of Mitzi's father hanging over him), was not easily intimidated by her. On the other hand, Ludmer, though a determined and smart man confident of his own capabilities, seemed to have lacked interpersonal as well as diplomatic skills. How could he have underestimated the strength of Mitzi's ambitions to steer Steinberg Inc. herself? How could he have believed that Mitzi would let him go unpunished after he pushed her out of the company? It is even more incomprehensible that he could commit the strategic mistake of forcing Marilyn's son out of the company when he was in bitter need of her goodwill as Mitzi's main contender.

In retrospect, it seems that there was nobody at all who could have succeeded in taking over the leadership role after Sam. Such were the innate dynamics of Steinberg Inc. and the will of Mitzi Steinberg. If she could not have the helm, nobody should be able to have it. Better to let the organization perish. Steinberg Inc. was thus caught in a downward spiral after Sam's death. The company's destruction started much earlier, however, in Sam's own attitudes and actions. In hindsight, there is not much that could have saved the company from the time of Sam's death on. The seeds for Steinberg Inc.'s destruction were sown during its ascent. The education of Sam's daughters – although well meant – was not directed at creating capable, thoughtful successors.

When the die was cast, there was nobody around strong enough to play a countervailing power role. There was no one to set clear boundaries and convey to Sam the implications of selecting certain candidates. Could *anyone* have been strong enough? It was as if Sam had made up his mind from day one that the husband of his favorite daughter would run the company.

Eventually, one man's dream perished with him because he was not willing to share it with others. Perhaps this story will serve as a valuable example for other entrepreneurs in preventing their growing businesses from going the route of Steinberg Inc.

Epilogue

The epilogue is rather sad. Michel Gaucher's regime was not to last for long. In retrospect, his takeover of Steinberg's was a disastrous move. He did not know anything about supermarkets (his company having originally been a small shipping enterprise). Furthermore, he terminated many of Steinberg Inc.'s key executives. Under his regime, the stores went downhill fast.

Gaucher went bankrupt only three years after the takeover, having financially overextended himself. The stores were sold off to various chains before the bankruptcy. While this was going on, thousands of employees lost their jobs. The politically charged decision of the *Caisse de Dépôts et Placement* (with its eyes on the company's real estate holdings) turned out to be a costly one. It is estimated that the *Caisse* lost around half a billion dollars' worth of pension fund money, and the banks that were involved never recovered all their funds. In hindsight, it is clear that the price paid for the company to its shareholders was in considerable excess of its value. And the ultimate cost? There is no longer any store with the name of Steinberg.[1]

Note

1   A number of primary and secondary sources were used in preparing this case. The main reference source was the book A. Gibbon and P. Hadekel, *Steinberg: The Breakup of a Family Empire*. Toronto: Macmillan, 1990. This engaging and exhaustively researched study by two Canadian journalists was the recipient of a national business writing award and is highly recommended to anyone interested in the Steinberg saga. Arnold Steinberg, former executive vice president at Steinberg Inc. and now a principal at the merchant bank Cleman Ludmer Steinberg Inc. in Montreal was also a valuable resource. As both a Steinberg executive and a nephew of Sam Steinberg, his insights were most helpful. Other sources include the National Film Board of Canada's documentary *The Corporation: After Sam*; H. Mintzberg and J. A. Waters's article "Tracking Strategy in an Entrepreneurial Firm." *Academy of Management Journal*, 1982, *25*(3), 465–499; Steinberg Inc.'s annual reports and corporate communication materials; and press clippings from the *Financial Post*, *Globe and Mail*, *Financial Times of Canada*, and *The Gazette* (a Montreal newspaper). Thanks, too, to the *Financial Post* Corporation for granting access to the clippings files of its corporate library.

Case 9

Medea revisited
Valtex Inc.

No one could envy Jacques Dormant, the senior partner of Valtex's accountancy firm. He may have been trained as an accountant, but now he is being asked to play the role of a family counselor. He would do well to keep in mind Shakespeare's words of wisdom, "Hell hath no furie like a woman scorned." How can he bring some tranquillity to a very explosive situation? How should he react to the request by two major shareholders of Valtex that he help fire the president of the company – a person who, given the difficult times the company is facing, would be extremely hard to replace? How can Dormant, a rational man, recommend a bad management decision based on irrational thinking?

When you read this case, ask yourself what you would do if you were in Jacques Dormant's position. What are his options, given the developments in both the company and the family?

VALTEX INC.

Jacques Dormant, senior partner of the Vandienne & Co. accountancy firm, was rowing in his classic wooden scull on the river Wammel not too far from Tilburg, a city in the southern Netherlands. As he stared over the landscape, his mind went back to the board meeting the previous day with the top management and shareholders of the Valtex Corporation, a medium-sized family-owned textile firm that had been Jacques's first client. In his thirty-five-year career as an accountant, Jacques had never attended such a chaotic and acrimonious meeting. (And he had thought he had seen it all!) Over the years, and especially lately, he had become quite used to the fact that board meetings at Valtex could be tense. In addition to corporate issues, disputes among the family members and other matters seemingly not directly related to Valtex appeared on the table all too often.

Dormant knew that there were at least two reasons for the increasingly stressful board meetings. First, the personal relationship between management and shareholders had seriously deteriorated. Second, a difference of opinion about the overall direction of the company had come to a head. The dispute centered around the employment of corporate funds: management preferred to invest available funds in promising opportunities in the United States, while shareholders preferred a fast payback on their loans.

Yesterday's meeting had ended with a two-week adjournment. Immediately afterwards, Jacques had been approached by two shareholders – the only two non-executive shareholders – who wanted to talk in private. The two sisters (who together held 67 percent of the Valtex shares) told him that they had completely lost confidence in Valtex's management and wanted to sell. They felt that they no longer had any control over the company or its executives. They saw recent investments in a plant in South Carolina, made against their explicit wishes, as a clear example of this unacceptable state of affairs. The sisters' comments still rang clearly in Jacques' ears: "What can we do? We don't know anyone capable of immediately replacing these executives. We lack the skills to manage the company ourselves. We realize that full management cooperation – a sine qua non if we ever hope to sell our shares – is highly uncertain at this point." To them, management's monopoly on knowledge and contacts was a major cause of their lack of options.

At their wits' end, the sisters asked Jacques – who had become quite accustomed to playing the role of family counselor – if he could come up with some kind of solution. Would it be possible to sell the company or partially replace top management? They also asked Jacques to keep the content of their conversation confidential. A premature disclosure, the sisters felt, would only cause further deterioration, which would be dangerous for the survival of the firm.

Rowing slowly down river, Jacques tried to analyze what had happened at the last board meeting. He felt badly torn between the parties. What really bothered him was that he had been asked to hide certain information from the executives at Valtex. These people were more than just clients; they were his longtime friends. He was also troubled by the content of the request itself. Was selling really the only solution? It seemed to be what the sisters wanted. Previous attempts at reconciliation had proven unsuccessful, and after the acrimony of the day before, things did not look promising now. What should he do?

Company background

Valtex Inc. was founded in 1922 by Theodor de Valk, an energetic and domineering entrepreneur who saw potentially profitable trade opportunities in the international yarn and wool markets. He managed to borrow some money and opened an office in Amsterdam as an independent sales agent for yarn companies. His efforts met with success, and within a year he began to trade for himself.

In the following years, the sales volume increased and the product range widened. What helped make the business grow was a new employee, Joseph Romein, who turned out to be a star salesman and purchaser. Gradually, Valtex became a diversified import-export textile firm. In 1933, the company acquired a small fish smokery in Berkel-on-Wammel close to Tilburg, converted it into a textile mill, and Valtex's first production plant was established. The following year, the head office was moved to Berkel. The new production facility boosted Valtex's growth. Soon the first two foreign sales offices, in Boston and in Antwerp, were opened.

In 1940, Holland entered the war. The German occupation, the international trade blockade, and increasing transportation difficulties made international business activity almost impossible. Fortunately, Valtex managed to avoid complete ruin at the hands of the Germans by hiding a substantial part of the company's stock behind a fake wall. Soon after the war ended, Valtex was able to resume its activities. This early recuperation gave the company the opportunity to benefit substantially from the postwar boom period. Within two years, sales and profits had returned to prewar levels, and it was business as usual once again.

Theodor de Valk died in 1950. His three children, Eleonor (aged twenty-six), Melanie (aged twenty-four), and the much younger Peter (aged thirteen) each inherited 33 percent of the shares. De Valk's will had a clause that gave Peter the right to buy out his sisters when he reached the age of twenty-five. When the time came, however, he did not exercise this option (and even stated that he would never do so). At that time – that is, when Peter turned twenty-five – the three heirs made an agreement concerning the sale of shares: if ever one of the shareholders wanted to sell out, the two remaining shareholders had the right of first refusal on the shares being offered. Offering shares to non-family members was unacceptable to all of them.

At de Valk's death, the presidency of Valtex went to Joseph Romein (aged forty) who by that time had been working at Valtex for more than twenty-three years and had become de Valk's right-hand man. Romein had promised de Valk on his deathbed to take care of the older man's family. In running the company, Romein was assisted by the team from de Valk's days and later also by the two sisters' husbands, Alphons Claessens (a division manager) and Henricus Brocker, who were brought into the company by their wives. Romein's management style could be described as rather autocratic and patriarchal. His remuneration was based on a profit-sharing formula as the idea of giving shares was abhorrent to the owners.

Being an experienced and gifted entrepreneur, Romein (later assisted by Brocker in the role of vice president) increased Valtex's rate of expansion. Under his presidency, the company flourished. At the end of the 1960s, Valtex had eleven national and five international divisions, a total staff of 1,200 employees, and a consolidated turnover of $150 million (US). This expansion was made possible partly by an extremely conservative dividend policy: all the profits were plowed back into the company and reinvested in stock and modern production equipment. This policy proved to be very successful. It enabled Valtex to survive at a time when competition from the Far East forced many Western competitors into bankruptcy.

The policy of establishing reserves and investing in modern equipment was "sold" by Romein (in his role as mediator) to the three shareholders as the most tax-efficient approach for them, because it minimized their personal income tax. However, this argument did not remove their lingering resentment toward the policy, especially from 1975 onward. The capital gains tax introduced in Holland that year led to a negative attitude on the part of the female shareholders toward their Valtex investment. It was their opinion that the only "benefit" they derived from their non-liquid shares was increased taxes.

The main characters

Eleonor, the oldest de Valk (and judged to be the least intelligent), was never really involved in the company. Like her husband (Alphons Claessens), who had a mainly ceremonial role at Valtex, she was more interested in the social life of Tilburg and preferred to let the company be run by others. Her influence at board meetings was minimal. On the rare occasions when she spoke out about corporate matters, the others considered her contributions irrelevant and ignored her input. As a result, she became even less inclined to speak at these meetings. In most instances, Eleonor took her sister's side. (In the case of a tie, the president had the deciding vote.)

Melanie, on the other hand, was always quietly involved with the business. Being Theodor's favorite child, she was frequently taken along on business trips and was appointed as his personal assistant at age nineteen. After her father's death, and according to his will, she was the only family member on an interim board (together with Romein and some of her father's friends). Later, after her marriage and the birth of her children, her involvement decreased temporarily. When the children became teenagers, however, she again focused her energy on the company. Her prior experience, her concrete ideas, and the fact that she was perceived to be the most intelligent of the three heirs made her the dominant shareholder. She could be quite manipulative and was also known to be extremely stubborn.

Peter, the youngest of the de Valk heirs, was the only shareholder who decided to make his career at Valtex. Although Peter had a strong technical background and a good head for business, he was perceived as lacking a sense of overall perspective and therefore as not being capable of taking on the role of president. In spite of this stigma, his most important ambition was to hold his father's position in the company – a desire that strongly influenced his behavior, especially after his sisters judged that he was not presidential material. This disagreement estranged Peter somewhat from his sisters and subsequently made him decide at times to vote for management and against his sisters. When the company's internal problems came to a head, Peter was only fifty years old and had stated repeatedly and unequivocally that he had no intention of retiring.

Henricus Brocker, Melanie's husband, already had business experience when he joined Valtex. At age twenty, he had started a small textile firm in southern Holland. The company was not very successful, however, and Henricus just managed to break even. Soon after, he started another firm with two partners, and this time he met with more success. After being taken on at Valtex, he sold his stake in his own company. At Valtex, a much larger firm, Brocker's entrepreneurial and interpersonal talents quickly became evident. They led Romein to select him as his vice president.

Recent events

In 1977, Joseph Romein reached retirement age. Although he expressed a strong interest in staying on for another five years, be it as president or as adviser, the three shareholders insisted that he leave and be replaced by Henricus Brocker (a point of view put forward mainly by the most outspoken shareholder, Melanie de Valk). The shareholders' intention was to gain effective control over the company by installing a member of the family as president (and thus to change its dividend policy). After an administrative battle of some weeks, Romein left angrily. He felt extremely bitter at being forced out of the company he had built up and worked for for more than half a century. His entrepreneurial zeal could not be dampened, however: soon after his departure, he set up his own company, which, supported by one of his sons, became quite successful and turned into a strong Valtex competitor.

Romein was succeeded by Henricus Brocker, who had by then been vice president for nearly twenty years and was eager to take over the top position. The new management team consisted of Brocker (president and CEO), Gilles Tromp (the newly appointed finance director), and Peter de Valk (shareholder, vice president, and technical director). Directly under the three top people were the various division managers (including Alphons Claessens). Their power was limited, however, because of top management's strong involvement in all decisions.

Having shared an office with Romein and worked closely with him for almost twenty years, Brocker had a leadership style and business approach that were nearly identical to those of his predecessor. In addition, Brocker possessed many of Romein's entrepreneurial talents. In general, he maintained Romein's formula for success: a wide range of products, large stock, and flexible manufacturing processes. This policy appeared to be successful, both from a profits and from a sales perspective.

Because of pressure from the shareholders, however, the financial policy of the firm was changed fundamentally. This did not mean that Valtex started to pay out dividends. Instead, the old structure, whereby the shareholders owned every subsidiary personally, was changed into a holding structure – a change suggested by Brocker's wife, Melanie, having been advised on the matter by her tax accountant. This meant that the newly created holding company, fully owned by the three original shareholders, acquired the shares of all of the individual subsidiaries. Since the new holding company did not have the financial resources to pay cash for the shares, the shareholders were paid with a deferred subordinate debt position in the holding company, to be paid back out of future profits. This maneuver improved both the risk and the liquidity position of the shareholders, since loans could either be paid back in part or be sold.

During the 1980s, Valtex's growth reached a plateau. Competition was more intense, margins were decreasing, and some of the big chemical and textile companies (Valtex's main suppliers) decided to drop some items or to sell their products through their own sales channels. Clearly, this had a negative impact on profit performance. When Brocker decided that Valtex needed to explore new markets and new products, the company adopted a diversification strategy with a main concentration on the US market. The biggest project in 1983 was investing in a distribution network for carpets in the United States. Due to an unanticipated drop in the value of the dollar, however, the project failed dramatically. Other projects turned out to be more successful, but the returns took time to materialize.

The declining profits and various investments had a substantial negative impact on Valtex's liquidity position, tying up funds that could have been used to pay back the subordinate debt. The rapid rate at which the company had been reimbursing the loan had to be modified. This seriously annoyed the two non-active shareholders, in spite of the fact that 45 percent of the subordinate debt had already been paid back in only three years.

Panicked by the increasingly volatile business environment, the shareholders (led by Melanie) demanded full payment of their loan immediately. Brocker refused, arguing that immediate redemption could endanger the growth of the firm or even threaten its survival. He added that the bank would not permit a payback that would bring the company's risk exposure to an unacceptably high level.

This rejection caused a serious deterioration in the originally good relationship between management and shareholders. But an even more serious conflict was triggered by the Brockers' divorce in 1984. Melanie loudly and publicly blamed the company and everything that had to do with it (her brother and sister included) for her marital unhappiness.

With the breakup of her marriage, Melanie insisted upon the immediate dismissal of Brocker, now her former husband, at whatever cost. Peter and Eleonor, both realizing that such drastic action would seriously endanger the company (and thus their own financial interests), refused to support their sister. Eleonor, who usually' backed Melanie, decided against her this time. Peter had no doubts about the matter and pressed Melanie to try to understand the difference between personal and business affairs. A stalemate developed, thwarting Melanie. After some time, however, she was able to convince Eleonor that it would be in Eleonor's best interests – for purely financial reasons – if there were substantial changes in the management of the company. Eleonor put her doubts about Melanie's motives vis-à-vis her exhusband aside and gave full vent to her frustration at the lack of shareholder income from Valtex. Once she sided with Melanie, things became intolerably tense between the sisters (as one faction) and the rest of the people in the organization (as the other). This tension led to the recent explosive meeting and the sisters' subsequent secret discussion with Jacques Dormant.

COMMENTARY

Perhaps Jacques Dormant would have done well to read up on his Greek mythology in order to understand the appeal of revenge. He might have come across the story of Medea, a sorceress who was the wife of Jason, the leader of the Argonauts. Her infamous reputation is based on the fact that she cut the throats of her own children to avenge herself on Jason after he deserted her. The developments at Valtex, although not so gruesome, show many parallels to Medea's story.

Jacques Dormant, struggling with a serious conflict of loyalties, was uncertain how to manage the situation in which he found himself. He had to either support firing someone with whom he had had a good working relationship for many years or let down two of his fellow board members, who were also longtime friends.

Since he did not like to do things behind a client's back, Dormant decided to be up-front: he made a valiant effort to reconcile the different parties. But his attempt at resolving the conflict failed because the Brockers were fighting their postmarital battles in the boardroom.

Eventually, Dormant decided he had no choice but to look at options other than reconciliation. His first approach was to attempt to identify a potential replacement for Brocker. While finding general managers was no problem, finding people with knowledge of this particular industry was almost impossible. Proposed candidates had neither the expertise nor the contacts to survive in a difficult market. Dormant thought that someone with their experience would need at least two years to become familiar with Valtex's particular business segment, but two years was much too long. Besides, the potential candidates would be very expensive, and they were demanding shares in the company. Giving shares to outsiders, as Romein had discovered long ago, was unacceptable to the shareholders.

Dormant's second approach was to look for a buyer for the company, since the sisters had a clear preference for selling. In seeking a buyer, Dormant was aware that he had to operate with the utmost care. Bids for family firms were traditionally under market value to begin with, and the mere rumor of a forced sale could depress the price considerably.

Dormant received various bids, but they were all unacceptably low. He wondered whether he had underestimated the speed with which bad news traveled. None of the bids fitted the demands. Consequently, Dormant was back at square one.

At this point, Dormant got in touch with one of Brocker's sons, a recent economics graduate. The son, being very familiar with the problems at Valtex, advised Dormant to look into the possibility of a leveraged buyout. That option looked promising, particularly since management, after being informed of this possibility, seemed interested. Initially, even the two sisters seemed eager. Moreover, financing turned out to be not too problematic.

Management chose an arrangement whereby Brocker would get 51 percent and Peter de Valk 49 percent. Both executives were enthusiastic about the proposal; not only would the conflict be solved and the company saved, but there was the possibility of making some money in the process as well. The plan was this: Brocker would stay on for a couple of years; then, upon Brocker's retirement, Peter de Valk would take over (and in due course pass the power on to one of Brocker's sons, who was already working at Valtex). Dormant's mission seemed to be completed.

Then Melanie changed her mind. Given her spitefulness, she could not cope with the fact that her exhusband would end up owning a substantial part of *her* company, the company *her* father had founded. So she put pressure on Eleonor and managed to convince her that it was ridiculous that their brother should end up owning the company. Her arguments were convincing enough; her sister joined her in blocking the deal.

Eventually, tired of all the fights and eager for a solution, the family agreed to sell the company to an outsider for a smaller sum than the leveraged buyout would have generated.

Brocker, who had initially agreed to stay with Valtex for another two years, left within half a year following a serious argument with the new owner about dividend matters and financial policies. He and two of his sons (they were soon joined by the third son, who had been working at Valtex) started a new company in the same industry, as Romein had done – a company that became quite successful. Peter de Valk and Alphons Claessens continued working at Valtex.

The new owner, a banker who had very little knowledge of the industry, turned out to be an asset-stripper. He reorganized the company and put the buildings in a separate corporation that rented them back to Valtex. When he got into liquidity problems due to the high cost of the bank loans and started to have difficulties paying his suppliers, he considered bankruptcy. In the end, he arranged with the unhappy suppliers to pay them off over an extended period of time. This incident was hard on Valtex's reputation. As clients and suppliers started to drift to Brocker's and Romein's companies, and Valtex reorganized on a much smaller scale, many of the old Valtex employees found themselves without a job.

There is very little to add to this self-explanatory story. A successful company became a Greek tragedy because its founder, Theodor de Valk, thought only about his son as a potential successor, though his second daughter, Melanie, seemed the most capable of the three children. Melanie had heard the same dinner-table conversation about the business as Peter during childhood and adolescence; she had always been interested in the business. But Peter was the anointed successor, probably because Theodor de Valk considered the kind of business he was in too tough for his "little girl." Consequently, Melanie was never considered, let alone trained, for a senior position in the company. This situation must have aroused a considerable amount of both resentment toward and envy of her brother. Although she tried to manage Valtex by proxy, through her husband, this clearly did not provide Melanie with the satisfaction she would have had from being directly involved in the company.

As things turned out, Theodor de Valk's choice was unfortunate. As we know, many entrepreneurial fathers can make life difficult for their sons, causing serious self-esteem problems in their male offspring. This seems to have been the case with Peter, who could not have been described as a competent, self-assured executive. Frequently, entrepreneurs such as Theodor see their sons, at least unconsciously, as threats. They fear (and rightly so) that with their own physical decline, their sons will become competitors and want to take their power away. Entrepreneurial fathers worry that their sons want to take control of the "family jewels." Intrapsychically, growing sons become threats to their fathers' masculinity.

In some parts of the animal kingdom, males eventually kill their fathers and possess the females in the pack. An analogy can be made to the world of human beings. If an aging entrepreneur's Oedipus complex has not been adequately resolved, his primal fears are complicated by a lingering desire to have exclusive possession of his own mother and overthrow his own father. Since the successful entrepreneur may feel that he achieved a symbolic Oedipal victory over his father (by being his mother's favorite), he must be on guard to avoid having the same thing happen to him. Consequently, many entrepreneurs are like the Greek king Laius, trying to kill (at least symbolically) their sons. Many entrepreneurial fathers go to great lengths to put their sons in their place, to keep them down. Such an attitude toward training and development, however, does not make for capable, self-confident sons.

In contrast, male entrepreneurs tend to see their daughters as unthreatening; daughters generally do not arouse strong competitive feelings. In hindsight, we can see that Theodor would have done well to have considered Melanie as a possible successor. Instead, he created a woman tortured by envy as she saw her brother getting the opportunities that had passed her by.

For a while, Melanie was able to express her interest in the company through her husband. With the divorce, however, her envious feelings toward her brother and exhusband came to the fore. Envy turned into vindictiveness. Attempts were made at triangulation, whereby Melanie and Tobias Brocker tried to involve their children in their fights. In the end, Melanie destroyed the possibility that her own children could become the third generation of family members to run Valtex. The sad thing is that her children were very interested in the company and had educated themselves accordingly.

Ironically, Melanie's brother, her rival, continued to work for the company in a subordinate position, while her former husband and children became direct competitors of Valtex. The old president, Joseph Romein, who had built up Valtex with de Valk, became another competitor. If the members of the family had been wiser in their attitudes toward ownership and management, the scenario could have been a much happier one. Not only could many of the employees at Valtex have remained in their jobs, but Melanie would have had an opportunity to build a special relationship with her sons by passing the business on to them. After all, a son does not easily forget what his mother does to or for him.

D. MULTIGENERATIONAL ISSUES

Case 10

Superman with feet of clay

Anton Dreesmann

Understanding, managing, or advising a multigenerational family firm offers special challenges. As the family forks out into various branches, family dynamics become increasingly complex and maintaining harmony between the different factions becomes trickier. At the same time, civilized relationships among all the relatives are essential if the family is to develop a common perspective on the business and plan for continuity.

In the Dreesmann case, we will look at key success factors that have kept this family firm functioning for an exceptionally long time. It is unusual to find a thriving firm that has remained in the same *two* families for four generations. Despite the increasing number of shareholder-owners, the Vroom and Dreesmann families have handed down the firm to successive generations with relatively little fuss. As you read, think about what elements have fostered smooth transfers of power along the way and what went wrong in the succession process in the present generation.

Research has shown that family firms need a structure that lets them create a shared outlook for the future. Does that sort of structure exist formally at Vendex, or has the corporate culture at each stage of the company's development been based on the current Chief Executive Officer's leadership style and vision? What will happen in the future, now that there is no longer a family member at the head of the organization?

Another important factor in ensuring continuity is the selection process for key positions in the company. How has this issue been handled at Vendex? What kind of mechanisms have been used to ensure "meritocratic nepotism"?

In such a large family firm – one with hundreds of owners – is remaining privately owned really the overriding issue? With so many different agendas on the table, other options may be valid. After reading this case, think about whether the family made the right choice in taking the firm public. Should the family have considered other ways to create a greater concentration of ownership? Was their decision based on sound reasoning, or were family members too focused on their own financial gain?

Think too about the leadership style of the main protagonist, Anton Dreesmann. What were the principal characteristics of his leadership style?

Can you make some inferences about his inner world, about the things that motivated him?

The centerpiece of this case is the search for a successor for "Master Anton." From the information available, do you feel that the process was handled properly? What can you say of the role of the various dramatis personae? What insights do you have about Anton's chosen successor, Arie Van der Zwan? Was the succession crisis at Vendex inevitable? What do you think of the role of the supervisory board in this drama? Could the succession issue have been handled differently?

ANTON DREESMANN: THE RISE AND FALL OF A DEPARTMENT STORE DYNASTY

"Lying ill in intensive care, I saw my last will opened. I was already in my grave, and I saw the power struggle develop in front of my eyes. However, I was able to pull myself up, using my tombstone. They had not counted on that."[1]

It was July 30, 1988, and Anton Dreesmann, who had been Chief Executive Officer and largest minority shareholder in Vendex International (formerly Vroom & Dreesmann) for seventeen years, was making a statement to the Dutch press from his villa in Laren, where he was recovering from his second stroke. Dreesmann had been responsible for the growth of Vendex from a domestic Dutch department store conglomerate into an international service corporation. In 1988, the company was among the largest family-owned corporations in the world, with a turnover of 15 billion Dutch guilders ($9 billion US).

Anton Dreesmann made his statement public through Johan Nathans, the representative of Vendex's employees and president of the Central Works Council of the company. (See Figure C10.1 for an explanation of company and stakeholder structure in the Netherlands and Figure C10.2 for Vendex International Holdings in 1988.) With the press release, Anton Dreesmann declared war on his supervisory board, presided over by his long-time friend Gerrit Van Driel, and on his own hand-picked successor, Arie Van der Zwan. Van der Zwan had been vice chairman of Vendex International for only seven months. The press statement was the final outburst in a period of considerable tension and uncertainty that had lasted for months. It was to result in a bloody war of succession that would see no winners and many casualties.

The Dreesmann family: a department store dynasty

First generation (1875–1934)

In 1875, a young German immigrant, Anton Caspar Rudolph Dreesmann, arrived in Amsterdam. With the moral support of the Tombrocks (another immigrant family from Haseluhne) and a loan from the bank, he selected a small, attractive location in the center of old Amsterdam and rolled up his sleeves. A few weeks

Supervisory Board: This board is responsible for the "quality" of management. It has to give approval for major company decisions such as those regarding acquisitions, reorganizations, and layoffs. Furthermore, it is supposed to check the appropriateness of company policy as made by the board of management; in other words, it is a controlling body, not a policy-making body. The supervisory board appoints and dismisses the members of the board of management and appoints its own members (sometimes on nomination by the board of management or the Central Works Council). Supervisory boards usually consist of CEOs of other companies and leading academics.

Board of Management: Also translated as executive committee or executive board, this body actually runs the company. It usually consists of financial, commercial, production and personnel directors and the CEO. This board is directly accountable for its actions to the supervisory board and, in a more complicated way, to the Central Works Council and the shareholders.

Central Works Council: Every Dutch company with more than 100 employees is obliged by law to install a works council that represents the employees. The rights of the council to be informed on company policy, especially social policy, are extensive. The board of management often has to consult with or get the approval of the works council for company decisions. This council has no formal appointment or dismissal power over the board of management, however.

Shareholders: The rights of the shareholders to influence company policy are very limited in the Netherlands. Usually, these rights are further restricted by company measures intended to prevent hostile takeovers (limited or non-existent voting rights, for example). Shareholders' interests are supposed to be defended by the supervisory board.

Figure C10.1 Corporate structure in the Netherlands

later, the draper shop "De Zon" was in business. The shop was an immediate success. Dreesmann offered a large choice of textiles to his customers, and he was a hard worker, determined to make his venture a lasting business.

During that time, he met Willem Vroom, who, with his father, ran a similar shop in Amsterdam. The two friends visited the Tombrock family regularly on Sundays, and they eventually married two of the Tombrock daughters. Closely linked through marriage and business, Anton and Willem decided to merge their shops in 1887 and predictably christened the new shop Vroom & Dreesmann. Each partner took 50 percent of the shares.

The following years were prosperous for Vroom & Dreesmann. The partners' hard work and keen sense of business made the Amsterdam draper shop grow into a real department store with a wide range of goods. By 1900, Vroom & Dreesmann already consisted of twelve separate stores throughout the

RETAIL	SERVICE
Distilleries	Information service companies
Furniture stores	Brand protection agency
Housing supermarkets	Corporate law firm
Fashion stores	Laundry chain
Sports clothing chain	Software house
Showrooms	Film financing house
Photography shops	Cleaning company chain
White goods shops	Transportation firms
Jewelry shops	Health care centers
Supermarket chains	Small restaurants
Mail-order firms	Distributors and consultancies
Opticians	Real estate holding companies
Department stores	Temporary agencies
Bank	Training companies
Trailer parks	Golf courses

Figure C10.2 Vendex International's Holdings, December 1988

Netherlands. Directors for new branches were recruited solely among family members – brothers, sons, and sons-in-law of the original founders. A director got 50 percent of the shares of his new store, and Anton Dreesmann and Willem Vroom each got 25 percent and a seat on the supervisory board. Every department store had its own characteristics, but the basic selection was purchased centrally, thus creating economies of scale. The broad selection of goods, well-trained personnel, and affordable prices made the name V&D synonymous with "department store" in the Netherlands for many years.

From the accounts of family members and others who still remember Anton Dreesmann emerges the image of a dynamic and amiable character. Dreesmann was a pious man and a hard worker, but he also enjoyed life. The luxurious family villa – the Loverhof, with its many roses – was a favorite family gathering place. Dreesmann took an active interest in art, amassing several art collections during his lifetime. He also gave large donations to the Roman Catholic Church and to charity. One of his many admirers described how, after a long day's work, he spent his evenings collecting money for charity in the upper-class neighborhood where he lived. By the end of his life, he had been named

Roman Count and Chamberlain of the Pope, the highest "civilian" distinctions one can receive in the Roman Catholic Church.

Second generation (1934–1954)

Willem Dreesmann, by then Anton's only surviving son, inherited most of his father's shares and all the board of directors' seats in the branches after his father's death in 1934, making him the largest minority shareholder and the de facto leader of the family. The power base of the Vrooms was much more diluted, because Willem Vroom had had many sons. Under Willem Dreesmann's management, the newly created department store empire was consolidated.

Third generation (1954–1995)

The children of Willem Dreesmann and his wife, Anna Peek, grew up in luxury but by no means in idleness. They had a strict and rather formal upbringing. The boys went to the best Catholic boarding schools, which was unusual for Dutch children, and could visit their family at home only once a month. The girls were educated by nuns. The Dreesmann family credo was, "It doesn't matter what you become, as long as you become the best." An unofficial credo also circulated among the children – one they referred to as "closing the tap": all the children were free to do as they wanted, as long as they were prepared to face the possibility of disinheritance if their acts did not meet with family approval.

Upon Willem Dreesmann's death in 1954, his shares of Vroom & Dreesmann ended up in the hands of two of his seven children: Willem Jr. and his brother Anton, ten years younger. The oldest brother, Theo, had never shown any affinity for department store management and lived a quiet life as CEO of a bank. The youngest brother, Bernard, traded his shares in Vroom & Dreesmann for the company's possessions in England, the Morley's stores, perhaps because he foresaw a power struggle among the brothers and decided in favor of a career of his own in a different country. In the patriarchal view of Willem Sr, girls could never have a say in the company; thus, like Theo, the three daughters inherited only property, not shares.

The two Dreesmann brothers involved in the business were very ambitious and had an enormous capacity for work and perseverance. Their personalities differed considerably, however. Willem Jr (1913–71) had been brought up to run the company. He was trained on the job, as was every Dreesmann, Vroom, or other family member who wanted to enter the business. He had never bothered to finish the university program he had begun, starting instead as an assistant sales clerk in one of the provincial branches of Vroom & Dreesmann. At the time of his father's death, he was serving as director of the store in The Hague. In many ways he resembled his grandfather Anton: he was an amiable though autocratic man and a good listener with a passion for department stores. With his keen eye for detail, he transformed Vroom & Dreesman The Hague into the showpiece of the company – indeed, the best and most profitable department store in the country. This success and his many seats on the supervisory boards of the other branches made him the leading figure in Vroom & Dreesmann in the 1950s and 1960s.

The younger brother, Anton, had his mother's disposition: fierce, impulsive, and extroverted. In a cameo appearance in a *roman-à-clef* written by his sister Cecile, he was described as follows: "Of all the Dreesmann children, Anton certainly has the most brilliant mind and an almost insatiable thirst for knowledge, a general curiosity that makes him consider his work for the department store as only part of his program in life."[2] Anton received two master's degrees from the University of Amsterdam, one in law (1947) and one in economics (1949), a considerable intellectual achievement given the fact that studying was virtually impossible during the war period of 1940 to 1945. After two years of training on the job in Leiden and Breda, he joined the store in The Hague in 1952 as an assistant director to his brother Willem. He was twenty-nine years old. Two years later, he became a full director. This did not mean that he was on the same level as Willem, however, because the latter also held a seat on the supervisory board of every Vroom & Dreesmann branch.

Anton was more interested in broad general economic developments than in the details that never escaped the attention of Willem (such as a locked cupboard on display with the keys missing). Anton was looked on as the scholar, while Willem saw himself as the "person out in the field."[3] Willem used Anton's skills mainly to solve complicated legal matters and to compose important letters. In addition to his work for the company, Anton was working at that time on an 1,800 page PhD thesis in economics, with a focus on department stores. Its title was *Evolution and Expansion: Research into the Synergy of Structure, Function, and Pricing Policies in Retailing*. In his thesis, Anton pointed out that since the First World War, the position of the department store worldwide had been dominated by new and extremely aggressive forms of retailing. He stressed the necessity of extending or renewing the lifecycle of merchandising formulas as a continuous process. In 1963, he received his doctorate in economics with honors.

Anton's broad outlook went further than the retail floor; in fact, it extended beyond the Dutch border, an exception in those days. His main interest was North America. Every year he and his wife crossed the ocean to explore the United States in a rented car. Anton also attended international trade fairs and conferences on the retail trade, often as a lecturer. His speeches were peppered with American colloquialisms and references to US developments that had not yet arrived in the Netherlands.

Then tragedy struck: Willem, the brother most active in the company, died as the result of injuries sustained in a car crash in southern France. It was 1971, and Anton was forty-eight years old.

A portrait of Anton Dreesmann

At the time of his brother's death, Anton Dreesmann was striking, both physically and intellectually. Weighing over 200 pounds, he described himself as the living contradiction of a Dutch proverb that claims, "Fat executives do not carry weight." His knowledge, memory, and manner of expressing himself were at least as impressive as his stature.

Anton was an obsessive reader and claimed to have devoured more than 5,000 books before he was sixteen years old. Over ninety-five daily, weekly, and monthly periodicals arrived at his Vendex office regularly, and he read and understood them all (or so he said), devoting barely more than a few minutes to each. He liked to impress people with his deep understanding of numerous subjects, challenging them to test his knowledge. The corridors of his villa were crammed with books – more than 50,000 in all on subjects varying from works of art to medical literature.

Anton said this of himself: "I realize that I'm rather manic; I need to know everything, to follow all the important developments, to be prepared. I want to know the world in which Vendex is developing. Books, periodicals, papers, languages, science, works of art, or companies – I can't get enough of them. I memorize the essentials of every book through extracts. Don't ask me about details, however."[4]

Visitors to the villa were astonished by his ability to remember without hesitation the location of any particular book in his extensive library. In a television interview, Anton even claimed that his photographic memory enabled him to "remember every comma in every letter I have ever written."[5] (Unfortunately, in the same interview his memory seemed far from perfect.) His emphasis on learning also came through in his vision of management and running a business. According to him, most people get set in their ways when they reach age thirty-five. They need continuous challenges in order to keep on learning.

The chance to learn something was often one of the reasons Anton gave for buying or taking a stake in a given company. He considered the ability to combine theory with practice to be his specialty. A director of one of the companies Vendex acquired commented: "During our first meeting I did not know what was happening to me. I am used to a glassy stare whenever I try to explain our complicated activities to someone. Dreesmann did not understand at first either, but he immediately reacted: could you explain that again . . . and again . . . and again? He forced me to rephrase until we were communicating on the same wave length. Subsequently, he hit the essentials in great detail. He asked precisely those questions that matter in our line of business. There are high-placed officials in this company that have only succeeded in doing this after several years. Colleagues at Vendex tell me that this kind of conversation is the rule rather than the exception: Dreesmann is rarely off the mark."[6]

Although Anton Dreesmann was frequently seen in public, he was no socialite. During cocktail receptions, he often retired to his office, sometimes staying on the phone for hours with someone in the United States or reading the latest business reports. He often worked fourteen-hour days or more. He had many contacts but very few close friends. Most of the friends he did have were fervent art collectors like himself, not businessmen. He claimed to have two marriages: one to his company and one to his wife.

Yet Anton Dreesmann valued his family life highly. His children could always call him for support during office hours or in the middle of the night. Ties remained strong in the immediate family as the children grew up: even when most of the children were grown, they still frequently had dinner together at home in Laren.

Anton Dreesmann's ties with his brothers and sisters were less close. He had hardly any contact at all with most of them. His sister Cecile, who was well known in the Netherlands for her embroidery art and her six marriages, often criticized Anton in the media for his lack of modesty, and she found him short on gratitude to his forefathers. The rest of the family led a more secluded life. His only remaining brother, Bernard, said about his relationship with Anton, "We lost contact. The rest of the family I see regularly, but my brother I don't see any more. He talks so much. I don't seem to hold his attention. In the long run, you don't feel like keeping in touch anymore. However, I do like my brother, very much indeed."[7]

The era of Master Anton (1971–95)

Taking charge (1971–1973)

In 1971 – the year of Willem Dreesmann's death – Vroom & Dreesmann was more commonly thought of as a series of separate department stores than as a cohesive corporation with one face and one vision. Vroom & Dreesmann consisted then of twenty-three independent companies responsible for sixty department stores, each largely differing in style, selection of goods, and profitability. There were sophisticated, thriving businesses like the one in The Hague, and there were ailing local stores in the provinces. The practice of appointing only family members as directors had provided security and lifelong employment for many a Vroom and Dreesmann, but it had not supplied the company with excellent management talent.

Furthermore, ownership of the shares had become extremely complicated. The Roman Catholic descendants of Willem Vroom and the first Anton Dreesmann had had many children, and many of those offspring had intermarried. The dispersion of shares and power was greater in the Vroom branch and less diluted among the Dreesmann descendants (the "Loverhof group" as they called themselves, referring to the old family homestead). Despite the Dreesmanns' smaller numbers, they were in possession of the majority of the shares. At his brother Willem's death, the younger Anton suddenly found himself in the position of a large minority shareholder and potentially the most influential person in the company.

Anton took charge with a surprising swiftness and determination. He based his strategy on these four points:

1   No other family member could guide Vroom & Dreesmann through the 1970s better than he could.
2   The twenty-three separate companies had to be united under one central and decisive manager.
3   The practices of nepotism had to be ended.
4   Because the margins in the retail trade in the Netherlands were too small to allow long-term survival, internationalization and diversification were necessary.

In 1971, the power – shares and profit – was concentrated in three regional blocks, all of whose directors were members of the Loverhof group. Anton did not waste any time. According to Rudi Vroom, the leader of one of the blocks, Anton struck a deal with the leader of another block at Willem's funeral, giving Anton the votes and support that would enable him to assume control of the whole company.

In order to unify the separate stores under his command, Anton first had to persuade people in his own family to trade their shares in one of the smaller companies for shares in a new holding company so as to consolidate the first two regional blocks of the company. Doing so created few difficulties: Anton was convincing as the new leader in the company. Moreover, not every store was profitable; the trading of these shares for a stake in the total company was in many cases an attractive proposal. Unwilling family members/shareholders were bought out, and several family members/directors were persuaded to resign. (Anton's seat on the supervisory boards of all twenty-three companies made this possible.) In cases of resistance, Anton incited the shareholders of the firms in question to demand dividends that would cause a cash crisis. He then offered his help – if the shareholders were willing to transfer their shares to the holding company.

It took Anton less than two years to unite the Loverhof group behind him. In 1973, he was ready to deal with Rudi Vroom and his sphere of influence in the company. One Sunday afternoon, the two men met to discuss the future and agreed that Anton was the man to lead the company. In an interview in 1983, Rudi Vroom remembered that conversation: "The first item on Anton's list was, Who is going to be the boss? Anton had that ambition, and I thought him more capable than anybody else."[8] Hence, in 1973, the twenty-three separate companies of Vroom & Dreesmann were transformed into one holding company with subsidiaries, headed by a single board of management presided over by one Chief Executive Officer: Anton Dreesmann. Anton recruited an outsider, Gerrit van Driel, then CEO of Wessanen, to be president of the new supervisory board. (Wessanen was originally a family-owned company that had grown into an industrial food conglomerate traded on the stock exchange.)

Evolution and expansion (1973–86)

During the next fifteen years, Anton put the theories of his 1963 doctoral thesis into practice, and the company prospered under his leadership. He made many acquisitions, looking for "small, close-to-the-market companies with low technology, low capital investment, no manufacturing, high growth potential, and small overhead."[9] He described his formula as "financial support for accelerated growth while respecting the values and culture of the newly acquired company."[10] Many entrepreneurial owners of businesses with a lack of financial strength to expand were attracted by Anton's method of building an empire; in 1986, the company was said to receive a new acquisition offer every three days.

The company's transformation from department store chain to major international corporation in the service industry progressed gradually. The name of the new corporation was changed to Vendex International in 1982, while the original department store chain, which now represented only 15 percent of the total turnover, kept the name Vroom & Dreesmann. In addition, Vendex took extensive measures to prevent hostile takeovers by making it absolutely impossible for one shareholder to take control of the whole company.

During the entire period of Anton Dreesmann's leadership, Vendex continued to be a flat organization – "as flat as a pancake," as he himself stated. The head office did not employ more than thirty people. For every acquisition, outside experts were hired, some of whom had had connections with Vendex for over ten years. One of them explained, "If the decision to acquire a company is taken, a contract can be produced extremely fast. The board of management hardly needs to explain: three words and a phone call are enough to start the outside experts working."[11]

Dreesmann expressed his idea of how the board of management should work: "We members of the board of management are transmitters; we persuade, motivate, and find new ways. Our sixty mostly youthful entrepreneurs are by no means held back. According to our company policy, we want them to act given our decentralized environment and our *short* communication lines. Since I'm short-tempered, I sometimes think, Good God, sir, I would have done that in three minutes. Entrepreneurs, however, have to act independently. At the most a small stimulus now and then, intervention if necessary; but usually only coaching is needed. The board of management's foremost task is to inspire and innovate."[12]

The only outsider on the board of management was N. E. Keller, recruited by Anton Dreesmann in 1982. After an impressive career with Unilever, Keller had started his own consulting firm in Switzerland. When he visited Anton Dreesmann to propose his services, he was offered a seat on the board of management as director of service industry and international business development. Anton Dreesmann had just suffered a minor stroke and needed help in the two areas he usually covered himself. The relationship lasted until May 1987, when Keller resigned.

In a 1988 interview, Keller gave this reason for his departure: "If you're hired as a chauffeur and you never drive, because the boss is always driving, what's the use?"[13] From Anton Dreesmann's perspective, Keller lacked sufficient knowledge of numbers. Not surprisingly, then, their differences of opinion were generally about numbers. Keller said, "I always quarreled about numbers with Dreesmann. I would say, 'All we do here is screw around with numbers. What's lacking are concepts.' Conceptual thinking is foreign to Vendex. I was the only strategic thinker."[14] After his short career at Vendex, Keller went back to Geneva, quite bitter about his years with the company.

By the 1980s, Anton Dreesmann had grown into a national celebrity. There was hardly a conference or television program on entrepreneurship or management in general without his energetic presence. One journalist has suggested that Dreesmann realized the impact that the media can have only after an incident with the unions in 1982. That journalist wrote: "The financial results of the department store chain Vroom & Dreesmann had decreased over a period of time and Dreesmann had proposed a salary cutback. In protest the employees went on strike, a rarity in the industry. Fifteen hundred employees gathered in a location in Amsterdam to travel by bus to the 'Spaklerweg'[15] with the intention of paying a visit to the head office. Dreesmann had learned of this. At the door to the meeting hall, 'Master Anton' asked permission to enter. Union leaders were addressing the crowd and television cameras were filming what was happening. As soon as Anton saw that the cameras were there, he ran on stage and demanded the floor to explain that the measures were meant to benefit everybody in the end. He was denied the chance to speak and the meeting was ended. That evening, millions of viewers heard the department store tycoon loudly voice his dissatisfaction because he could not address his people – his people!"[16]

By shouting "Bloody cowards, that's what you are!" Anton had succeeded in focusing most of the media coverage on himself instead of on the unions.

Succession

The quest for a "crown prince"

In 1986, when Anton Dreesmann reached the age of sixty-three, he was at the height of his career. He directed his still-expanding empire from a small and efficient head office. Vendex International was bigger and more profitable than ever; Anton was one of the most respected and frequently quoted industrialists the Netherlands had ever seen, and he had made his family the wealthy shareholders of an international service empire.

That year Anton Dreesmann concentrated his energy on two areas: preparing Vendex International for the stock exchange and finding a successor. Both the public stock issue and his retirement were planned for 1990. Dreesmann wanted his successor to be vice chairman of the Vendex board of management in order to get to know the company before he himself retired. He knew that his search for a successor would not be easy. He was looking for an exceptional person with exceptional qualities: "a long-term vision of the global market, sufficient imagination, intellectual capacity, and the ability to recognize innovative concepts and combinations – a general outlook and at the same time a keen eye for details as to the financial aspects of the company."[17]

Anton Dreesmann could not find such a person within Vendex. He considered his senior managers to be excellent retailers and service providers, but there were no crown princes. "I'm looking for a man with a huge intellectual grasp. I can't find such a person in my direct environment. It sounds pedantic, but I'm looking for someone above standard."[18]

The reputation of his successor was also of vital importance, since the new leader would be running a public company. Part of Vendex's initial share price would be determined by the market's faith in the leadership qualities of the new Chief Executive Officer.

Anton Dreesmann thus directed his attention toward the financial world. He focused on Arie Van der Zwan, then CEO of the National Investment Bank (NIB). Van der Zwan proved to fit most of Dreesmann's criteria: he was a professor of economics, an independent thinker and non-conformist, a banker, and an entrepreneur. Anton Dreesmann wooed his candidate successfully, and in autumn of 1986, Arie Van der Zwan accepted his offer to become CEO of Vendex International in 1990. In 1987, Van der Zwan would start to attend the meetings of the board of management and the supervisory board. In January 1988, he would start his official career with Vendex International in the position of vice chairman of the board of management.

Arie Van der Zwan

Van der Zwan's management style has been described as follows: "As a manager, he likes clarity. Meetings have to be well prepared, negotiating partners have to be well informed, and appointments and agreements need to be put down in writing. He is not as much a strategist or diplomat as an analyst with a good sense for the (possible) motives of adversaries. He likes action. He likes to act quickly on the basis of rationality."[19]

Anton Dreesmann and Arie Van der Zwan met as early as 1968 at a conference on the economics of distribution. Later they became colleagues, teaching the same subject at the universities of Amsterdam and Rotterdam. Their ideas on the service industry were very similar, and – in the words of Van der Zwan – a "state of understanding" grew.

The announcement

Now that he had found his successor, Anton Dreesmann had to convince his supervisory board that he had selected the right candidate. After fairly perfunctory consideration, the board willingly gave its blessing. Anton

Dreesmann subsequently wrote a letter to all the shareholders in which he praised Van der Zwan's knowledge and accomplishments extensively. He informed the other members of the board of management as well, and on December 17, 1986, he made his announcement to the press.

Later on, in July 1987, he explained his choice and timing to a journalist: "Van der Zwan and I speak the same language. We both have an academic background and a thorough knowledge of the business environment. We consider that a sound basis for entrepreneurship. . . . Your point about Van der Zwan's lacking international background is correct. My intention is to travel a lot with Van der Zwan. He will have to build personal relationships as well as business relationships, just as I did. Get to know people. That's a tremendous asset. However, it's an unusual approach in the business world. . . . In my opinion, the job that Van der Zwan has to do is among the five toughest in Dutch industry. I myself will complete the 'going public' of the family business with a stock issue in 1990. The suitable corporate image will be accomplished primarily by Van der Zwan. His appointment can be seen as the final step in the development of a family business into a public corporation."[20]

Crisis

In December 1987, Anton Dreesmann suffered a second stroke. This time it was a severe one, and he had to be hospitalized.

Arie Van der Zwan's first day as vice chairman of Vendex's board of management was January 1, 1988. Anton Dreesmann had not yet recovered, so Van der Zwan took charge immediately, concentrating on the valuation of Vendex in view of the coming stock issue. Interests in foreign companies had to be assessed and possible losses located and ended. His first task was to revalue the department store chain. In addition, Van der Zwan introduced a more formal decision-making process.

During the first three months of 1988, Anton Dreesmann was officially recovering at home, although occasionally he dropped in at the office on his way to another appointment. In April, the shareholders were informed by letter that Dreesmann had recovered and was going to take charge again as CEO.

In March and April, a rumor spread through the company to the effect that several subsidiary managers were getting increasingly frustrated with Van der Zwan's different management approach. (Van der Zwan had, for example, postponed – and in some cases virtually stopped – all acquisition plans.)

In May 1988, the company's annual report revealed that net income had dropped 25 percent in 1987, from 302 million guilders to 226 million guilders, while gross sales continued to grow. The board of management explained the situation by referring to market distortions due to the emergence of new competitors, which caused a disequilibrium between Vendex's operating income and costs. That portion of the decline of profitability not due to market distortions seemed to be attributable to the Vroom & Dreesmann department stores.

The annual shareholders' meeting went smoothly on July 16, 1988, although the family was informed that the department stores were not performing as they should be and had to be restructured. On June 25, the supervisory board and the board of management met to make a decision about the restructuring of the department store chain. The proposed reorganization was ratified by those boards without undue conflict. On June 28, Vendex issued a press release stating that the restructuring of the Vroom & Dreesmann department stores would require the layoff of 1,400 people.

Early in 1988, Vendex began using a different accounting method in computing corporate results. Instead of deducting the actual rent that the department stores paid to the holding company, they now deducted the opportunity costs of renting the store buildings on a commercial basis. According to this new accounting method (based on the actual rent), Vroom & Dreesmann was losing 35 million guilders per year instead of gaining 9 million guilders. Although the unions and the family did not seem alarmed at this development, since it was no secret that things were not going well at Vroom & Dreesmann, tension developed in the company because of the problems that the decreasing profits seemed to highlight. Despite the tense situation, however, Anton Dreesmann left his office for a two-and-a-half-week business trip to Brazil and the United States.

On July 29, the *NRC/Handelsblad*, the Netherlands' leading newspaper, published an article suggesting a possible power struggle between the Dreesmann family and the board of management. The article stated that family members were increasingly doubtful about Van der Zwan's policies and their possible consequences for the future price of shares. According to the article, neither Van der Zwan nor Anton Dreesmann wanted to comment.[21] That evening, Anton Dreesmann received Johan Nathans, president of the Central Works Council, at his home in Laren. The essence of their conversation was that Dreesmann would not tolerate the continued employment of Van der Zwan. Dreesmann declared, among other things: "During my illness, Van der Zwan has taken control. To my misery and horror, the man is selling out the whole business. I told the supervisory board that Van der Zwan had to leave as far back as February. He's not the right man. Our American partners can't deal with Van der Zwan at all – they hate his guts. I wasn't there when they cooked up these layoffs. I wasn't informed. I flatly refuse to turn 1,400 people into the streets. We have sufficient time and money, damn it! I, Dreesmann, have the social duty to take care of these people."[22]

Anton Dreesmann stated that he had no objection to Nathans's going to the press with this information, which Nathans did. The following day, Anton Dreesmann's declaration of war made headlines in all the papers, as described in the opening of this case. That same evening, Anton Dreesmann sent out a personal communiqué declaring that Van der Zwan's reorganization plan had been withdrawn.

Turbulent weeks followed. Some family members took sides with Anton

Dreesmann, but others did not. Journalists speculated heavily on the outcome of the situation. Van der Zwan stayed away from the media completely. Everybody waited intently for the supervisory board to save the situation. But would the board be able to exercise its formal power in a situation where the informal power was very solidly in the hands of Anton Dreesmann, largest minority shareholder and opinion leader for the rest of the shareholders?

On August 16, the supervisory board issued a statement outlining its decision concerning Dreesmann and Van der Zwan. The Board said that Anton Dreesmann would step down as Chief Executive Officer for health reasons, becoming vice president of the supervisory board. The new CEO would be Abraham Verhoef, one of Anton's trusted advisers, who had been with the firm since 1946. Anton referred to him as his fiscal and financial conscience. Arie Van der Zwan would remain vice chairman of the board of management.

On August 15, Van der Zwan received a letter signed by Van Driel, chairman of the supervisory board, confirming that he would be the next CEO after Verhoef. He would get the plum he had been promised, but it would be deferred.

At the end of 1988, members of the dominant branch of the Dreesmann family made one more attempt to regain their lost power base. They tried to arrange a leveraged buyout of the shares of the other factions, financed through junk bonds, with the debt paid through the sales of parts of Vendex International. Anton Dreesmann seemed to be so obsessed with being in charge once more and showing what he could do with the department stores (and perhaps getting back at certain supervisory board members, such as Van Driel) that he was prepared to disassemble parts of his empire. According to the statutory rules of Vendex, however, such an action needed the approval of the supervisory board. This approval was withheld because the board felt – probably rightly so – that owners in the various branches of the family would not be able to come to an agreement on the proposed reorganization.[23]

On January 1, 1990, Jan Michiel Hessels, formerly of McKinsey, Akzo, and Deli Universal, succeeded Verhoef as the new CEO of Vendex International. To improve the profitability of the department stores, he implemented a program of cost cutting, delayering, and rethinking the rationalization of the product mix. Given Vendex's poor financial results, the planned stock offer was postponed to give Hessels's efforts a chance to work. This new program was executed carefully, because Hessels was aware of Dreesmann's emotional attachment to the stores. Vendex's new strategy became one of maximum organic growth, focusing on service and retailing.

In 1995, a substantial part of the company's shares (held by approximately 800 members of the founding families) were offered on the Amsterdam stock exchange. Many of the Dreesmann family members expressed their satisfaction that they finally would be able to cash in their holdings in the family firm.

Van der Zwan never became CEO. The reshuffling of the board of directors by the supervisory board was merely a face-saving measure. Van der Zwan left in February 1989 with a "golden handshake."

Anton Dreesmann's failing health forced him to withdraw from public life. He remained a member of the supervisory board until 1995, but for the most part, his family tried to protect him from outside interference.

COMMENTARY

Before Anton Dreesmann's entry on the scene, Vroom & Dreesmann was a rather sleepy, highly decentralized enterprise consisting of twenty-three different companies responsible for sixty department stores. Although they shared the Vroom & Dreesmann name, the stores varied in character, and profitability was uneven. The prevailing attitude in the company was "If it ain't broke, don't fix it." Innovative human resource management practices were unheard of. Many of the stores provided a "home" for family members, an assured place of employment. Unfortunately, the dark side of Vroom & Dreesmann's nepotistic practices was a paucity of capable executive talent, with predictable repercussions for successful management. Developing a vision for the future of the family firm did not seem to be a high priority; rather, a "more of the same" mindset prevailed. The company seemed to be stuck in a time warp, locally oriented and unaware of dramatic changes in retailing in other countries.

"Rags to rags in three generations" could have become the fate of this family firm. As the number of owners in the company increased explosively, more and more factions developed, each with its own view of where the company should be going. The Catholic religion, which had originally been the glue that kept the families together, lost its hold. The long-standing practice of giving each son a store to run proved to be less and less effective, as the unevenness of the results demonstrated. Something had to be done to make for a more unified family vision; planning for continuity required action. With the death of Willem Dreesmann, a *deus ex machina* in the form of Anton Dreesmann set this process into motion.

The tale of Anton Dreesmann is an interesting one; it contains enough material for a best-seller about the making of a successful business tycoon. But like many tales, this story contains an aspect of Greek myth: a man engaged in a race against time who only late in life gets the opportunity to prove his capabilities. Tragically, however, his body is becoming increasingly frail. He is all too aware that his time is running out.

After Anton's second stroke and his withdrawal from active management, his carefully built masterpiece was shown to be less stable than he had imagined. Many of the "crown jewels" of his empire had to be sold to stave off liquidity problems. Vendex International had become overextended, and its flagship, Vroom & Dreesmann, had become unprofitable. The company had to slim down considerably. It was not until 1995 that Vendex International was ready to implement what Anton Dreesmann had been striving for all along: a public stock offering.

In its crisis years, Vendex shattered the hopes and expectations of many of its people, starting with those of Anton himself. The monument he had tried to create increasingly resembled a tombstone. Vendex's decline destroyed the plans of Arie Van der Zwan, whose career and public image both suffered serious damage. Furthermore, the many family shareholders had to wait much longer than they had hoped or expected for their paper shares to be transformed into real money. Last but not least, the employees of Vendex International, who once were proud to be working for a celebrated company, were subjected to difficult and uncertain times. How could these things have happened? And could they have been prevented?

One way to begin this analysis is to take a closer look at the individual who revitalized a company that, at the time of his ascension to power, seemed to be merely drifting along. What observations can be made about the person who changed all that? What can be said about Anton Dreesmann?

The making of a leader

Anton was raised in a family where expectations were high (remember the motto: "It doesn't matter what you become, as long as you become the best"), especially for the boys. The family atmosphere as described by Anton's sister Cecile was formal and not very warm. Anton's father, Willem, appears to have been a detached man, more involved with his art treasures than with his family. He settled disputes between his wife and the children in his office; the child involved in any dispute waited outside the office until a red light came on. Anna Peek, Anton's mother, has been described as a society hostess who ran a perfect household and often paraded her children in front of guests during cocktails. Appearances were what counted, not the child's individual experience. Education was harsh and took place away from the family home; the boys all went to boarding school, an unusual form of education in the Dutch context. (In the Netherlands, normally only problem children were sent away to boarding school at that time.)

One may conclude that Anton was expected to strive for the best but got little warmth or encouragement from his parents. We can only speculate about the effects of a parental outlook that defined normal achievements as failure and excellence as the only acceptable result.

Anton's professional approach reflected the appreciation of hard work and excellence instilled by the elders in the Dreesmann family. Like the other children, he knew that "the tap would be closed" for offspring who did not uphold these values. Certainly this environment (which discouraged the making of "spoiled kids") and this work ethic influenced both Anton's personality and the way he made decisions.

In Chapter 4, I discussed reactive narcissism, a form of narcissism often caused by unresponsive, cold, or rejecting parents. In some instances, children whose capabilities are not encouraged are left with a shaky sense of self-esteem and a legacy of insecurity. As a way of coping with these feelings of inadequacy, they may develop a craving for self-affirmation; they may be haunted by a constant need to reassure themselves that they are special. This often results in extremes of grandiosity, exploitation, or exhibitionism. The information available about Anton Dreesmann's personality indicates that he may have had some of these characteristics.

Another factor that must have contributed to Dreesmann's peculiar personality makeup was the close link between the idea of success for the male members of the Dreesmann family and their efforts in the department stores. Anton's older brother Willem was by far the "best" son in this regard, the living image of his grandfather. We may hypothesize that a major theme in Anton's inner world was how to live up to his brother's image. What could he do to better his brother? The importance of this theme is reflected in the fact that Anton – although more of an intellectual than a "sales type" – still chose a career in the family business. How much he was allowed to do in the family business initially is another matter altogether. Clearly he was not overtaxed: he had the time to write an unusually long dissertation and read numerous books, newspapers, weeklies, and monthly magazines while on the job.

Nearly twenty years of domination by his brother Willem must have had a great impact on Anton's feelings about himself. The fact that within the family his ideas were never taken seriously must have frustrated him greatly. His need to prove his worth to the rest of the family must have been enormous. The extraordinary length of his thesis is one indication of this. His brother's death, which led to Anton's assuming the helm of Vendex, was the catalyst that released Anton's pent-up energy.

Anton's leadership style can be described as dramatic. As discussed in Chapter 4, the guiding theme of a dramatic leader is grandiosity: "I want to get attention from and impress the people who count in my life." As soon as Anton got his hands on the family business, he plunged into a frenzy of activity to show what he could do. He wanted first to impress his family, then to have an impact on the rest of the world. There was hardly any television program or seminar on business to which he did not give his opinions. He succeeded in being in the spotlight continually, with ever more daring, controversial statements. That media attention added to Anton's inherent sense of narcissism; knowing that every word one says can be read the next day on the front page of the newspaper is a heady experience.

We can only guess at the person or people Anton really wanted to impress. His brother surely would have been one of the prime candidates, followed by his father. Anton had never been able to convince these two people that he was a serious businessman. Instead, he was stereotyped in the family. He was considered to be an intellectual, a bookworm – in short, something of a failure (according to the criteria of his family). We can assume that Anton, after Willem's death, desperately needed to live up to his father's and brother's memory and prove that he was at least as good a "department store man" as Willem – and maybe even better. (In fact, Willem's restricted views would likely have caused Vroom & Dreesmann serious problems during the recession in the 1970s, had he lived and remained in charge that long.) Anton's wish to be taken seriously by his father and Willem can be seen as one of the explanations for his dramatic need to expand the business. He was driven to transform the company, to make it his own creation.

The need to prove his superiority gave Anton wings. The combination of his considerable intellectual capacity and his dramatic style worked to his advantage, especially in the beginning. And since he ably took care of the dependency needs of his family, he managed to get their support and be accepted as their "strong leader." Because he envisioned a strong future for the family business, he was able to unify a very dispersed, tottering empire. Later, a similar process occurred with his subordinates, especially the executives of the businesses he took over. The comments of colleagues that are quoted in this case reflect those executives' idealization of their leader: he had unlimited knowledge, enthusiasm, and business sense.

Like most dramatic leaders, Dreesmann needed constant activity, excitement, and stimulation – elements provided him by his hectic, overactive way of doing business. He bought Staal Bankiers in an afternoon, and he offered a baffled Keller a seat on the board of management the first time they met. These examples also reflect the typically dramatic character of his strategy: diversification and growth, often based on impulse. He himself claimed that he had *no* strategy: the divisions were not planned, he said, but evolved over the years.

Anton Dreesmann seems to have really cared for his employees. His personality, however, did not allow easy intimacy. In all his interactions – even those with his close subordinate Verhoef and his own brothers and sisters – he kept his distance. He was not a great listener; nevertheless, he was perceived by many people as a genuinely warm and charismatic person. The executives of his various business units "mirrored" themselves in him and set out to expand their own businesses in the Dreesmann way.

In the 1980s, the darker side of this dramatic leader became more visible. Although Anton said all the right things about what makes for excellent leadership practices and how to design vanguard companies, it is not evident that he practiced what he preached. Did he really empower his executives? Vendex's headquarters were kept extremely small and the subsidiaries were left very much on their own, but nobody was in doubt about who made the important decisions in the company: there was only one boss, and that was Anton Dreesmann. Only Verhoef and perhaps Van Driel seem to have had some influence (albeit marginal) on his decisions.

Continuous success made Anton more and more convinced of his superior personality. His statements became dangerously grandiose, culminating in the claim during an interview on VPRO television that he remembered "every comma in every letter he had ever written." (He made a similar statement on a television program once, only to forget the question asked by the interviewer.)

In later years, the extremely small head office, the absence of a consistent strategy, and the lack of efficient information systems became a problem. Anton ran from deal to seminar to deal and seemed to spend hardly any time on existing businesses. Strategic direction was missing, as was control. Losses started to pile up, but it was not clear why or where (and nobody had or took the time to look into the matter).

Anton Dreesmann's executive team consisted mainly of homegrown sycophants. The corporate ambience was not conducive to the development of the next generation of executives. Keller attempted to transform Vendex into a "real" corporation but was thrown out for his pains. Here we see a typical example of the earlier-mentioned defense mechanism of "splitting." A narcissistic person employing this defense may change his or her opinion about somebody from extremely positive to extremely negative if things do not work out as expected. Criticism is not taken lightly by leaders who "split," who feel that people are either for or against them. Anton referred to the once-revered Keller as an incompetent fool as soon as Keller stopped playing Anton's game. The Van der Zwan episode – the crown prince's fall from glory – was a repetition of this phenomenon. And Van Driel, the chairman of the supervisory board, became yet another victim of this behavior pattern.

Succession

By 1986, Anton Dreesmann was ready for the end game. For almost fifteen years, he had been building his company, which had become the symbol of both his success and his unique personality. He was the most admired executive in Holland. Vendex had become an extension of his personality: *he* had done it all; it was *his* masterpiece. He rarely referred to his grandfather's, father's, or brother's role in making the company what it was. He had given birth to it and to himself; he was his own man.

Anton's feeling of grandiosity was also reflected in the criteria required for his successor: only a very special person would be able to follow in his footsteps. Of course, such a person could not be found among the sycophants in his immediate environment. Although his standards were high, Anton seems to have been sincere in looking for a successor. He did not attempt to postpone the decision, unlike those leaders who cling to power in a futile attempt to deny their own mortality. Anton wanted to end his show with fireworks: a public stock issue that would enrich the family and highlight the fact that the perfect successor was already in place.

However, in his quest for a crown prince, Anton looked to his own image: his criteria reflected his own perceived characteristics. His selection of Van der Zwan seems to have been a comedy of errors of perception. Each man looked into the other's face and, as in a magic mirror, saw himself. "We speak the same language," said Dreesmann. Yet as soon as Van der Zwan took the director's seat and Dreesmann realized that his power base had changed, the mirror broke.

The fall

In theory, Van der Zwan and Dreesmann came from the same mold: both were intellectuals and entrepreneurs; both were non-conformist professors. In reality, however, their personalities and leadership styles were very different.

From early on, Van der Zwan had fought a battle against the establishment of which he later became part (but which he never took to heart). The early lessons he learned about who is in and who is out might have had an influence on his leadership style. Rather detached, he did not feel comfortable with personal relations and preferred to rely on facts. Van der Zwan mistrusted ideas and visions based on intuition; he relied instead on well-prepared meetings, exact numbers, and clear procedures. He had an analytic personality that was often perceived by other people as cold. He disliked being contradicted, because he usually perceived his own ideas as having more validity than anyone else's.

The change of leadership when Van der Zwan (in his role of vice chairman of the board of management) took over for the ailing Dreesmann came as a shock to the company. Within a month there was trouble. A former business unit manager I interviewed described the change as follows: "We used to look forward to our monthly meeting with the CEO. We would catch up on the business with Dreesmann and propose our new acquisition strategies to him. With Van der Zwan, everything changed completely. It was as if there were ice in the room; even his handshake was cold. All our investment plans were cancelled because Van der Zwan thought them not sufficiently backed by facts."

It is difficult to know Van der Zwan's intentions as he entered the company, but he probably intended to organize things his way quickly and prepare Vendex for a stock offering. When he arrived at Vendex, he brought along an outside analyst and secretary. Obviously, he felt that he could rely on only facts collected by people who were not yet part of the establishment.

Van der Zwan chose the department stores as the first object of his scrutiny, thereby aiming at the heart of the company, the flagship on which Anton had built his empire. It was the cash flow from the department stores that had made many of the acquisitions possible. Unfortunately, little had been invested in the stores themselves.

Within one month, Anton realized what was going on. Perhaps he was informed by members of the board of management, perhaps by his American business partners (who immediately got into trouble with Van der Zwan over dividend matters). He tried to get rid of Van der Zwan by informing members of the supervisory board (which in the past had always complied with Anton's wishes) that they should fire him. Like a modern King Lear, however, Anton was forced to see that one cannot give away the office while keeping the power. The supervisory board stuck with Van der Zwan because its members felt that they could not dismiss a person of sterling reputation after their having appointed him only one month earlier. After the June board meeting, Anton must have realized how much power he had already lost. Van der Zwan was in the process of destroying Dreesmann's grand finale in the worst possible way: his actions were showing that Anton had mismanaged the core of his inheritance, the Vroom & Dreesmann department stores.

We may infer that Anton perceived the layoffs at V&D as a personal attack. Whatever other factors may have been involved, the fact remains that the department stores were Anton Dreesmann's emotional Achilles' heel. After all those years of grandiosity, he may have dreaded the possibility that he would be exposed as a failure (thereby proving that Willem had been right all along). Maybe the despair that this caused in him inspired his last appeal to the press, which has a Lear-like madness in it. Or perhaps that statement was a carefully planned action, set up after a visit with his most powerful allies in Brazil and the United States. Whatever the background, the fact is that, as in the story of King Lear, nobody really "survived."

The moral of the tale

The supervisory board can be criticized on two fronts: for not having played a more dominant role in the appointment of Anton's successor and for letting the situation, once Van der Zwan was appointed, get out of hand. As some studies have shown, appointing one's own successor is a process fraught with unconscious conflict.[24] Too many executives selecting a successor are motivated by the hidden wish that the appointee will fail, proving that they themselves are irreplaceable.

When Dreesmann announced the appointment of Van der Zwan as his successor, some Dutch newspapers expressed doubts about the choice.

If the supervisory board had the same doubts, they did not act on them. They should have been alerted to the potential for problems by the fact that Anton had made no effort to build a second layer of top management. But many years of Anton's successful decisions (and perhaps a too-close relationship between Anton and the chairman of the board, Van Driel) had made that board insufficiently effective as a controlling body. The CEO's role as an important shareholder made matters more complicated, but that does not excuse the board.

Why Van der Zwan chose to step into this minefield is not obvious. The dangers he faced were foreshadowed by the Keller incident, but perhaps Van der Zwan's own feelings of grandiosity gave him the idea that he could pull things off despite Anton Dreesmann. Van der Zwan seemed to be good at identifying rational factors while ignoring (or not recognizing) the more elusive emotional issues. He should have known that he was playing with fire in restructuring the department stores. Van der Zwan might have succeeded in downsizing some of the companies in England, the States, or Brazil, but to touch *Anton's* people in *Anton's* stores was another matter altogether. Van der Zwan's assessment that Vendex was not in top financial condition when he took over was correct; but it is also a fact that the departure of discontented managers and the reversal of acquisition plans worsened things. Van der Zwan as the immediate successor was not a good choice.

The idea of an interim leader – someone like Verhoef – for a limited period of time (two years, perhaps) is often a valid solution in cases like this. The organization can then "mourn" the departure of the old leader without having to adapt to a totally new one at the same time. Whether Anton would have accepted this solution is difficult to assess.

From the point of view of planning for continuity in a complex family firm, Anton Dreesmann made many right moves. His opening salvo after the death of his brother Willem was to unite a very diverse group of family members. Explicitly or implicitly he recognized the importance of a family council, and in turn the family members supported him because he offered a vision for the future. While the theme that united the many branches of the family was the planned stock offer – which would mean that they could finally cash in their shares – Anton also created a new pride in the family firm (thereby reinforcing his power base) by making it grow into the darling of the Dutch business community.

Anton Dreesmann also recognized that if the company was to thrive, the existing nepotistic practices had to be jettisoned. Although family pressure to put sons in prominent positions was constant, Dreesmann realized that the price of nepotism was excessively high and that bringing in professional management was essential. As a management professor, he knew very well what makes for a high-performance workplace. Although he did not always "walk the talk" (his grandiosity sometimes got in the way), Anton's management philosophy was instrumental in attracting a large number of highly competent executives to the family firm.

Finally, Anton Dreesmann recognized the value of a strong supervisory board. He realized that family firms in particular need strong sparring partners. The kind of people he selected for the supervisory board show that he was not looking for yea-sayers. The selection of Van Driel, for example, was astute, since he already had experience with a large family-owned firm.

Anton Dreesmann was a man with many angels and many demons in his inner theater. His native intelligence, drive, and charisma enabled him to overcome his feeling of insignificance and won him the top position at the family firm. He was a remarkable and original leader. However, his self-esteem proved to be too closely linked with his position as CEO, and when the time came, he could not let go. This phenomenon is prevalent in family firms where the leader has virtually unlimited control during his or her career. Anton had prepared carefully for a successor. It is unfortunate that his demons controlled the stage in the last act of his career.

Notes

1 P. Fentrop, "Tot mijn ellende is Van der Zwan bezig de hele zaak uit te verkopen" (To my misery Van der Zwan is busy selling out the whole business). *NCR/Handelsblad*, July 30, 1988, p. 1.
2 C. Dreesmann, *De Mandersens* (Amsterdam: de Boekerij, 1988), p. 115.
3 A. Kok, "The Last Tycoon." *Quote*, April 1988, pp. 44–45.
4 D. Kuin and H. Maarsen, "Ik heb 1,000 uur in Van Gend & Loos gestopt" (I put a 1000 hours in Van Gend & Loos), a discussion with Dreesmann III. *Het Financieele Dagblad*, June 18, 1987, p. 13.

5   Interview on VPRO television, The Netherlands, 1987.
6   Kok, "The Last Tycoon," p. 55.
7   H. Kops, A. Van Bergen, and C. Graafsma, "Holle Bolle Gijs: het laatste gevecht van Anton Dreesmann" (The "big gobbler": the last fight of Anton Dreesmann). *Elseviers Magazine*, August 13, 1988, p. 14.
8   Ibid.
9   D. Kuin and H. Maarsen, "Een oesterschelp gaat langzaam open" (An oystershell is opening slowly), a discussion with Dreesmann I. *Het Financieele Dagblad*, June 16, 1987, p. 11.
10 J. Mulder, "De vlucht van Vendex" (The take-off of Vendex). *Elseviers Magazine*, December 20, 1986, p. 34.
11 Ibid., p. 39.
12 Ibid., p. 31.
13 "Keller (ex-Vendex) haalt uit naar Anton Dreesmann" (Keller hits back at Anton Dreesmann). *Het Financieele Dagblad*, August 13, 1988, p. 4.
14 Ibid.
15 This is the way the head office was referred to.
16 Kok, "The Last Tycoon," p. 53.
17 D. Kuin and H. Maarsen, "Vendex wil verder groeien met een nieuwe zon" (Vendex will continue to grow with a new sun), a discussion with Dreesmann IV. *Het Financieele Dagblad*, June 20, 1987, p. 16.
18 Ibid.
19 Ibid.
20 Kuin and Maarsen, "Vendex wil verder groeien," p. 16.
21 P. Fentrop, "Binnen Vendex dreigt machtstrijd tussen families en directie" (Inside Vendex there is the threat of a powerstruggle between the families and management). *NRC/Handelsblad*, July 29, 1988, p. 1.
22 Fentrop, "Tot mijn ellende is Van der Zwan bezig," p. 1.
23 J. Terlingen, "De geheime couppoging van Anton Dreesmann" (The secret takeover attempt of Anton Dreesmann). *Vrij Nederland*, January 4, 1992, pp. 17–19.
24 (Levinson, 1981; Sonnenfeld, 1988; Kets de Vries, 1989).

Managing for continuity
The Bonnier Group

The last case in the book, an overview of the history of the Bonnier Group, is a rare and remarkable example of a hundred-and-ninety-year-old family business that has for six generations been run by the founder's family and recently was turned over to the seventh. In spite of the image of stability the company has projected outwards throughout its existence it had to ride out many storms and was faced with calamity more than once. Today it is thriving again, ready to meet new challenges under the next generation of Bonniers. As a case in point it is an instructive example of the successful management of a family conglomerate.

The case is written from the point of view of Margot Delacroix, a French management consultant whose firm had been asked to do a strategic audit of the company. At the time, for a number of reasons (not the least being the impulsivity of its then president, Abbe, and the Swedish tax system), Bonnier was in possession of a rather mixed portfolio of companies. Something had to be done to rationalize it. Apart from the strategic quandary of the company, the most interesting question presented by the case is how the family managed to stay in business for so many generations. What did they do to make that possible? Were there any (written or unwritten) rules that evolved over the years that facilitated this process? As the reader, try to identify the major factors that contributed to Bonnier's success in planning for continuity.

THE BONNIER GROUP

Albert "Abbe" Bonnier II died in April 1989, at the age of eighty-one. Aware of his imminent death, Abbe had nominated his younger brother, Lukas, to replace him as chairman of the Bonnier Group. His nomination was accepted by the board which was composed mostly of family members, and in January 1989, Lukas, at the age of sixty-six, took over the reins of the family-owned media and industrial conglomerate that in many ways was Abbe's brainchild.

The Bonnier family business was now in the hands of a man who had spent all of his working life in the magazine company and whose spare-time passion was growing roses. At his side was Olle Måberg, who during his thirty-five years of service with the company, had risen from a financial job in the family book publishing house to the Group presidency.

Some three years later, Margot Delacroix, a French management consultant, arrived in Stockholm to conduct preliminary interviews with the Bonnier family and representatives of the Group's management team in preparation for a consulting assignment. Delacroix was intrigued about what she would find. She knew that the Bonnier company was a rarity – a family concern that had survived into its sixth generation when few make it to the third. The questions that occupied her mind were these: How had Bonnier managed the transition process, and was the company going to make it to the seventh generation?

The background information provided to Delacroix by her research department recounted the romantic beginnings of the Bonnier dynasty. The thick folder of clippings and notes made for interesting reading.

The founding of the Bonnier dynasty

Gutkind Hirschel, the cultured son of a prosperous Dresden banker and a French mother, was inspired by the French Revolution to leave home to start a new life in Copenhagen, where he would not be constrained by his Jewish origins. Arriving in 1801, he took the name Gerhard Bonnier – a name possibly inspired by Gerhard's mother, who had worked as a milliner or *bonnetière*. Upon his arrival, Gerhard supported himself by teaching French; later, he opened a bookstore, dabbled in publishing, and briefly produced a newspaper.

Gerhard's three sons, Adolf, Albert, and David, moved to Stockholm, where prospects for a cultured and creative family were deemed better. Adolf imitated his father and opened a bookstore, one that later became a meeting place for the literary establishment; David launched a newspaper; and Albert, in 1837, founded the book publishing house that bears his name and remains the heart of the family business. Albert's success reputedly stemmed from a combination of commercial astuteness and a genuine interest in literature, writers, and the creative process. His authors became his friends and protégés, encouraged and stimulated by him and by subsequent generations of Bonniers. In 1864, Albert made an investment that was to have a significant impact on the Bonnier business dynasty: he assisted a young journalist to found Sweden's first daily morning newspaper – *Dagens Nyheter* ("News of the Day") – modeled on Paris's *Le Petit Journal*. Albert initially took a 5 percent shareholding of what has become Sweden's second largest daily newspaper.

Karl Otto and his sons

At the end of the nineteenth century, Karl Otto, Albert's oldest son, inherited a well-established family business with a prominent place in Sweden's cultural and publishing circles. As the publishers of many Swedish classics (including the works of Nobel laureates), commercial and genealogical directories, and new novels, the company (and its ubiquitous products) promoted the Bonnier name at all levels of Swedish society. In addition, the family was seen as the guiding light behind the prospering *Dagens Nyheter*, having acquired a majority shareholding when Karl Otto took over the chairmanship of the newspaper. (The acquisition of that paper was possible only in return for a pledge not to influence editorial policy, a commitment maintained to the present day.)

Karl Otto had six children: two girls, who (in keeping with the patriarchal tradition of the family) were not expected to play an active role in the business, and four sons, one of whom wished to pursue a scientific career and who, as a consequence, was disinherited, creating resentment among his descendants that lingers to this day. The remaining sons, Tor (the eldest child,) Åke, and Kaj, were trained to take a place in the company and in due course inherited shares. They and their families became known as the "branches," of which the Tor branch, since Tor was the first-born and that branch therefore had the largest shareholding, was the most senior. It was also the most prolific: Tor married three times and had six sons in all, the youngest when Tor was in his sixties. (See Figure C11.1 for a family tree.)

Tor's chairmanship saw another significant acquisition – one on a par with the *Dagens Nyheter* investment. In 1929, Bonnier purchased Sweden's largest magazine publisher, – Åhlén & Åkerlund. Tor recalled his eldest son, Albert II – known as Abbe – from the United States, where he had been undergoing training, to take part in this new venture.

The "loving dictator"

The twenty-two year-old young man who received the summons to return home had been sent to the United States as part of the then time-honored custom of sending young Bonniers overseas to be trained in preparation for a role in the family business. Young Abbe had left high school to learn book publishing with companies in Berlin, Paris, and London, newspaper publishing in Fleet Street, and finally graphics and printing in New York. The latter was included when it became clear that Abbe wanted a career in journalism and newspapers rather than book publishing. Abbe started as purchasing manager at Åhlén & Åkerlund and then moved on to become technical manager. He began to show evidence of an entrepreneurial spirit, taking the initiative in the purchase of other companies with complementary activities. By 1940, when his uncle Åke moved to the United States, Abbe had become president of Åhlén & Åkerlund. In the same year, he was appointed to the *Dagens Nyheter* board.

The Second World War saw Sweden isolated in its neutrality, but for Abbe it was a spur to his commercial and creative drive. Without competition from foreign publications, radio, or TV, the magazine business flourished, introducing new titles, pushing up circulation, and producing massive profits (which Abbe invested in other companies). However, for a prominent family of Jewish origins, success in the media industry during a time of international hostilities was a mixed blessing. Sweden had its share of anti-Semitic elements that questioned the role of the Bonniers in such an important national publication as *Dagens Nyheter*. Abbe's response was forthright: he spoke publicly against fascist regimes and, on one notable occasion, led a large gathering in the singing of patriotic Swedish songs. But his stand could not eliminate all indignities. His brother Johan was forced to quit his job at *Dagens Nyheter*, for example, because one journalist refused to work with him.

By 1953, when Abbe became president and Chief Executive Officer of the Bonnier Group under chairman Tor, the company, based on a rationale of synergy and self-sufficiency, had moved into ink production, printing press manufacture, packaging, paper mills, and shipping. Moreover, the *Dagens Nyheter* company, at Abbe's urging, had launched a sister journal, *Expressen*, a daily evening newspaper that today has the largest circulation in Sweden.

The expansion continued as Abbe, with his reputation for having his finger on the pulse of things, continued his pursuit of commercial adventures during the 1950s and 1960s. He took the company into areas as diverse as the farming of shrimp, the publishing of magazines in Colombia, the production of meat tenderizers and swimming pools, and the importing of televisions. Not all of these activities were profitable, but they fulfilled two aims: they introduced stimulating new ideas for development to reduce the risks Abbe believed the company faced; and they gave the opportunity, through legitimate tax minimization schemes, for family members to enhance their revenue and protect their capital base – a major consideration in social democratic Sweden, with its high tax rates. A further consideration was the threat in 1968 of state investigations into the concentration of media ownership. The Bonnier Group was made to understand that its activities should be modified, forcing the divestment of some of the company's media interests. In this climate, the expansion of the company's industrial divisions was politically more acceptable.

Because of Abbe's past success, enthusiasm, drive, and force of personality he rarely encountered strong opposition to any of his ideas, and his dominance does not appear to have been generally resented among family members and staff. Looking back on their time working with Abbe, many of them recall the inspirational excitement that he engendered. His younger brother Lukas refers to him as the "loving dictator," a judgment that others share.

While Abbe was building a career in magazines and new ventures, his cousin Gerard, only child of Åke, was being trained in book publishing. Born in 1917, Gerard was drawn by temperament and inclination toward literature and the arts. From the time he left high school until his death, he worked happily in the family book firm (initially under his uncle Kaj), where he indulged his love of poetry and relished the contact with Sweden's leading authors. He became president of the book company in 1953, going on to create his own domain, which contrasted with Abbe's industrial and media interests. This, according to Abbe's younger daughter, Jeanette, became a source for "a lot of disagreements in my father's

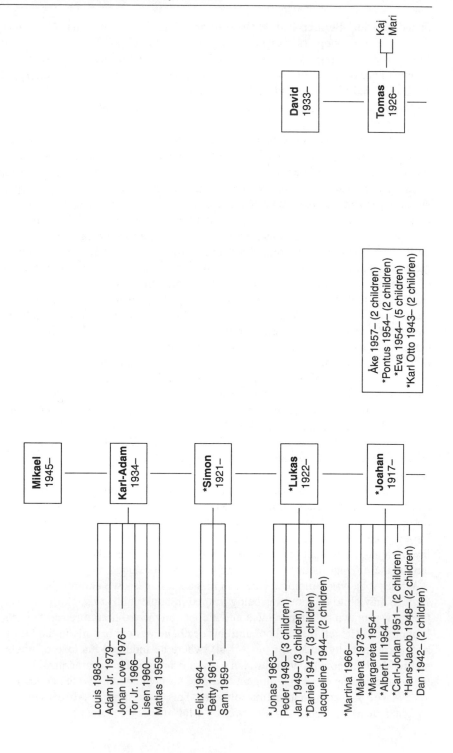

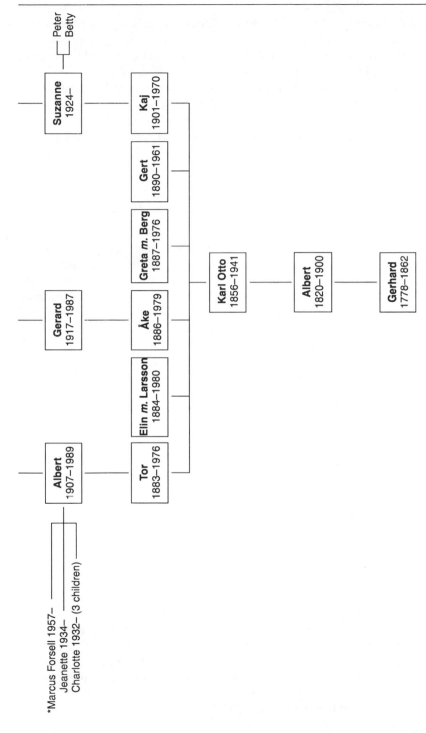

Figure C11.1 The Bonnier family tree. * designate now active in the company

time, unlike today, when the younger generation realize it is important to stick together and not to quarrel."

Gerard is seen as the member of his generation who continued the Bonnier tradition of patronage of artists and writers, his love of modern art being evidenced by the abundance of artworks in all the Bonnier buildings. It was under Gerard's presidency that the book company, under financial pressure, moved into book clubs as a way of selling its publications, a highly successful move both in Sweden and later in other Scandinavian countries. Today Bonnier is a dominant force in book-club marketing, achieving 70 percent of its book sales through this outlet.

Flotation of *Dagens Nyheter* and *Expressen*: Marieberg

The year 1953 was a milestone in ways other than the elevation of Abbe and Gerard to their respective presidencies. This was also the year when the shareholdings in the business passed from the fourth to the fifth generation and when Kaj, in dispute with Tor over strategy, decided that he wanted to sell his interest in the company. This was achieved by launching a new company, Marieberg, that became owner of *Dagens Nyheter* and *Expressen* and was floated on the Stockholm exchange. Shares in Marieberg were held by the Bonnier Group (through the Group's holding company, Bonnierföretagen), Boninvest (the family equity investment company), and Deni (a private investment partnership specifically created to hold shares in Marieberg for Bonnier family members), as well as new subscribing shareholders. A complex series of share transfers left the Kaj branch with cash and a substantial holding in Deni but no interest in the Bonnier Group.

After the transaction, the Åke and Tor branches were free to pass on their increased holdings in the Bonnier Group. For Åke, there was little difficulty; he had one son and, at that time, two grandchildren. For Tor, however, matters were not so straightforward. Six sons by three wives and nine grandchildren (with probably more to follow) created a difficult inheritance with long-term implications. He had previously decided, however, that his three oldest sons, who worked in the business, should inherit his Bonnier shares and that his younger sons would be provided for by other interests.

The "Agreement" and the family board

The senior family members of all branches realized that this was a problem later generations would probably be confronted with repeatedly. They decided that some generally accepted rules were required to avoid future disputes over inheritance. This led to the "Agreement," a written document with the fundamental objective of retaining family control and management of the company: it set out basic principles concerning the sale or transfer of shares between family members (see Figure C11.2).

The Agreement has the fundamental objective of retaining family control and management of the Bonnier Group. The key elements of the Agreement are listed below:

1 Instigated: 1959
  Valid to: 2000
  Modified: 1960, 1983, 1987, 1990.
2 Sales between brothers and sisters are valued by the buyer and seller and are relatively unconstrained, as are sales between cousins in the same family branch.
3 Sales between branches have limits placed on them.
4 Sales made back to the company are valued at a low rate so as to discourage this type of transaction.
5 If an owner wants to sell but cannot find a buyer in the immediate branch, he or she is obliged to sell to all other owners in proportion to their stake and at the company's price.
6 Bonnier spouses are excluded from inheriting shares because of the expectation that the children are the rightful long-term beneficiaries.

Figure C11.2 Key elements of the "Agreement"

The importance of the Agreement for the family can be judged by the impact of the occasional breach of the letter or spirit of its conditions. Such breaches continue to provoke discussions on the relevance and effectiveness of the Agreement and the merits of modifying it. A continuous debate about modifications is conducted among the family members at all levels but is addressed in detail by the family board. The idea of a kind of family council was conceived in the 1950s. Indeed, the original Agreement provided for the establishment of a council on which any family member could sit, provided that person was at least twenty-five years old and had worked at least five years in the company. The provision was not immediately put into practice, however. In the early 1980s the idea was resurrected and debated; in 1987, after Gerard (who died that year), Abbe, Johan, and Lukas completed the transfer of their shares to the sixth generation, it became reality. Today, the family board includes Pontus (chairman), Jeanette, Carl-Johan, Hans-Jacob, and Daniel, all of whom were elected by the Bonnier owners to the holding partnership board that controls the Bonnier Group. Johan and Lukas are honorary members of the Board; Olle Måberg is its only non-family member (see Figure C11.3 for a schematic overview of shareholdings in Bonnier sphere companies).

Olle Måberg

In reading the annual reports and the background information provided by the research department, Delacroix had noted the trend toward divestment of the

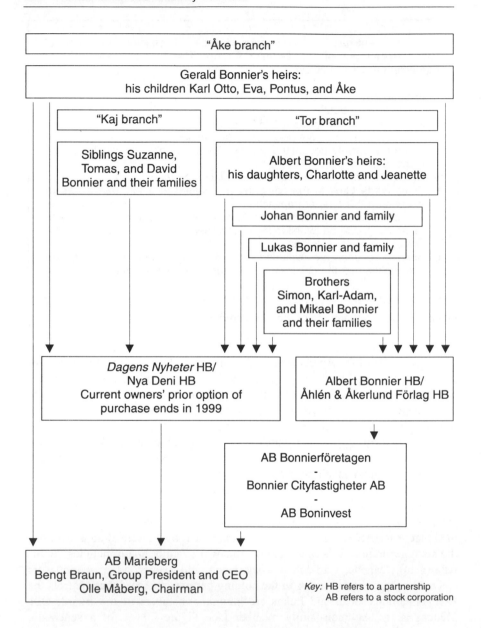

Figure C11.3 Schematic of shareholdings in Bonnier companies

industrial divisions and the trading of industrial interests for media holdings (see Figure C11.4 and C11.5 for a summary of the Bonnier Group activities and an overview of the company's organization and ownership). This trend had its roots in the difficult and costly 1987 acquisition of additional holdings in two printing and packaging companies that had previously been divisions of the Bonnier Group (divisions that had been floated on the Stockholm exchange in 1977). The difficult acquisition experience finally convinced Abbe, who in previous annual reports had spoken glowingly of the potential of the industrial divisions, that the time for change was at hand. The problems associated with the acquisition accelerated a rethinking of the corporate strategy – a strategy that focused increasingly on the media industry, particularly on international expansion.

Arriving from the Stockholm airport to meet Olle Måberg at his office in 1992, Delacroix was struck by the originality of the modern complex of buildings that housed the Bonnier headquarters and some of its divisions. She was not surprised to learn later that its conception had been the subject of a prestigious architectural competition in the 1940s. Dominated by a high-rise tower carrying the distinctive B of the Bonnier logo, the buildings seemed to symbolize the energy, creativity, and self-confidence of the company at that time.

Ushered into Måberg's office, Delacroix found a man in his late fifties, who was polite and slightly ponderous when speaking English. Prompted by questions from Delacroix, Måberg described some of the history of the Bonnier Group and the highlights of his professional experience within it. Joining the book company in 1956, he rose to become its president in 1974, complementing chairman Gerard Bonnier's artistic predilection with his own financial expertise. Måberg mentioned two turning points in his career with Bonnier. The first, during the sixties, occurred when the book company faced bankruptcy. He himself was at the center of the rescue plan that required a dramatic and in many ways traumatic reorganization. For Olle Måberg, this crisis was, according to one family member, "his breakthrough in the group." The other major event was part of an attempt at internationalization on the part of the book company. A joint venture was formed to found a book club in the United Kingdom – a venture that eventually failed, leaving Bonnier with a disastrous loss. By 1990, however, the company was market leader again, with a third of the Swedish market.

In 1979, when Abbe had stepped from the presidency of the Group to its chairmanship, he had decided to replace himself with two men who would alternate every two years between the posts of president and vice president. Olle Måberg was one of the two, and when his alter ego resigned in dissatisfaction over the arrangement, he took on the presidency full time. From this base, he subsequently adopted other influential positions in the different Bonnier companies, acquiring considerable standing in the commercial world of Sweden. Delacroix was intrigued about how a non-family member could have risen that high, what motivated him to stay, and how he managed to maintain the delicate balance between the various siblings, aunts, uncles, and cousins. Indeed, she later heard one family member half-jokingly refer to Måberg as "the man who

Division	Activity	Invoice sales SKr M		Profit after net financial items SKr M		% returns on total assets		Comments
		89	90	89	90	89	90	
Book	Book publishing, book and music clubs, business information services, and stationery products.	1,134	1,441	975	993	16	15	This division accounts for a third of Swedish book sales, a sixth of new titles in a stagnant market. It was restructured in 1991 into 2 companies – one containing small publishing houses, the other given the original name of Albert Bonnier Förlag (and intended to be the powerhouse of old).
Bonnier Publications	Scandinavia's largest publisher of special-interest and monthly magazines, reference books, and handbooks; book club.	899	991	110	118	22	24	In 1990, all the magazine interests were brought together under Erik Skipper Larsen, president of Bonnier Publications in Denmark. Nordification of the Swedish special-interest magazines is intended to extend their markets to Norway, Denmark, and Finland. Publications Bonnier in France will be a beachhead for expansion into the rest of Europe.
Bonnier Business Press	Business periodicals, trade press, and information services (printed and electrical).	737	897	87	100	22	21	Most periodicals are market leaders but were affected by the advertising downturn. Information services were the main source of expansion.
Semic International	Publishing, manufacture of entertainment products for the young (comics and magazines). A key product is the Phantom comic based on a US model from 1950.	680	741	39	30	11	10	This division has suffered from a decline in comic books in Nordic markets over two years due to competition from other media. Eastern Europe is targeted for growth, and investment focuses on teenage magazines.
Film	Cinema chain, video and film distribution, TV channels (part owner), and film production.	844	749	42	–56	16	0	Video and cinema attendance declined sharply when the state TV monopoly was broken up and private channels were introduced. Operating margins were reduced by weak film launches and losses incurred on Swedish-language productions. Restructuring is expected to continue in the Scandinavian film industry.

Note: SKr M = million Swedish Kronor

Publications Bonnier	Special-interest magazines in France: *Mon Jardin et Ma Maison*, *Le Journal de la Maison*, *Maison Bricolages*, *Saveurs*.	147	175	-2	-5	0	0	This group experienced losses due to weak advertising market, the launch of *Saveurs*, and excessive costs arising from switching to the until-further-notice Scandinavian-style subscription system.
Åhlen & Åkerlund Förlag	Publisher of 8 general popular magazines (3 weekly, 3 monthly, and 2 quarterly), including Sweden's largest circulation family magazine, *Året Runt*; operator of Sweden's largest advertising sales company, Annons Bolaget.	508	598	3	-28	–	0	1990 was a year when a new company was formed to offer journalistic and editorial consultancy services to Bonnier Publications. Å & Å was restructured, which led to the formation of the Bonnier Media University to signal commitment to the media industry as well as to provide training for Bonnier staff.
Furniture Gp.	Manufacturer of furniture and components, particularly made of polyurethane.	614	578	37	50	14	18	This division has a stable volume and profit forecast.
Medical Gp.	Manufacturer of kits for diagnostic blood testing (since most other medical interests were divested in 1989).	33	38	0	0	23	15	R&D is the focus of this division. Germany remained the largest market.
Dental Gp.	Marketer and distributor of high-volume medical supplies to dentists.	553	339	4	-6	–	0	This division has six subsidiaries in Denmark, Norway, Great Britain, the US, and France. The latter two were divested during 1990, converting operating loss into a profit of SKr 2 M.
Bonnier Technology	Manufacturer of capital equipment, mainly for the pulp and paper industry.	490	465	73	55	20	15	The Bonnier Technology Group was sold in 1991.
Data Group Auriga	Leading Swedish company in automated data network retrieval source from paper-based documents (e.g., tax returns, credit card slips).	183	92	6	-3	–	0	Developments in paperless transaction analysis are the focus of this division.
Press Data (75% interest)	Subscription service for publishing companies.	98	38	17	9	–	–	Associated companies include Marieberg, Grafton, Idab, Pressens, Samdistribution, Priab, Publishers Equipment Co., and Stroede.

Figure C11.4 Summary of Bonnier group activities

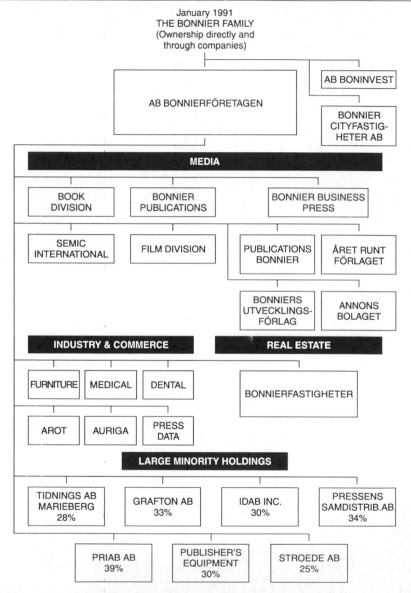

January 1991
THE BONNIER FAMILY
(Ownership directly and
through companies)

AB BONNIERFÖRETAGEN

AB BONINVEST

BONNIER
CITYFASTIG-
HETER AB

MEDIA

BOOK
DIVISION

BONNIER
PUBLICATIONS

BONNIER BUSINESS
PRESS

SEMIC
INTERNATIONAL

FILM DIVISION

PUBLICATIONS
BONNIER

ÅRET RUNT
FÖRLAGET

BONNIERS
UTVECKLINGS-
FÖRLAG

ANNONS
BOLAGET

INDUSTRY & COMMERCE

REAL ESTATE

FURNITURE | MEDICAL | DENTAL

BONNIERFASTIGHETER

AROT | AURIGA | PRESS
DATA

LARGE MINORITY HOLDINGS

TIDNINGS AB
MARIEBERG
28%

GRAFTON AB
33%

IDAB INC.
30%

PRESSENS
SAMDISTRIB.AB
34%

PRIAB AB
39%

PUBLISHER'S
EQUIPMENT
30%

STROEDE AB
25%

Notes:
Bonnier Cityfastigheter: Property company not consolidated in the Bonnier Group but controlling the Bonnier Group family property portfolio. Market value of property: SKr 1.225M.

Boninvest: Investment company of the Bonnier family which owns and manages the Bonnier Sphere's listed share holdings. Market value at end of 1990, SKr 439M. Boninvest is not consolidated in the Bonnier Group.

Source: The Bonnier Group 1990 annual report.

Figure C11.5 Company organization

could play the family like a piano," a talent that Måberg had tacitly acknowledged in an interview on Swedish television a few years previously, when he said that he worked for a very Swedish company "with fifty-six problems -- nine divisions and forty-seven owners!" This remark reminded Delacroix of the family's current rapid growth (compared with the previous generation), and she wondered about the implications.

The Åke Branch

Inquiring from Måberg about the evolution of the various family branches, Delacroix discovered that the Kaj branch had withdrawn from Bonnier Group activities and now concentrated its interests in the Marieberg company. In the Åke branch, only one of Gerard's children had not entered the family business, dedicating his life to the priesthood instead. The other children, Karl Otto, Eva, and Pontus, had all found positions in the company. Eva had come on board a little later than the others: influenced by the radical movements of the 1960s, she had initially spurned a role in the family business, preferring to train in social work and marrying young to start a family. She eventually joined the book company, however, and rose to become a publisher, carrying on her father's tradition of developing and nurturing writers. Her brother, Karl Otto, also inherited his father's love of literature and the arts and joined the book company after university, to also work in publishing. A reserved man, comfortable in the book publishing world, Karl Otto had expressed no ambition to take on a greater executive role in the management of the Bonnier Group: now, however, he sits on various Bonnier boards. (When Delacroix later met Karl Otto, he reminded her of a professor, an impression reinforced by the rather cloistered atmosphere of the book publishing house on Sveavägen.) In contrast to his siblings, Pontus Bonnier pursued a more business-oriented training and career. After studying at the Stockholm School of Economics, he joined a major Swedish industrial company as a financial controller. Returning to the family business six years later to use his financial expertise in strategic and investment roles for the company, he also took on the mantle of champion for the Åke branch. This was a natural development, given that he was the largest individual shareholder in Bonnier and (by virtue of his presence on many Bonnier boards) held a position of considerable influence. By 1990, he had become president of Boninvest, the family investment company.

The Tor Branch

The Tor branch enjoyed none of the simple coherence of the Åke branch. From the 1950s on, Tor's sons, grandchildren, and great-grandchildren gradually came into their inheritance (which inevitably, had become increasingly reduced in individual terms as it was passed down through the generations). About half of Tor's descendants achieved executive roles in the company, creating a network of brothers, uncles, and cousins with a broad spectrum of responsibilities. Tor's son

Lukas, for example, the magazine specialist, rose to the highest position in the Bonnier Group. A man with an informal air (Delacroix never saw him wear a tie or jacket), Lukas adopted a more consensual approach to the management of the company than Abbe's "loving dictatorship." He was expected to retire later in the year of her visit, when he reached the age of seventy. Another of Tor's sons, Johan, who was long the self-acknowledged playboy of the family, now sits on many boards of the Bonnier Group (and of other organizations where Bonniers have interests), acting as an elder statesman and taking a strategic view of the company's development. Trained as a journalist, Johan started his own clothing and retail business. When it eventually failed, it was taken over in part by the Bonnier Group. Tor's son Simon also took an active role in the company, serving as the US-based "foreign ambassador" for the industrial divisions.

Many of Tor's grandchildren, Måberg explained to Delacroix, had been taken on by the company, forming a disparate group of people of differing ages, aspirations, and ambitions. For example, Charlotte and Jeanette, Abbe's daughters, had seniority in terms of age, but their executive role was minimal (limited to serving on various boards and monitoring the activities of their cousins, who had charge of the day-to-day operations). Carl-Johan and his brother Hans-Jacob, both sons from Johan's third marriage, were by contrast heavily involved in the company's management. Carl-Johan, another graduate of the Stockholm School of Economics, joined Bonnier at graduation, training in executive roles in various divisions and later becoming executive vice-president of the Bonnier Group, reporting to Måberg. Hans-Jacob was vice-president in the business press division.

Måberg went on to refer to other grandchildren and great-grandchildren of Tor's: Daniel, Lukas's son, the *Francophile* who was running Publications Bonnier in Paris, publishing four French-language special-interest magazines; Jonas, Daniel's younger brother, who was an author and the editor of a book-club magazine; the twins, Margareta and Albert III, who were respectively an architect/interior designer with the Bonnier property company and the editor of "Facts Books"; Marcus Forsell (Charlotte's son), who was president of a video distribution subsidiary. These and other cousins, collectively and individually, were the human stock that would carry on the Bonnier tradition, irrespective of their particular branch.

Returning to the subject of his own career and his rise in the company, Måberg offered a simple reply: "I don't know what Abbe liked about me, but he knew that I was loyal to the family and to himself; we had the same goals and culture. He was fantastic and brilliant; he loved new products and people. His maternal grandparents were actors, and he was a showman. When we were alone together, I would have to remind him that there were only two of us in the room."

Commenting on his relations with some of the younger generation, Måberg was thoughtful: "I've observed them for many years. I met Carl-Johan, for instance, because he was in the family and we had business together when he was one of the divisional heads. It was I – not Abbe, not the family – who brought him into the company as vice president, although often it's their parents who want them to join. Hans-Jacob, on the other hand, came to work for me as my personal assistant after working in Paris and then heading up the Norwegian operations of Duni, a Bonnier paper products company. I suggested to Abbe that Hans-Jacob was the most media-minded of the younger generation, and now he's one of a team of three in the business press management. I had a discussion with Pontus in 1978 in which I suggested that he would be best advised to first make a career for himself outside, which he did, and he then joined the company in 1983" (See Figure C11.6 for a list of Bonnier family members with executive roles in the Bonnier Group.)

Meeting the family

As the interviews unfolded, Delacroix began to mentally categorize the people she was meeting. For simplicity, on her return to Paris she intended to describe to

---

AB Bonnierföretagen (holding company)
- Lukas Bonnier, chairman
- Carl-Johan Bonnier, executive vice president

Boninvest
- Pontus Bonnier, president

Bonnier Cityfastigheter
- Margareta Bonnier, interior designer

Book Division
- Karl Otto Bonnier, vice president and publisher
- Eva Bonnier, publisher
- Albert Bonnier III, editor, Facts Books
- Jonas Bonnier, editor, book-club magazine

Bonnier Publications
- Betty Bonnier, marketing director, special-interest magazines, Sweden
- Martina Bonnier, fashion editor, Damernas Värld

Bonnier Business Press
- Hans-Jacob Bonnier, vice president, international division

Film Division
- Marcus Forsell, president, video subsidiary

Publications Bonnier
- Daniel Bonnier, president

Figure C11.6 Bonnier family members with executive roles in the Bonnier Group

her colleague, Paul Dupré (who was leading the Bonnier consultancy) the two groups of family members that seemed to emerge: the *éminences grises* (those exerting power only unofficially) and the *éminences blondes*. The first were Abbe's daughters, those of Tor's surviving sons who had retired from active management in the firm, and those of Tor's surviving sons who had never been in executive roles; they acted as elders, mentors, and confidants to the younger generation. The second group consisted of next-generation cousins with executive roles in the business.

Hans-Jacob Bonnier

Delacroix's first meeting was with Hans-Jacob, the son of Abbe's younger brother Johan (and one of the *éminences blondes*). A member of the board of the Bonnier Group, he gave Delacroix the impression of being a person who reflects carefully before speaking in a low-key way. Hans-Jacob explained to Delacroix the prime Bonnier strategy for entering new media markets: simply stated, this involved finding a local partner who had compatible expertise, good local contacts, and possibly a distribution set-up and financing. If these requirements were satisfied, Bonnier would introduce its product or concept. As evidence of the success of this tactic, Hans-Jacob referred to two recent ventures that seemed to be solid but still had to be proven successful. He also expressed his conviction that Bonnier was right to build on its main strength – 150 years of publishing. Hans-Jacob had no concept of how Abbe had intended to finance a family-owned diversified conglomerate, although he said that he agreed with the rationale of spreading risks, which he felt could be achieved without venturing outside the broad media sphere.

Hans-Jacob remembered his uncle Abbe as the mentor who brought him into the business, noting that the attention that he and his male cousins in his family branch received was probably due to Abbe's not having a son himself. For Hans-Jacob, Abbe was a "serious" man with a strong sense of family obligation: a man who led and dominated his generation of Bonniers; a revolutionary. In fact, Hans-Jacob detected a general theme in the development of the family: different generations were either revolutionary or evolutionary, with one type following the other. The revolutionaries were entrepreneurial and lived through a period of rapid change with "fights behind closed doors," whereas the evolutionaries were consolidators, building on the work of the previous generation. In these terms, Abbe's generation was clearly revolutionary and, if Hans-Jacob's theory holds, his own will be evolutionary.

Hans-Jacob's non-confrontational approach struck Delacroix as well suited for a creative business in Sweden's egalitarian society. In fact, with only a few exceptions, Delacroix found this low-key, held-back manner to be a Bonnier (or perhaps a Swedish) trait.

Charlotte Bonnier

Delacroix's next interviewee – Abbe's oldest daughter, Charlotte – was one of these exceptions. Charlotte, now in her fifties, always seemed prepared to speak her mind. This tendency probably developed during her professional career at the magazine company (where she rose to become editor of the leading women's magazine, *Husmodern*) and was reinforced by long-term residence in New York. From what Delacroix had heard about Abbe, she saw in Charlotte some of the characteristics that he must have possessed: energy, restlessness, and dynamism. When asked about her father and the issue of succession, Charlotte replied, "My father had fantasy, creativity, and an adventurous spirit – everything that's needed to lead the Bonnier Group, today as well as yesterday. He built up the company and, whatever they say today, some of it was very successful and kept the family together. If we can't find somebody in the younger generation to do the same thing, then we should get someone from outside who can make us the most money."

Delacroix learned that Charlotte was disappointed that the industrial divisions could not be retained but had apparently come to accept that circumstances dictated their disposal. Charlotte felt that lack of effort in finding the right management rather than lack of family interest was the cause: "It's much easier to have an opinion about the newspapers and movies."

Jeanette Bonnier

Charlotte's younger sister, Jeanette, trained as a journalist after leaving high school, and for a time she ran the Bonnier department store in Manhattan as well as an art gallery. From the early 1980s, on she chose to concentrate on her directorships on several Bonnier company boards. Described by one of her cousins as someone who has good business sense, she was an active member of the family board, which met "to discuss problems in the business about five times a year." Given her background in and passion for the film business, she saw as one of the firm's main problems the lack of a "definite philosophy and decisiveness": she saw these characteristics as necessary to clear away the "loss-making small businesses and get a firmer control," thereby enabling the strategy of converting to a purely media-oriented company to be successfully implemented. She too was anxious about who from among the next generation should take over, noting that she had a strong preference for a family member rather than "someone from outside."

Delacroix found Jeanette slightly less forthright than her sister, though interested in discussing some of the personal issues facing women in family companies. She was enthusiastic about the advantages of working for a family firm, with "its freedom to act, informality, and fast decisions – a fun place to work that inspires commitment and a sense of belonging if you have a strong owner." She recognized, however, that family dominance can deter able people from making a career in such a company – particularly one such as Bonnier, which relies on creativity and a degree of artistic independence. Being a Bonnier meant, for Jeanette, "that the minute you're born you have something to work for, although being a woman means having a tough time wherever you are."

Lukas Bonnier

The next person Delacroix interviewed was Lukas Bonnier, chairman of the Bonnier Group. A magazine enthusiast all his working life, Lukas was instrumental in introducing a string of new publications over the years. These either originated in Scandinavian markets to suit local tastes or were adaptations of foreign (often US) ideas. Bonnier was now attempting to introduce its own products in a number of European countries or, as Lukas said, "doing successfully what Bonnier is good at – finding niches in the media field." Lukas believed this approach to be in keeping with his objective to create a pan-European media company with the same publications and products reproduced in many countries.

Lukas said that he was anxious to "keep the family together, to keep the flame alight for the next generation." To help that generation, he drafted what he called an "Owners' Philosophy," a document that set out the Bonniers' "liberal philosophy, tolerance and honesty, our preference for natural growth rather than acquisitions." This benign outlook extended to continuing Abbe's tradition of giving family members a place in the company if they want one, but Lukas did not expect to fill every key position with a Bonnier: "A degree of ruthlessness has to be accepted to keep the not-so-good apples from the pie."

Eva Bonnier

Eva Bonnier, Gerard's only daughter (whose stated personal ambition was to be "a very good publisher to carry on my father's inheritance") was Delacroix's next interviewee. She struck Delacroix as a sympathetic person with whom authors, both established and emerging, would probably develop an easy rapport. Her professional development took her from being a reader of children's books to the role of senior publisher at the time of the interview; on the way, she created Eva Bonnier publications, a specialist publishing house for women's publications. Very conscious herself of the role of women in society and business, and particularly in a renowned family firm, Eva said, "I was glad to lose the Bonnier name when I married; it made me a normal person." She reverted to the Bonnier name on her divorce, however, feeling closer to the family and its traditions when she occupied a place in the business. With hindsight, she was somewhat annoyed that opportunities in the family firm were deemed to be for males only, but she accepted the fact that if her only daughter eventually wants to work in the Bonnier organization, a university training and talent will be prerequisites in the changing Bonnier environment.

Eva was concerned about many issues not yet addressed by the company: "a company that has changed so much since the death of Abbe and my father, who, despite a sometimes difficult relationship (when Abbe's projects lost money) worked together to support the book company when it was in difficulty." She happily supported the move towards specialization in media provided the remodeled company focused on being "the best in Sweden first." Despite being a major owner through her shareholding and that of her children, Eva did not actively participate in discussions about the strategic orientation of the company (her brother Pontus, Delacroix's next interviewee, fulfilling that role for her branch).

Pontus Bonnier

Given Pontus's training and his role in the company and in family affairs (as chairman of the family board), Delacroix's conversation with him focused on the financial and strategic aspects of the Bonnier Group's plans. Pontus's concerns centered around the "uncertainty and confusion" in the company – an organization that he was nevertheless proud to describe as "having a face in a rather faceless Swedish society." He said, though, that he would like to see a more rigorous attempt at resolving problems quickly: "We haven't been that tough." He suggested that the creation of a small group of directors from among the holding company board would speed up the decision-making process.

The strategy to concentrate on the media had Pontus' full support, but he believed the re-orientation needed to be done in a considered and pragmatic way. Prices for industrial companies had fallen, and the divestment of Bonnier's industrial assets at poor prices could result in insufficient equity finance for the media divisions. Pontus also wondered, in anticipating the longer term, whether the book and business press divisions would continue to provide the cash flow needed to fund new ventures. Like Hans-Jacob, Pontus never understood how Abbe, someone he remembered with affection (but "not as a mentor, as he was for, say, Hans-Jacob"), intended to ensure the long-term financing of an industrial, media, and property conglomerate.

Simon Bonnier

Among the *éminences grises* Delacroix included Simon Bonnier, despite his residence in the United States. Simon had trained in agriculture, and Delacroix sensed that this had given him a down-to-earth pragmatism in his business career – a career that had begun at Bonnier nearly forty years earlier when Abbe had offered him a job in South America. "Being close to Abbe was a lot of fun," said Simon. He recalled his half-brother with affection, ascribing to him much of the success of Bonnier since the Second World War: "What we did right is obvious – we're still here! But the cash we made in the 1950s and 1960s was only short-term wealth. We did things for tax reasons – shipping instead of paying taxes and building wealth on the balance sheet. Also, Abbe believed we should internationalize the company, but that wasn't possible through the publications business with its small language base, so we went into industrial activities."

Johan Bonnier

Johan Bonnier, Abbe's younger brother, was the only family member whom Delacroix met at home. He was living with his fourth wife and young daughter in the family mansion, *Nedre Manilla* ("Gunpowder House"), overlooking Stockholm harbor. Johan's family shared the house with Jytte, Tor's third wife, who occasionally lived in the apartment above the family art gallery – a suite of rooms that housed an impressive display of Swedish artists, particularly portraits of famous Swedish writers whose work the company had published.

To some extent, Johan shared Charlotte's reservations about the plans to concentrate exclusively on the media at the expense of the industrial divisions. He would have preferred to see the maintenance of the broad fifty-fifty split envisaged by Abbe, with a third of the revenue being generated in Sweden and the rest overseas. With his seniority and knowledge of the labyrinthine interests of the Bonnier family, Johan noted that he was eager to fulfill the role of elder to the younger generation, an arrangement that he wanted to formalize in the shape of a council of elders to advise the holding company board and the family board. This council, which would consist of distinguished business leaders and academics known to Johan, would (as one of its principal functions) guide and support the new chairman of the Bonnier Group in times of transition.

After her meeting with Johan Bonnier, Delacroix left the senior members of Abbe's generation in anticipation of meeting some more of Abbe's descendants, but she went to talk to his only grandson first.

Marcus Forsell

Delacroix's interview with Charlotte's son, Marcus, was in sharp contrast to her discussions with Johan Bonnier. One of the youngest of the new generation working in the company, Marcus was a film and business graduate of New York University and a former intern at *The New York Times*. He returned to Sweden upon Abbe's urging "to grow up and make a choice before the barriers were too great. My grandfather was pleased I returned." Marcus remarked that he was proud of his Bonnier heritage: "It's easy for a child to feel secure with such a lineage; belonging to this family gives me a sense of mission." He commented that he was ambitious for the company and wanted to play his part in the new strategy, despite his frustration when his ideas did not get an airing: "Carl-Johan should listen more to the dynamic elements in the family."

Marcus acknowledged to Delacroix that he still had to prove himself – he was, after all, only in his thirties – and that he might be considered brash and impulsive. (Delacroix later described him to Dupré as a young man in a hurry, but she did not doubt that he had inherited some of Abbe's drive and determination – traits that the Bonnier company could profitably employ.) Indeed, Marcus claimed some success already, having increased the market share of the video distribution subsidiary from 18 percent to 34 percent. Some of his ideas that he described to Delacroix – the creation of a radio station in the newly liberalized Swedish broadcasting market, for example – seemed at first sight to fit logically with the overall Bonnier strategy.

Karl Otto

Of Abbe's other descendants, Delacroix first met Gerard's oldest son, Karl Otto – Abbe's first cousin once removed – and a further contrast became immediately apparent to her. A self-styled "peaceable man," Karl Otto recounted his views of the Bonnier Group and its future in a self-effacing way, seeking no new role for himself in this period of transition: "I would be wrong for president, and I wonder whether even the best family member is necessarily the right person for the job."

Daniel Bonnier

Delacroix interviewed Daniel Bonnier, Lukas's son, on the run; he was leaving to get a plane to Paris. After graduating in economics from Stockholm University, Daniel had worked in merchandising for three years at Semic, the comics division of the Bonnier Group. Later, to broaden his experience, he left Bonnier and went to the United States to work in advertising and research at *Business Week* magazine, although he was called back to Paris in 1975 to take on a temporary assignment with Bonnier in the acquisition and transitional management of a small magazine. Because he and his family grew to like the French way of life, they decided to stay.

Reporting directly to his father (Lukas), Daniel was at the time of the interview president of Publications Bonnier, a magazine company that issued four monthly French-language publications specializing in household and cuisine topics. Delacroix understood from their conversation that it was important for Daniel to demonstrate to the Bonnier Group that his subsidiary could operate autonomously from within a market rather than transferring existing titles from Scandinavia. Bonnier Publications, for example – a company separate from Publications Bonnier – had its headquarters in Copenhagen, but it marketed two magazines in France independent of the French subsidiary, because, in Daniel's word, "there is no synergy".

Although physically remote from the center of the family business, Daniel seemed to be aware of recent developments. He mentioned to Delacroix that he had been giving much thought to the prospect of his father's expected retirement and the choice of his successor.

Carl-Johan Bonnier

Delacroix had her final interview with Johan Bonnier's son Carl-Johan, who, as the executive vice president of the Bonnier Group, occupied the most senior position held by a member of the younger generation. Delacroix was in no doubt that Carl-Johan, at forty-one, was a rising star at Bonnier; this much had become apparent during her previous interviews. He was the most likely candidate for president. However, she needed to clarify his exact role and intended future responsibilities.

Carl-Johan explained that he saw himself as the deal-maker in the restructuring process and in organizational and management development, preparing the company for its new future. The daily operations and strategic review of the company were in the hands of Olle Måberg, someone with whom Carl-Johan said he had a "good relationship" (although he did not see Måberg as a mentor). Along with a small group of top executive officers, he and Måberg were members of the recently formed executive board, set up to provide an operational counter-balance to the non-executive board and the family group.

Carl-Johan's ongoing observation of the European media industry had convinced him that Bonnier should aim to "remain the dominant media company in the Nordic countries while exploiting niche opportunities in the rest of Europe." He added the following: "There are very few acquisitions where we would gain; there are not many strategic options open to us. We don't have the financial strength to do a lot of things. We've spent 1 billion kronor on the restructuring and closure of our printing press business and another 1 billion kronor on buying stock in Marieberg, a long-term strategic investment."

Giving more detail on the strategy of re-focusing on the media industry, Carl-Johan cautioned Delacroix against seeing the process as simply one of raising cash quickly through the divestment of all industrial holdings for instant reinvestment in the media. There were industrial activities strategically ready for divestment and others where a sale would be made only if the price were right. There were also industrial companies that could be retained and might even merit further investment. In other words, he said, the re-focusing strategy was being implemented through a rationale of opportunism, strategic priorities, and financial constraints. Carl-Johan was sanguine about this approach; he expected the family company "to still be here in 150 years. We're in no hurry. The only thing we can't do is speculate whether we should keep the company or not."

Commenting on his own rise in the company, Carl-Johan compared how his generation had been trained and integrated into the family firm with the generation of Abbe, Lukas, Johan, and Gerard: "The older generation worked as family company managers from the beginning of their careers, whereas my generation started in the company as ordinary people and had to work their way up. I always knew that even though I was an owner, I had a boss who could sack me. I'm more interested in managers choosing someone because of his or her abilities; because of our professional approach, managers can see the possibilities of hiring a family member. There are no written rules or formal selection processes (for bringing the younger generation into the business), and the reason I'm executive vice president today is because of my own abilities. I may have been observed, but it wasn't a formal process."

After her meeting with Carl-Johan, Delacroix felt that she had met enough family members with a key role in or influence over the company to give her a flavor of its history, current status, and future plans. Olle Måberg suggested, however, that certain non-family senior executives – some with long tenure in the company – would also be worth talking to, and Delacroix agreed.

Meeting the non-family executives

Torsten Ekström

Torsten Ekström, described by Carl-Johan as the most senior non-family executive, joined Bonnier in 1953. Having worked in the company under the chairmanships of Tor, Abbe, and Lukas, Ekström had watched the organization evolve from a "partnership between Tor and his brothers to a family-owned corporation under Abbe – a corporation that the younger generation want to develop over the next couple of years." Most of Ekström's professional life coincided with that of the leadership of Abbe, a "likeable and ambitious man with an entrepreneurial talent that, combined with his international training, gave him a world vision that fitted well into the post war period in Europe."

Asked by Delacroix to comment on any issues of concern, Ekström said that neighboring markets in Scandinavia and Germany had not in the past received the attention they deserved. He regretted that so much effort had been expended in the United States given how little the firm had to show for that effort – nothing more than perhaps the discovery of products (for example, comics, napkins, plastics) that could be transferred to Sweden. He said he found it "difficult to accept the fact that the United States is better as a source than as a market."

Moving from strategic concerns toward organizational problems, Ekström told Delacroix that the company, in his opinion, needed to address the question of entrepreneurial drive, to prompt the exploration of new ideas and markets from within the company rather than by a small group of senior management. Some progress had been made in encouraging divisions to become more entrepreneurial in their own fields, but much more would be possible if incentive systems were in place: "Abbe was always ready to offer a piece of the pie."

Delacroix found Torsten Ekström to be an affable man who clearly enjoyed the family's trust and who felt confident enough to, as he said, "always be blunt with everyone."

Hans-Olav Johansson

Another long-serving executive Delacroix spoke with was Hans-Olav Johansson, executive vice president for finance, reporting to Carl-Johan. He was the person Delacroix hoped would clarify some of Bonnier's financial philosophy. A graduate of the Stockholm School of Economics and a financial specialist, Johansson joined Bonnier in 1964. He described his current position to Delacroix as the Bonnier Group's "major policeman": each divisional financial controller was accountable functionally to him, providing the figures and forecasts for forward planning and capital expenditure but leaving the business decisions to the divisions' boards.

The substantial capital investment of 1 billion kronor in Marieberg had Johansson's support, because he judged that without the Marieberg connection, the "Bonniers' role as publishers would be seriously diminished." However, he felt that establishing "some kind of target return on equity in a family business" would be a difficult process, since the criteria for investment decisions are not necessarily those of a public corporation or the stock market. (A family investment decision can, for example, be influenced by such emotive factors as tradition or be set against a time horizon that is much longer than that of the professional investment analyst. Personal tax efficiency can also have a bearing – if, for instance, it affects the next generation's inheritance.)

Having received these explanations, which clarified some of Carl-Johan's remarks on the divestment and reinvestment process, Delacroix felt that she had a greater understanding of some of the strategic and investment priorities at Bonnier.

Erik Skipper Larsen

Delacroix's last interviewee was Erik Skipper Larsen, president of Bonnier Publications. Following a reorganization of Åhlén & Åkerlund, Bonnier Publications, with headquarters in Copenhagen, incorporated all the special- and general-interest magazines. Larsen, a life-long journalist, joined Bonnier indirectly after rising to the position of managing director in a Danish family-owned magazine company in which Bonnier acquired a 50 percent interest in 1971 and of which it took full control in 1983.

Given Bonnier's ambitions in the written media, Delacroix was especially interested to hear the views of the person at the forefront of implementing a major part of the new strategy and asked him whether he thought Bonnier could meet the goals the organization had set itself. He responded that he was confident, and for one important reason: "Bonnier can make money on very small-circulation magazines since the company has traditionally survived in small markets and has learned how to create, launch, and develop new products with a minimum of staff and investment. In Denmark, for instance, Bonnier is making money on a magazine with a circulation of 40,000 – a circulation level that for large organizations like Bertelsmann in Germany would not be attractive. Similarly, plans to launch a general-interest magazine in Germany with a target circulation of 100,000 would be met with local incredulity because people there would not believe that we could make money at this level."

Larsen's confidence was, however, tempered by a few caveats. He noted that he did not believe that further expansion in magazines and newspapers in Sweden alone should be Bonnier's first priority. Rather, he would prefer to see Scandinavia as a homogeneous home market of seventeen million consumers, providing a strong base for penetrating markets elsewhere in Europe. This penetration would be led by what Larsen called the "multi-national magazines" – magazines with a common theme and visual layout that require only text translation to be launched in another country. *Illustrated Science* was one of five Bonnier magazines of this type and a good model for Larsen's concept. Already published in the Nordic countries and France with a circulation of over 600,000, this magazine was about to be introduced in Germany. Whether this approach can be continued throughout Europe, to countries more culturally remote from Scandinavia, Larsen is still unsure. In the medium term, he would not be surprised if Bonnier decided to open an office in southern Germany or France to serve the central and southern European markets, employing local staff rather than Danes or Swedes.

After Abbe

Delacroix relaxed in her airplane seat on the way back to Paris and considered the myriad of new impressions, facts, ideas, and people that had been presented to her in the previous few days.

She felt she understood what had happened "after Abbe," but she was not sure what should happen now. Having familiarized herself with top fifty European media owners and the current situation of the media in Europe, Delacroix understood the rationale behind the Bonnier strategy. But would it work? And what of the issues to be faced? How would any unforeseen events in the family affect the business? Clearly, making recommendations to Bonnier was not going to be an easy task.

The Bonnier Group Epilogue

In late 1994, for the first time in its one-hundred-and-ninety-year history, the Bonnier family became the subject of a public scandal that was to rock the impeccable reputation it had enjoyed up until then. Johan Bonnier, at the age of seventy-seven, fired off a series of personal attacks against Olle Wästberg, the editor-in-chief of *Expressen*, the Bonnier-owned evening paper with Sweden's largest circulation. For a while, Wästberg took up the fight, but he finally had to resign in February 1995. Although Johan Bonnier may have had some good reasons for questioning the editor-in-chief's way of running the newspaper, the media quickly blew up the incident to such inordinate proportions, that four days later, Johan saw himself forced to leave all his seats on the different boards of directors of Marieberg. With the full backing of the family, he remained, however, as chairman of Deni, the private Bonnier company owning shares in Marieberg.

From having been able to closely guard their privacy and personal affairs and keep their "skeletons" deep inside the family closet, the Bonniers suddenly became public property and Johan the *non plus ultra* of bad conduct. Characteristic of the strong bonds existing within the family is the fact that in spite of earlier, minor faux pas, family members had always showed a united front and stood up for Johan. Johan's staying on the board of Deni was another demonstration of the family's real stand in the matter.

The Bonnier Group is now facing difficulties on other fronts as well. The number of shareholders has reached fifty-four and is growing. Twelve out of thirty-six adult family members are active today in the company, in accordance with the stated principle to offer a position to every Bonnier who wishes to work for it. More and more shareholders live outside Sweden, however, and have less and less contact with the company's activities. The holding company is a partnership, implying that every owner is personally responsible for it with his or her own private capital. This might result in unforeseeable consequences should anything happen to the profitability of the business, and the family is in the process of changing the legal structure of the company (effective by the year 2000).

Another controversial issue is the fact that every percentage in the Bonnier Group is worth 60 to 70 million kronor but the yearly dividend paid to shareholders equals 250.000 kronor for each percentage they own in the company. This amounts to one-third of the habitual dividend paid out by publicly owned companies, the main reason for the low dividend being Swedish tax law. Apart from such issues, however, the greatest threat to the Bonnier family today comes from the Swedish government, in the form of a newly established media council that will study the implications of the Bonnier Group's position of power – obtained through the sale of 1.2 million daily newspapers, 22,000 cinema tickets, 41,000 books (and many other goods) every day.

In spite of the events of the past year and the threats that Bonnier faces today, the company is standing on more stable feet than one might expect. In 1993, the holding company made a net profit of 307 or 420 million kronor (depending on the way it is calculated), with a turnover of 6.5 billion kronor.[1] Overall costs have been cut by 50 percent. Clear goals have been set and are already being implemented. All in all, the Bonnier Group seems to be well prepared for the future and will, with some luck, master the difficulties it is faced with now and in the future, just as it has done throughout six previous generations.

Note

1 In 1993 Swedish *krona* 1 = US$ 0.13.

COMMENTARY

In looking back at the origins of a family business, we can distinguish a variety of reasons behind the founder's motivation to build an enterprise. One of the most common is the wish for a support system that will provide his or her family with the necessary means to survive under new or difficult circumstances. This wish may be accompanied by fantasies of subsequent great prosperity and of the ability to give family and relatives complete financial security (and perhaps even luxury later on). Other entrepreneurs, as mentioned before, create their own business as a means to satisfy their deeply rooted intrapsychic needs. As we have seen, various motives may play a role -- among them, a desire to be loved, the urge to assert one's independence, or the longing to get even or to repair. For many entrepreneurs, the firm is an extension of the self, representing a way of attaining some form of immortality. The company may also take on the role of a transitional object (discussed in Chapter 4), providing the sought-after illusion of safety and stability. Another common reason for wanting to tackle a business on one's own seems to be the strong urge to venture into new, unknown territory and to satisfy an incessant drive toward exploration and discovery.

In the case of the Bonnier Group, the latter seems to have been one of the salient factors. The founder, Gutkind Hirschel (alias Gerhard Bonnier), was certainly also guided by the wish to escape unfavorable conditions for people of Jewish origin in his native Germany. The need for a support system for his family, however, was not of primary importance to the son of a wealthy banker and jeweler. Venturing into a new and unfamiliar business in a foreign country, sending his three sons to Sweden to try their luck there instead of keeping them close to consolidate the existing business – this indicates a strong drive toward exploration in Gerhard Bonnier. This same sense of adventure, though accompanied by a prevailing need for risk reduction, appears to have been the guiding light throughout Abbe's reign in the company.

When a business does not exist exclusively to fill the owner's various financial and psychological needs, as Bonnier does not, outsiders have a greater chance to play an important part in the leadership of the company. In the Bonnier family, this openness to welcoming non-family members to high positions has always had strong support. Consider, for example, the following non-family members, who occupy (or have occupied) senior executive positions: Olle Måberg, the former Chief Executive Officer and present president of the Bonnier Group; Hans-Olav Johansson, the executive vice president for finance; Erik Skipper Larsen, the president of Bonnier Publications; and Bengt Braun, the president and CEO of Marieberg. The support of non-family members was explicitly confirmed by Karl Otto Bonnier's query, whether even the best Bonnier would necessarily be the right person to become president of the company. The company's motto today seems to be, "The right person in the right place," regardless of whether this person is a Bonnier or not.

The presence of non-family members in executive positions carries several advantages to both the firm and the family. As outsiders, these people have not been indoctrinated with the family myths from early childhood on and are thus better able to view the business with fresh eyes. Less influenced by family considerations, they detect dysfunctional biases more easily and, if the situation in the company is such that it encourages this kind of behavior, act on their convictions. Sometimes, as is the case with Olle Måberg, these outsiders can take on the role of official representatives of the company, with all the attention focused on them, while the family quietly pulls the strings from behind.

Non-family members are likely to have a more neutral view than relatives concerning decision making about family affairs, especially in difficult situations. This too is apparent in the case of Bonnier. The way the company is run illustrates management's ability to maintain a pattern of relatively objective strategic thinking. This contrasts strongly with the all too common failing of family-owned and family-driven companies to regress to a very partisan decision-making process ruled completely by emotions. Many times Måberg has been the mediator between family members in moments of friction, succeeding more often than not to calm stormy family waters.

The beneficial impact of non-family executives in helping the family members to make sound, well-reasoned decisions has assumed particular significance for Bonnier during the most recent decade, when bringing the company back to its core competences (diverted by Abbe's sometimes emotional, impulse-driven decisions) has been a priority. The losses and overdiversification that resulted from Abbe's investments could have led to the splitting up of the company, with unforeseeable results, had management not recognized the necessity of returning to the firm's principal business activity: the media. Luckily, as Eva Bonnier noted, the company has changed very much since Abbe's death. Management today is deeply involved in the restructuring of its business activities, strongly concentrating on expanding into what Bonnier has always been best at. Characteristic of the sound management practices at Bonnier is the way this reorganization process is conducted: assets not being utilized in the core business are sold off gradually, with a sale effected only when the best price can be assured.

Abbe's death, while putting a stop to a potentially dangerous diversification process, brought other pressing issues into the open. First and foremost, it left the company without an obvious leader from within the family. This "handicap," however, lost significance when Måberg took over as CEO and then went on to become president, eventually ceding his place to Carl-Johan Bonnier. We can imagine how things would have turned out had Abbe had a son. Because he was a strong character with a firm and unshakeable belief in the validity of his own ideas (he was not nicknamed "the loving dictator" for nothing), his relationship with grown-up sons trying to assert their own ideas and to establish different ways and means of running the company would most likely have been fraught with all sorts of tension. Instead, Abbe spent considerable energy mentoring his nephew Hans-Jacob. Their relationship was ideal in that it provided Hans-Jacob with the attention and guidance of an experienced and willing mentor, yet no identification, competitiveness, or fear of Oedipal victory marred their relationship or fouled the atmosphere of the company.

One of the factors playing an important part in the continuation of the Bonnier company is the strong sense of belonging that prevails among family members. The Bonnier family has always been known as a closely knit community of relatives who stand up for each other and support each other in the face of outside criticism. As one family member once said, "One for all, all for one." We can only speculate about how far this "myth of harmony" has been consciously cultivated to maintain an us-versus-them mentality that strengthens family unity in the face of a hostile outside world. With a family this large, individualism among its members can easily become destructive. Having recognized this, the leading figures of the family have good reason to try to create a desired state of "pseudomutuality" and to maintain the perceived harmony. If this kind of manipulation takes place, it is not obvious to the observer; there is, however, ample proof of the success of those efforts (if they are employed).

That family members are prepared to support each other fully became obvious when the *Expressen* scandal erupted and Johan became the target of a great deal of unfavorable public attention. His resignation from the boards of the Bonnier companies was unavoidable in that situation, but the fact that he was allowed to remain chairman of Deni, the family's private company holding shares in Marieberg, shows that the family is behind him, however grave his mistake in interfering with editorial matters. This bond between family members is further strengthened by their practice of religiously sticking to old family traditions – from meetings of the family council (in combination with social events), to regular get-togethers on festive occasions such as Christmas and Midsummer Night, to such unlikely events as family members playing in a pop orchestra together. One explanation for this unique coherence might be found in the family's Jewish roots. Even though the Bonniers have not practiced their Jewish religion for seven generations, and intermarriages and the wish to assimilate have weakened their Jewish identity (to the extent that one of Gerard's children became a minister in the Swedish Church), the term *family* to a Bonnier means not just the "core" family but everyone who wears the name; family members are aware that without the latter, the former would not be able to survive.

Besides the strong moral support that they give to each other during difficult times, other (more tangible) proof can be found of the loyalty of the family members toward each other and the company. From a financial point of view, loyalty makes a lot of sense, because the partnership structure of the holding company binds family members so closely together that no individual can possibly pull in a different direction without causing damage to the whole. If a Bonnier wants to sell his or her share of the company, it has to be offered to the others first, far below market value to discourage these kinds of transactions. This is a strong motivation for trying to avoid conflict and keeping up the harmony, as we saw during the financial crisis of the late 1980s in Sweden, a period when the Bonnier Group lost 200 million kronor on one single investment. Instead of looking for a scapegoat among those responsible for the disastrous decision, the family collectively went in with their own private capital to cover the losses.

One further pillar that was deliberately erected to strengthen family solidarity is the famous Agreement regulating the power balance between the different Bonnier branches. It obviously has a strong calming effect on possible conflicts, because it makes it clear to every family member that the balance is impossible to rock. In spite of frequent modifications and updates of the Agreement, its basic principles have not changed since it was drafted in 1959.

Another factor that helps maintain the power balance within the Bonnier Group becomes apparent when studying the organizational structure of the holding company and the various positions held by family members in the different Bonnier "branches." With two exceptions (the siblings Karl Otto and Eva, and Lukas and his son Daniel, who reports to his father from a different country), no two Bonniers with immediate family ties (parent–child, siblings) can be found in executive positions within the same company. The closest relatives working together are first or second cousins. The implications of this are obvious: none of the underlying, often unresolved interpersonal issues (such as sibling rivalry or parent–child competition among "core" family members) puts pressure on working relationships.

Entrepreneurs often make the crucial mistake of neglecting their children's education. That mistake is often the first steps toward the downfall of a company. There are various reasons behind this neglect. By concentrating all their attention on the business, entrepreneurs often have no time or energy left to take care of such matters. If the children of the (male) entrepreneur are female and he has a traditional view of women, he might not consider it suitable that his daughters have anything to do with the business. Another common reason is the entrepreneur's wish to provide the children with all manner of comfort and worldly goods and not to "torture" them with education. Fortunately for the Bonnier children, a solid education is a must in their family. For a Bonnier who has been brought up with the stated goal of entering the business in the future, university studies are by now a prerequisite, followed by a practical training abroad (usually within some kind of media field).

As a consequence of receiving a thorough training from early on, it has become more and more usual for young Bonniers to achieve high positions in the company at a relatively early age. This trend started with Abbe, who became president of Åhlén & Åkerlund at the age of thirty-seven and Chief Executive Officer and president of the Bonnier Group at forty-six; and it has continued to the present, with Carl-Johan taking over the position of executive vice president for the holding company at age thirty-six and that of president at age forty-one. In fact, none of the Bonniers in president and vice president positions in the company was over the age of fifty when he or she attained the position.

Being a Bonnier today does not mean automatic access to one of the top positions. Even being a well-educated Bonnier might not suffice. Besides a university degree, other things are needed for obtaining and keeping a high position in the company: talent and drive. At Bonnier, meritocracy has taken the place of nepotism. In addition to such obvious advantages as a company run by competent people, other positive implications can be discerned, including a high level of commitment from non-family members, who benefit from the impartial treatment within the company. (It has to be noted, however, that no Bonnier has ever been fired from any position, regardless of what he or she has done or failed to do.)

One of the prevailing patterns for the present generation of Bonniers occupying executive positions is that most of them started their post-education careers outside the company and joined Bonnier only after a few years' experience in related fields. The advantages of this are numerous. The error stakes are substantially lower, because mistakes caused by lack of experience are made at the cost of another firm and do not harm Bonnier. What's more, these people have the opportunity to gain valuable insight into the business within a different setting and to improve this knowledge and apply it later at Bonnier. A further advantage is the absence of the psychological pressure, real or imagined, of having to give top performance in order to prove oneself to the family. The opportunity of proving one's worth to oneself and others without that kind of pressure makes it easier for family members to gain acknowledgment in the family's eyes and to develop a firm sense of self-esteem. In addition, having worked in another company first, they are unlikely to view the family firm as a transitional object or to allow the birthright of being a Bonnier to constitute their sole identity. Family members who have proven themselves in a different setting retain the feeling of competency gained by the outside experience (together with the deep-seated inner conviction of their ability to succeed elsewhere, should the need arise).

Thus the Bonnier company is, as we have seen, a relatively well-run company (although its financial returns could be better), with competent executives who seem to be aware of most of the pitfalls threatening their firm and the ways and means to avoid them. Besides good leadership, however, outside circumstances have had their considerable impact on the firm; these seem to have been, in the case of the Bonnier Group, mostly favorable. The holding company today finds itself in a kind of oligopoly (if not quite monopoly) situation in Swedish media, with every third book sold and with 60 percent of the book-club market firmly under its control. The Group owns Sweden's number-one evening newspaper, morning newspaper, and business newspaper and southern Sweden's largest regional newspaper. They dominate the journal market and sell 50 to 60 percent of all cinema tickets in Sweden. This favorable position has had an extremely stabilizing effect on the Bonnier Group. Furthermore, the rapid expansion of the company with each subsequent generation seems to have helped provide the constantly growing number of Bonniers with enough breathing space and the opportunity to unfold their talents in the different branches and parts of the firm without treading on each other's toes.

In addition to the positive aspects, there are, of course, things that Bonniers do not easily talk about. Like any large family, the Bonnier family is made up of individuals who are alike in many things but differ in even more. Besides obvious leaders and patriarchs (such as Gerhard, Tor, and Abbe), the family had and has its share of less adaptive personalities whose potential for survival in the cold, harsh outside world, away from the protective realm of the family company, is questionable. Other family members have demonstrated all-too-human weaknesses; the family is not lacking in Don Juans, Don Quixotes, and would-be-Napoleons. What is impressive in the case of Bonnier is the family's ability to live with such faults, to overcome them as far as possible, and to unite in the pursuit of their overshadowing common goal: the successful continuation of the Bonnier Group.

Concluding remarks

The preceding cases and commentaries have highlighted the delicacy of the interplay between two systems: the family and the family business. We have seen how powerfully these two systems affect each other. Unless the tensions within the family system are resolved, the prospects for continuity of the family business are grim: family members become so busy fighting each other that there is little energy left to fight in the marketplace. Anyone having anything to do with a family business must quickly become acquainted with its unique psychodynamic problems, because without an understanding of these elusive processes, even the best lawyer, tax specialist, accountant, investment banker, or strategic consultant will not get far. Eventually, he (or she) will have to deal with the question of perceived irrationality, and unless he finds the rationale behind the actions, he will be up against a brick wall. When playing organizational detective in family businesses, it is important to realize that what is good for a business is not necessarily perceived by involved relatives as being good for the family.

Organizational diagnosis and intervention are far more likely to be successful when the family is functional. Under functional families, I categorize those in which the couple has a high degree of marital happiness, relationships between children and parents are satisfying, and relationships among the children are amicable. Basically, in functional families, the parties enjoy being together; they have an internal sense of belonging and are willing to make sacrifices if doing so will benefit the group as a whole. In these families, the members take care of each other's needs; they really communicate, and they go out of their way to help each other. These families can enjoy certain traditions, though without going down the pathway of rigidification.

Functional families do not find themselves slipping into the extremes of enmeshment and disengagement; instead, family members respect each other's space and boundaries. Each family member is viewed as an autonomous human being – someone not to be intruded upon. Differences of opinion are respected. Sibling rivalry is not excessive; all the children, each with unique preferences and abilities, are appreciated as individuals in their own right. The children in these families are not troubled by parental favoritism leading to lingering resentment.

Of course, even in the best-functioning families, children compete with each other for preferential treatment by their parents. Relationships will never be perfect; there will always be feelings of being treated unjustly (one major contributing factor being such a simple thing as difference in birth order). In well-functioning families, however, these feelings of unfairness are acknowledged and worked through. What is essential is that children develop mutual empathy while appreciating each other's differences.

FACING THE SUCCESSION HURDLE

The case studies in this book have shown us that many families with their own business do not fit the definition of "functional." One area in which problems often come to a head is family business succession. Succession often raises all the issues we have examined in the preceding cases: the internal theater of the entrepreneur himself, problems of symbolic parricide, issues stemming from sibling rivalry, and multigenerational issues. Often all these conflicts surface because of the very nature of the organization's leader. The words of Leon Danco, one of the world's foremost family business consultants, are appropriate here: "[Succession] disaster occurs because the owner of the business cannot face the fact that at some point he must . . . and will be replaced. If the successful business owner, who had the ability, vision, and guts to build the business from nothing, does not have the courage to face the problems of the future, then his banker and attorney will do it for him on the way back from his funeral . . . four cars back from the flowers" (Danco, 1982, p. 5).

Research has demonstrated that companies that have a succession plan tend to be more profitable after succession than companies that fail to create one (Christensen, 1953; Trow, 1961; Ward, 1987). To have well-spelled-out succession plans creates a sense of focus, clarifies expectations, and reduces the level of anxiety. The question becomes how we, as outsiders, can facilitate this process.

Of course, there are a number of technical factors that may nudge business owners in the right direction. Tax legislation is a good example. Unless the estate is to be burdened by high inheritance taxes – which could endanger the continuation of the company – business owners need to take preventive steps (such as transferring ownership in good time to the next generation). However, in spite of the implicit logic of these suggestions, they are not often followed. Why? In the context of succession, many irrational matters come into play.

Facilitating forces

For effective succession planning, it helps to be dealing with relatively healthy families. Families that are not engaged in unholy triangles or bogged down by vindictive games are more likely to effectively transfer the business (Dyer, 1986; Malone, 1989).

Most important in this process of transition is the quality of the relationship between the leader of the business and the potential successor; trust, open communication, and mutual support are primary. The leader and the successor (as well as the other family members) must be willing to explore differences of opinion. People who listen to each other's opinion and acknowledge each other's achievements are more likely to work out their differences.

In planning for succession, it helps if a mentoring relationship develops between the entrepreneur or family business owner-manager and the successor. Instead of being envious of the younger generation, the leader of the company then can take vicarious pleasure in seeing the younger man or woman do things on his or her own, and both can gain a sense of continuity. In a mentor-protégé relationship, both parties can learn from one other. Such a relationship eases the owner's gradual withdrawal from the business and gives the next generation ample time to learn. For all this to take place, the present leader and other top executives have to be functioning in a generative mode, prepared to give guidance to the next generation rather than troubled by generational envy (Erikson, 1963).

Another important factor in ensuring smooth succession is the entrepreneur-owner's ability to transfer to the next generation a sense of fun and excitement about running the business. If the leader can generate enthusiasm about the future, other family members will not see the business as a millstone around their neck; they will not be troubled by a feeling of nemesis. If, on the other hand, the older leader considers the business to be a burden from which the children should be spared, the outcome is predictable.

Another factor contributing to a successful transfer of power relates to the leader's capacity for self-reflection. Unfortunately, too many entrepreneurs know only how to run; they are single-mindedly action-oriented. To stand still and ask themselves what they are running for (or where are they running to) is not part of their mindset. Truly effective executives, on the other hand, know how to act but also how to reflect. Such persons share the perspective of the Danish philosopher Kierkegaard, who said that the tragedy of life is that while you can understand it only backward, you have to live it forward. When people look at life as a continuity, they are more likely to plan for the future: to engage in estate planning, to think about succession and the ways power can be transferred. People who have this forward-looking mindset have a greater ability to disassociate themselves from their business to pursue other interests (both before and after retirement) and are better prepared to play the role of mentor to the next generation.

The final effective (but unwelcome) force in succession planning is the aging process. As one cynic put it, nothing helps unblock a stalemate about succession as effectively as a mild coronary. When one is lying in the hospital, it is difficult to deny the fact that one is mortal. In such situations, spouses, confidants, or board members can often give the extra push needed to help the person overcome his or her reluctance to let go of the business.

The theater of choice

In a family business, there are a considerable number of options available when deciding who should succeed the current organizational leader. Each option, however, has its own complications. For example, should the rule of primogeniture be applied? But what if the oldest child is not the most capable one or is not really interested in the business? If some form of nepotism is inevitable in family firms, it should at least be meritocratic nepotism. An effort should be made to pick the best family member available. It helps if the family has a variety of people to choose from.

Another prickly question is whether daughters should be eligible. Some family businesses still see the choice of a daughter as rather undesirable. The reasons are many. With daughters may come sons-in-law who want to get in on the act (or even take over). Furthermore, where there is marriage, there may be divorce: a leader may be concerned that if both a daughter and a son-in-law work in the firm, complicated problems might arise in the case of divorce. And then there is the problem of names: a married daughter will probably have changed her name, which can disrupt the symbolic, emotional value many people attach to the company label and identity. Because of these issues, daughters and sons-in-law are unwelcome in some family firms.

There are a number of imaginative, but not always practical, solutions for dealing with the problem of succession. If there are several children, shared management or some form of management rotation can be implemented. While this option can create organizational paralysis, in some instances it works very well; the pool of complementary individual skills yields enormous benefits for some companies. As always, though, for such an arrangement to work, trust and communication are essential.

If a new leader is needed before succession was anticipated or planned for, there are interim solutions. One is to put a trusted employee into an "acting" position for a specific period of time. This person may be appointed as trustee of the family patrimony until a family member can be groomed to take over. There is also the more dramatic option of bringing in professional management. Particularly in dysfunctional families, there are times when only a neutral non-family member can balance the interests of the different factions within the family unit.

Given the potential for family strife to spill over into the company, another popular and effective solution is to divide the business. One tactic puts each child in charge of a division or department, while a more draconian approach splits the business into separate companies and gives one to each family member. The value added to the company is frequently much higher if the latter option is chosen. Moreover, it is often the ideal solution for keeping potentially quarrelsome family members apart. Other possibilities are selling the business, going public, or liquidating.

The final issue, of course, is who should make the choice of successor. Should it be the outgoing president, a family council, the board of directors, or all the parties combined? Should the children be given the opportunity to choose among themselves? There is no perfect solution. However, because powerful psychological processes can affect the outgoing president's judgment, it is important that he or she not be the *sole* decision maker.

MANAGING FOR SURVIVAL

The cases and commentaries in this book have amply (and often dramatically) demonstrated the many problems that can arise in family businesses, particularly when the future of the company is at stake. At times, it may seem that short of being managed by a picture-perfect family (with no daughters), no business can have a rosy future. This is obviously not the case.

One technique that many families use is the family council. This option can be initiated even by healthy families – it need not be prompted by extensive trauma – and it does not imply reliance on outside advisers. In managing for survival, a family council can play an essential role in preventing the company from becoming a casualty to family drama. Such a council can formulate an attainable vision for the company's future, a task that is particularly important when succession is close at hand. Because the shared vision must be acceptable to the next generation – that is, it must be truly *shared* – the younger family members should be involved in its formulation. If left out, the next generation may inherit an impossible task: to live with constraints on running the business that they have not set and that to them are meaningless. Too many business owners forget that the vision of the younger generation is sometimes quite different from their own.

To be successful, such a family council must define the rules of the game for the whole family by setting the superordinate goals that are shared by all. For example, how do family members see the company's future? Are they aiming for continuity of the family regime? Do they want to go public? Do they want to sell the business? Do they want to divide the business? In an effective family council, the first task is to decide what its members want to accomplish.

The family council should also create built-in mechanisms for resolving conflict. Setting up certain rules that apply to everyone helps in building trust. For example, how should non-active family members be dealt with? How can people cash in their shares? Is there some kind of "shotgun" clause to ensure a fair price in the case of serious disagreements? The family council has to be the arbiter for equitable arrangements for entry and exit.

Moreover, this council should create a process whereby the continuity of the firm will be guaranteed, formulating steps as well as specific criteria for the selection of the successor. The transition process should likewise be clarified. What is the role of the present leader of the family firm in this process? Will he or she gradually move out, or will he or she leave quickly? Will this person stay on in an advisory capacity? On a related front, how are family members going to be selected for promotion? All these questions warrant answers.

The training and development of potential successors (indeed, of all participating family members) should also be clarified. What educational background best suits the job? What kind of on-the-job training is required? The potential successor should have a clear area of responsibility and thus an opportunity to demonstrate his or her competence. Salary levels should be spelled out and be made compatible with those of non-family members in comparable positions. Furthermore, a specific decision-making body needs to be designated to appoint the most suitable persons to occupy other senior positions. As we have seen, parents can be remarkably myopic when it comes to their offspring.

A carefully thought-through management development program can smooth succession planning. This kind of program should take into account two elements: what the company will require in the future and what the members of the next generation expect for themselves. In that context, the family council has to find answers to a number of key questions: How long, for example, should it take for a family member to assume a senior position? What experience should he or she have before assuming that role? Should future officers be required to acquire some outside experience before committing themselves to the family firm?

Experience shows that spending time outside the firm is essential for building up one's self-esteem and acquiring a sense of reality about one's abilities outside the family business environment (where it may be hard to test the candidate's real worth, given the specific nature of interpersonal relationships). It is important that potential successors explore their career interests to the fullest so that they can prove to themselves and their associates that they are capable of making it on their own, not just because they have family connections.

Although family councils are often the right forum for discussing key issues, I offer one caveat: the time will come when specific decisions have to be made rapidly. In business life, more than in many other situations, speed is a competitive advantage. Unfortunately, coalition politics can work to the detriment of quick decision making. Thus, although a certain amount of politicizing is an inevitable part of organizational life, it should be kept to a minimum in the family council setting. Unless there is a family member who dominates the council (due to personality or seniority) or a dominant coalition with common interests, there is a danger that the family council will begin to resemble elective politics, leading to situations where compromise candidates, not leaders, gain the upper hand.

In addition to creating a family council, the family firm can pick up a number of important lessons from practices in public companies. In order to prevent organizational myopia, outsiders must be welcomed and trusted. It will probably be necessary to hire non-family members to fill some of the key positions. If outsiders are not involved, it is unlikely that the best and the brightest from among the family will be willing to join the company (and those who are attracted to the firm may be exactly the kinds of people the organization does not want: very dependent personalities). True management professionalism can occur only when people have the feeling that non-family members are also eligible for senior management positions.

The human resource management systems in the family firm should be comparable to those of public companies. For reasons of equity, and in order to avoid destructive envy, it is particularly important to design fair incentive systems for non-family members. Other standard company practices, such as use of strategic planning, clearly defined rules and responsibilities, and division of labor, should be observed.

Family management should strive to build a corporate culture that is relatively open and minimally politicized − a culture in which people are not afraid to speak their minds and in which, through delegation, they have a certain amount of control over their lives. Companies ruled by fear are not characterized by the quality of their decision making.

In order to keep the company on course, an independent board of directors is needed. Not only should board members possess expertise on the more traditional tasks of boards (the selection, assessment, coaching, rewarding, and replacement of CEOs; major investment decisions; changes in corporate strategy; and the safeguarding of ethical and legal conduct), but they should also be knowledgeable about the dynamics of family life and its effect on the family business. Effective boards for family businesses are different from the boards of public companies in that they also play a bridging role between the family and the corporate system.

A good board of directors can be most helpful in facilitating management succession. In order to make a board effective and to create a relationship of trust and respect between the board and the family members, board members need to have an understanding of the relationship between the culture of the family and that of the company, and they must have empathy for the emotions of the various family members.

Professional advisers can also be important to family firms, taking on the role of guardians who help limit the enactment of family dramas on the company stage. And while there is something to be said for continuity, new advisers may be needed as the company goes through periods of rapid growth and transition. Owner-managers would do well to regularly assess their advisers' added value instead of relying on comfortable faces that may be out of touch with the present problems of the firm.

CHALLENGES AND REWARDS

Those readers who have experience with family firms know all too well that maintaining a separation between business and personal lives can be an uphill battle. Entrepreneurial and family firms are places where high drama is often the norm, where boredom is rare. When things are good, they are very, very good, but when they go bad, they are horrid. Given all the attendant drama, family firms offer a tremendous challenge. The excitement lies in making sense out of what is happening and arriving at viable solutions. There are endless combinations and permutations of patterns based on interpersonal relationships that must be considered, because they can create an array of different problems and possible solutions. In that respect, we might well recall the words of Tolstoy in *Anna Karenina*: "All happy families resemble one another; every unhappy family is unhappy in its own way."

Family business owners would do well to heed the adage that the challenge of life is to die young as late as possible. As the German architect Walter Gropius once said, "The human mind is like an umbrella: it functions best when open." Remaining curious and keeping an open attitude toward life and the possibilities for the future will take the family entrepreneur a long way. And when such an attitude is combined with a solid dose of humility, humanity, and humor, the destructive forces of envy, vindictiveness, and rigidity are less likely to gain a hold in the family firm.

References

American Psychiatric Association (1994) *Diagnostic and Statistical Handbook of Mental Disorders (DSM IV)*. Washington, DC: American Psychiatric Association.

Beckhard, R. and Dyer, W. (1983a) "Managing Change in the Family Firm: Issues and Strategies." *Sloan Management Review*, *24*, 59–65.

Beckhard, R. and Dyer, W. (1983b) "Managing Continuity in the Family-Owned Business." *Organizational Dynamics*, *12*, 5–12.

Benson, B., Crego, E. T. and Drucker, R. H. (1990) *Your Family Business: A Success Guide for Growth and Survival*. Homewood, Ill: Dow Jones-Irwin.

Betjeman, J. (1960) *Summoned by Bells*. London: John Murray.

Birch, D. L. (1988) "The Truth About Start-Ups." *Inc.*, January, p.14.

Böszörményi-Nagy, I. and Spark, G. M. (1973) *Invisible Loyalties*. New York: Brunner/Mazel.

Bowen, M. (1978) *Family Therapy in Clinical Practice*. New York: Aronson.

Casserly, J. (1993) *Scripps: The Divided Dynasty*. New York: Fine.

Castelnuovo-Tedesco, P. (1974) "Stealing, Revenge, and the Monte Cristo Complex." *International Journal of Psychoanalysis*, *55*, 169–177.

Christensen, C. R. (1953) *Management Succession in Small and Growing Enterprises*. Boston, Mass.: Graduate School of Business Administration, Harvard University.

Chutkow, P. (1988) "Her Nibs." *New York Times Magazine*, December 4, 1988, pp. 35–38, 47–49.

Cohen, L. P. (1994) "Daddy Dearest." *Wall Street Journal Europe*, October 14–15, pp. 1, 4.

Collins, O. F. and Moore, D. G. (1970) *The Organization Makers: A Study of Independent Entrepreneurs*. New York: Meredith.

Danco, L. (1982) *Beyond Survival: A Business Owner's Guide for Success*. Cleveland, Ohio: University Press.

Davies, A. F. (1980) *Skills, Outlooks, and Passions*. Cambridge, UK: Cambridge University Press.

De Pree, M. (1989) *Leadership is an Art*. New York: Doubleday.

Devereux, G. (1967) *From Anxiety to Method in the Behavioral Sciences*. New York: Humanities Press.

Donckels, R., and Fröhlich, E. (1991) "Are Family Businesses Really Different? European Experiences from Stratos." *Family Business Review*, Summer, *4*(2), 149–160.

du Toit, D. F. (1980) "Confessions of a Successful Entrepreneur." *Harvard Business Review*, November–December, pp. 44–48.

Dyer, W. G. (1986) *Cultural Change in Family Firms: Anticipating and Managing Business and Family Transitions*. San Francisco, Calif.: Jossey-Bass.

Dyer, W. G. (1992) *The Entrepreneurial Experience: Confronting Career Dilemmas of the Start-Up Executive*. San Francisco, Calif.: Jossey-Bass.

Edelson, M. (1984) *Hypothesis and Evidence in Psychoanalysis*. Chicago, Ill.: Chicago University Press.

Epstein, L. and Feiner, A. H. (eds) (1979) *Countertransference*. New York: Aronson.

Erikson, E. H. (1963) *Childhood and Society*. New York: Norton.

Ferreira, A. J. (1963) "Family Myths and Homeostasis." *Archives of General Psychiatry, 9*, 55–61.

Freud, S. (1912–13) *Totem and Taboo*. In J. Strachey (trans. and ed.), *The Standard Edition of the Complete Psychological Works of Sigmund Freud*, Vol. 13. London: Hogarth Press and the Institute of Psychoanalysis.

Freud, S. (1916) *Some Character-Types Met with in Psycho-Analytic Work*. In J. Strachey (trans. and ed.), *The Standard Edition of the Complete Psychological Works of Sigmund Freud*, Vol. 14. London: Hogarth Press and the Institute of Psychoanalysis.

Freud, S. (1917) *A Childhood Recollection from "Dichtung und Wahrheit."* In J. Strachey (trans. and ed.), *The Standard Edition of the Complete Psychological Works of Sigmund Freud*, Vol. 17. London: Hogarth Press and the Institute of Psychoanalysis.

Freud, S. (1933) *New Introductory Lectures on Psychoanalysis*. In J. Strachey (trans. and ed.), *The Standard Edition of the Complete Psychological Works of Sigmund Freud*, Vol. 22. London: Hogarth Press and the Institute of Psychoanalysis.

Geertz, C. (1973) *The Interpretation of Culture*. New York: Basic Books.

Geertz, C. (1983) *Local Knowledge*. New York: Basic Books.

George, A. L. (1969) "The Operational Code: A Neglected Approach to the Study of Political Leaders and Decision Making." *International Studies Quarterly, 13*, 190–222.

Glaser, B. and Strauss, A. (1967) *The Discovery of Grounded Theory*. Chicago, Ill.: Alpine.

Gomez, F. (1985) *On ne badine pas avec la politique* [One shouldn't joke about politics]. Paris: Lattès.

Gubernick, L. and King, R. J. (1987) "The Ultimate Family Feud." *Forbes*, 29 June, pp. 80–81.

Handler, W. C. (1994) "Succession in Family Business: A Review of the Research." *Family Business Review, 7*(2), 133–157.

Hirschhorn, L. (1988) *The Workplace Within: Psychodynamics of Organizational Life*. Cambridge, Mass.: MIT Press.

Hoffman, L. (1981) *Foundations of Family Therapy*. New York: Basic Books.

Hurstak, J., Raiser, J., and Pearson, A. (1991) *Salvatore Ferragamo, SpA*. Harvard Business School Case 9-392-034. Boston: Harvard University Business School.

Jardim, A. (1970) *The First Henry Ford: A Study in Personality and Business Leadership*. Cambridge, Mass.: MIT Press.

Kay, K. (1992) "The Kid Brother." *Family Business Review, 5*(3), 237–256.

Kent, C. A., Sexton, L., and Vesper, K. H. (eds) (1982) *Encyclopedia of Entrepreneurship*. Englewood Cliffs, NJ: Prentice-Hall.

Kepner, E. (1991) "The Family and the Firm: A Coevolutionary Perspective." *Family Business Review, 4*(4), 445–461.

Kernberg, O. (1975) *Borderline Conditions and Pathological Narcissism*. New York: Aronson.

Kets de Vries, M. F. R. (1975) *Power and the Corporate Mind*. Boston, Mass.: Houghton Mifflin.

Kets de Vries, M. F. R. (1977) "The Entrepreneurial Personality: A Person at the Crossroads." *Journal of Management Studies, 14*, 34–58.

Kets de Vries, M. F. R. (1979) "Managers Can Drive Their Subordinates Mad." *Harvard Business Review, 57*, 125–134.

Kets de Vries, M. F. R. (1984) *The Irrational Executive*. Madison, Conn.: International Universities Press.

Kets de Vries, M. F. R. (1989) *Prisoners of Leadership*. New York: Wiley.

Kets de Vries, M. F. R. (1992) "The Motivating Role of Envy: A Forgotten Factor in Management Theory." *Administration and Society, 24*(1), 41–60.

Kets de Vries, M. F. R. (1993) *Leaders, Fools, and Impostors: Essays on the Psychology of Leadership*. San Francisco, Calif.: Jossey Bass.

Kets de Vries, M. F. R. (1994) *Organizational Paradoxes: Clinical Approaches to Management* (rev. edn). London: Routledge.

Kets de Vries, M. F. R. (1995) *Life and Death in the Executive Fast Lane. Essays on Irrational Organizations and their Leaders*. San Francisco: Jossey Bass.

Kets de Vries, M. F. R. (1996) "The Anatomy of the Entrepreneur: Clinical Observations." *Human Relations*, forthcoming.

Kets de Vries, M. F. R. and Miller, D. (1984a) "Narcissism and Leadership: An Object Relations Perspective." *Human Relations, 38*(6), 583–601.

Kets de Vries, M. F. R. and Miller, D. (1984b) *The Neurotic Organization: Diagnosing and Changing Counterproductive Styles of Management*. San Francisco, Calif.: Jossey-Bass.

Kets de Vries, M. F. R. and Miller, D. (1987) *Unstable at the Top*. New York: New American Library/Penguin.

Kets de Vries, M. F. R. and Miller, D. (1988) *Unstable at the Top: Inside the Neurotic Organization*. New York: New American Library.

Kets de Vries, M. F. R. and Perzow, S. (1991) *Handbook of Character Studies*. Madison, Conn.: International Universities Press.

Kets de Vries, M. F. R., Baum, Howell S., Diamond, Michael A., Gilkey, Roderick, *et al.* (1991) *Organizations on the Couch: Clinical Perspectives on Organizational Behavior and Change*. San Francisco, Calif.: Jossey-Bass.

Klein, M. (1975) *Envy and Gratitude and Other Works, 1946–1963*. New York: Delta.

Kohut, H. (1971) *The Analysis of the Self*. Madison, Conn.: International Universities Press.

Kohut, H. (1977) *The Restoration of the Self*. Madison, Conn.: International Universities Press.

Kohut, H. and Wolf, E. S. (1978) "The Disorders of the Self and their Treatment: An Outline." *International Journal of Psychoanalysis, 59*, 413–426.

Labich, K. (1989) "Hot Company, Warm Culture." *Fortune*, Februrary 27, pp. 44–47.

Lacey, R. (1986) *Ford: The Men and the Machine*. Boston, Mass.: Little, Brown.

Langs, R. (1976) *The Therapeutic Interaction*. 2 vols. New York: Aronson.

Lansberg, I. (1988) "The Succession Conspiracy." *Family Business Review, 1*(2), 119–143.

Lasch, C. (1978) *The Culture of Narcissism*. New York: Norton.

Leites, N. (1953) *A Study of Bolshevism*. New York: Free Press.

Levinson, H. (1971) "Conflicts that Plague Family Businesses." *Harvard Business Review*, March–April, pp. 90–98.

Levinson, H. (1972) *Organizational Diagnosis*. Cambridge, Mass.: Harvard University Press.

Levinson, H. (1981) *Executive*. Cambridge, Mass.: Harvard University Press.

Levinson, H. (1984) *Corporate Leadership in Action*. New York: Basic Books.

Luborsky, L. (1984) *Principles of Psychoanalytic Psychotherapy*. New York: Basic Books.

Luborsky, L., Crits-Christoph, P., Minz, J. and Auerbach, A. (1988) *Who Will Benefit from Psychotherapy?* New York: Basic Books.

Mahler, M., Pine, F., and Bergman, A. (1975) *The Psychological Birth of the Human Infant*. New York: Basic Books.

Malone, S. (1989) "Selected Correlates of Business Continuity Planning in Family Business." *Family Business Review*, 2, 341–355.

McKnight, G. (1987) Gucci: A House Divided. New York: Donald J. Fine Inc.

Manchester, W. (1970) *The Arms of Krupp*, 2nd ed. Boston, Mass.: Bantam Books.

Millon T. (1981) Disorders of Personality, DSM III: Axis II. New York: Wiley.

Minuchin, S. (1974) *Families and Family Therapy*. Cambridge, Mass.: Harvard University Press.

Mintzberg, H. and Waters, J. A. (1982) "Tracking Strategy in an Entrepreneurial Firm." *Academy of Management Journal*, 25(3), 465–499.

Minuchin, S., Rosman, B. L. and Baker, L. (1978) *Psychosomatic Families*. Cambridge, Mass.: Harvard University Press.

Morais, R. (1991) *Pierre Cardin: The Man Who Became a Label*. New York: Bantam Books.

National Film Board of Canada (date unknown) *The Corporation: After Sam*. Documentary film.

Pillari, V. (1986) *Pathways to Family Myths*. New York: Brunner/Mazel.

Rosenblatt, P., de Mik, L., Anderson, R. M. and Johnson, P. A. (1985) *The Family in Business: Understanding and Dealing with the Challenges Entrepreneurial Families Face*. San Francisco, Calif.: Jossey-Bass.

Sandler, J. (ed.) (1987) *Projection, Identification, and Projective Identification*. New York: International Universities Press.

Schein, E. (1983) "The Role of the Founder in Creating Organizational Cultures." *Organizational Dynamics*, Summer, pp. 13–28.

Schein, E. (1985) *Organizational Culture and Leadership: A Dynamic View*. San Francisco, Calif.: Jossey-Bass.

Schein, E. (1987) *The Clinical Perspective in Field Work*. Newbury Park, Calif.: Sage.

Schoeck, H. (1969) *Envy: A Theory of Social Behavior*. Orlando, Fla.: Harcourt Brace Jovanovich.

Selvini Palazzoli, M., Boscolo, L., Cecchin, G. F. and Prata, G. (1978) *Paradox and Counterparadox*. New York: Jason Aronson.

Sexton, D., and Smilor, R. (eds) (1986) *The Art and Science of Entrepreneurship*. New York: Ballinger.

Smith, N. R. (1967) *The Entrepreneur and His Firm: The Relationship Between Type of Man and Type of Company*. East Lansing, Mich.: Michigan State University.

Sonnenfeld, J. (1988) *The Hero's Farewell*. New York: Oxford University Press.

Spence, D. P. (1982) *Narrative Truth and Historical Truth*. New York: Norton.

Stierlin, H. (1973) "Group Fantasies and Family Myths: Some Theoretical and Practical Aspects." *Family Process*, 12(2), 111–125.

Trow, D. B. (1961)"Executive Succession in Small Companies," *Administrative Science Quarterly*, 6, 228–239.

Turner, R. (1974) *Ethnomethodology*. Harmondsworth, UK: Penguin.

Waelder, R. (1936) "The Principle of Multiple Function." *Psychoanalytic Quarterly*, 5, 45–62.

Ward, J. (1987) *Keeping the Family Business Healthy: How to Plan for Continuing Growth, Profitability, and Family Leadership*. San Francisco, Calif.: Jossey-Bass.

Watson, T. J. Jr (1990) *Father, Son and Co: My Life at IBM and Beyond*. New York: Bantam.

Winnicott, D. W. (1971) *Playing and Reality*. New York: Basic Books.

Winnicott, D. W. (1975) *Through Paediatrics to Psychoanalysis*. New York: Basic Books.

Wynne, L. C., Ryckoff, I. M., Day, J. and Hirsch, S. I. (1958) "Pseudomutuality in the Family Relations of Schizophrenics." *Psychiatry*, 21, 205–220.

Zaleznik, A. (1966) *Human Dilemmas of Leadership*. New York: HarperCollins.

Zaleznik, A. (1989) *The Managerial Mystique.* New York: HarperCollins.

Zaleznik, A. and Kets de Vries, M. F. R. (1975) *Power and the Corporate Mind.* Boston, Mass.: Houghton-Mifflin.

Zeitlin, M. (1976) "Corporate Ownership and Control." *American Journal of Sociology,* 79, 1073–1119.

Index